Learning to read critically in

LEARNIN
SUPPO

Learning to read critically in educational leadership and management

Edited by
Mike Wallace and Louise Poulson

SAGE Publications
London ● Thousand Oaks ● New Delhi

First published 2003

SAGE Publications Ltd
6 Bonhill Street
London EC2A 4PU

SAGE Publications Inc
2455 Teller Road
Thousand Oaks, California 91320

SAGE Publications India Pvt Ltd
B–42 Panchsheel Enclave
Post Box 4109
New Delhi 100 017

Library of Congress Control Number: 2002110730

A catalogue record for this book is available from the
British Library

ISBN 0 7619-4795-7
ISBN 0 7619-4796-5 (pbk)

Typeset by Pantek Arts Ltd, Maidstone, Kent
Printed in Great Britain by Athenaeum Press Ltd,
Gateshead

Contents

Notes on Contributors

Mike Wallace is a Professor of Education at the University of Bath, UK.

Louise Poulson is a Senior Lecturer in Education at the University of Bath, UK.

Bill Mulford is a Professor and the Director of the Leadership for Learning Research Group, Faculty of Education, University of Tasmania, Australia.

Diana Kendall is a Research Associate at the Leadership of Learning Research Group, Faculty of Education, University of Tasmania, Australia.

Lawrie Kendall is a Research Associate at the Leadership for Learning Research Group, Faculty of Education, University of Tasmania, Australia.

Derek Glover is an Honorary Professor of Education at the University of Keele, UK.

Rosalind Levačić is the Professor of Economics and Finance of Education at the Institute of Education, University of London, UK.

Philip Hallinger is Executive Director of the College of Management, Mahidol University, Thailand.

Pornkasem Kantamara is the Management Program Leader at the Asian University of Science and Technology, Huay Yai, Banglamung, Thailand.

Raymond Bolam is a Visiting Professor of Education at the University of Bath, UK and University of Leicester, UK.

Chris Turner is a Lecturer in Education at the University of Wales, Swansea.

Sharon Kruse is an Associate Professor and the Chair of the Department of Educational Foundations and Leadership, University of Akron, Ohio, USA.

Karen Seashore Louis is Professor of Educational Policy and Administration, University of Minnesota, Minneapolis, USA.

Stephen Gough is a Lecturer in Education at the University of Bath, UK.

Kenneth Leithwood is a Professor at the Department of Educational Administration and Associate Dean (Research), Ontario Institute for Studies in Education, University of Toronto, Canada.

Doris Jantzi is a Senior Research Officer at the Department of Educational Administration, Ontario Institute for Studies in Education, University of Toronto, Canada.

Ronald H Heck is a Professor at the Department of Educational Administration, University of Hawaii at Manoa, USA.

Preface

The purpose of this book is to assist students working at an advanced level with learning what it might mean to be critical and how to become a more critical consumer of literature in a particular area of enquiry. It is addressed directly to students participating in masters and doctoral level programmes. The material may be studied independently by individuals and also incorporated into the formal input of a programme as a source of critical reading and writing exercises supported by tutors and supervisors. Undergraduate students, postgraduates pursuing vocational programmes and their tutors will also find useful the guidance on learning to be critical.

The book is a 'three-in-one' text, which students may use:

▶ to develop their critical understanding of research literature through a focus on reviewing empirical investigations in a particular field of enquiry;
▶ to increase their appreciation of what it is possible to achieve through professionally conducted research investigations of modest size or components of larger studies, informing their thinking about the scope and focus of their own dissertation or thesis;
▶ to learn about major findings, generalisations and concepts connected with a diversity of important topics in their field of enquiry.

Programme tutors and supervisors may also use the material as sources of critical review activities and assessed assignments, models of research, including some that are small-scale, to inform the planning of empirically based dissertations and theses, and research-based information on various substantive topics in the area covered.

The book is divided into three parts. Students are offered guidance in Part 1 on how critically to read literature in their area of study and how to build a critical approach to literature into their writing, whether of assignments, dissertation or thesis. A structured approach to the critical analysis of a single text is offered which is linked to two exercises in critically reviewing, respectively, either one or several texts on the same topic. Consideration is given to the process of conducting such small-scale research and of developing the written account of it that is eventually presented for examination. Throughout Part 1, we indicate where readers may find a relevant example among the accounts in Parts 2 and 3.

Part 2 consists of research reports written for publication (rather than examination) by leading academics in the field of enquiry. They provide extensive examples of an important type of literature. Students are invited to practise their critical reviewing skills on them. The research reports represent models of good practice in researching and report writing that may inform students' own investigations. But as with all research studies, it is legitimate for students and others to ask how convincing are these authors' arguments, their more detailed claims about what they have found out, and any recommendations they may offer for practice.

Part 3 consists of an exemplary critical literature review chapter, not only offering insights into a key aspect of the area of study but also demonstrating how a high quality literature review may be constructed. Here, too, it is legitimate to consider how far the reviewers' claims to knowledge embodied in their argument are convincing. Together, the reports and the review make up a collection that is international in scope, displaying different national contexts, foci, research designs, methods of data collection and analysis, and styles of reporting.

Finally, there are two appendices. The first provides reference to selected additional sources of information. The second consists of a blank form for analysing a single text that students may wish to photocopy or to use as the basis for creating a template on their computer.

We wish to acknowledge the contributions of all those whose collaborative efforts made this book possible. The authors of chapters for Parts 2 and 3 are all busy academics who were nevertheless willing to squeeze in the time required to draft and revise their chapters to a tight deadline. Ray Bolam's ideas strongly influenced our thinking in shaping the content of Part 1, though of course we take full responsibility for what we have done with them. Feedback from the students who have tried out materials connected with Part 1 within their coursework has proved invaluable in informing the development of this component of the book. Katherine Raithby, of the support staff at the University of Bath, provided very timely help with the exacting task of unifying the format of the many computer files that, in combination, constituted the manuscript.

Part 1

Becoming a critical consumer of the literature

Chapter 1

Critical reading for self-critical writing

Mike Wallace and Louise Poulson

If you are a student studying for a masters or doctoral degree, you are likely to notice that the word 'critical' crops up repeatedly in phrases like 'critical understanding', 'critical evaluation', 'critical engagement' or 'critical review', together with the closely associated words 'critique' and 'criticism' – whether in the student handbook, course unit outlines or assignment titles. These words and phrases are all connected with something that course designers value, and they are giving you the opportunity to learn how to do it to the literature in your chosen area of study. Assessors, supervisors and examiners also value 'critical' activity. Criteria for assessing your course assignments, dissertation or thesis all convey the expectation that you will be able to demonstrate how you have learned to perform this activity in whatever written work you submit, often through some form of literature review. Demonstrating your competence in critical reading of the literature through the critical academic writing you produce for assessment will be a condition for the award of your qualification. So you will have to be critical in your reading from the point where you begin preparing to write your first assignment.

But what does it actually mean to be critical as a reader of literature and to demonstrate being critical as a writer in your area of study? And if you do not already know what it means and how to do it, how are you to learn? In our experience, many students are unsure what is involved in being critical but are unwilling to say so because they assume that they are expected already to know. Some lack confidence in their ability as 'beginners' or 'amateurs' to challenge the arguments and evidence put forward by respected academics and other professional writers, often very persuasively. Others have strong opinions about practice born of their years as practitioners in the area they have chosen to study. But they frequently find difficulty in justifying why these opinions are worth holding and in coping with challenges to their views.

In some cases, students' previous academic training has emphasised deference to 'older and wiser' authority figures. Such students may naturally perceive that writers are expert purveyors of knowledge and wisdom that should not be questioned, but rather accepted and absorbed. The cultural adjustment to critical engagement with the ideas of those in 'authority' can be disorientating, but it must be achieved in order to meet the criteria for assessing postgraduate study in the western university tradition.

The process of academic enquiry reflected in postgraduate courses has its historical roots in this tradition. But with rapid globalisation it is increasingly being adopted in higher education institutions right across the world as a way of thinking and informing practical action. Here, while all individuals are entitled to respect as people, there is a cultural expectation that any person's work may legitimately be challenged, exposed to criticism, and even rejected if there are strong enough grounds for doing so. Therefore, it is quite acceptable for students to question the ideas of leading academic figures in their area of study, as long as they can give convincing reasons for their view.

Box 1.1
Being critical: great expectations

References to being critical are commonplace in official statements describing advanced courses. Anything that applies to masters level also applies to doctorates. Here is a selection from a masters course at the University of Bath offered in 2002:
  Aim
  ▶ to give participants opportunities to improve their skills of **critical** thinking and analysis.
  Learning Objective
  ▶ to identify, and engage **critically** with, appropriate and representative literature in the field . . .
  Assignment Assessment Criteria
  ▶ to what extent has the student made **critical** use of appropriate literature and professional experience to inform the focus of the study?
  ▶ to what extent has the student made **critical** use of the literature in the development of the study and its conclusions?

A national policy requirement
In 2001, the UK central government's national framework for all higher education qualifications included the following descriptors.
  Masters degrees are awarded to students who have demonstrated:
  ▶ a systematic understanding of knowledge, and a **critical** awareness of current problems and/or new insights, much of which is at, or informed by, the forefront of their academic discipline, field of study or area of professional practice;
  ▶ conceptual understanding that enables the student:
    – to evaluate **critically** current research and advanced scholarship in the discipline;
    – to evaluate methodologies and develop **critiques** of them and, where appropriate, to propose new hypotheses.

Indeed, the process of developing and refining knowledge and using it to inform efforts to improve practice proceeds through a never-ending sequence of claims to knowledge and counter-claims. There is a widely held belief among academics working in this tradition that no one can have a monopoly on what is to count as knowledge or on what will work in practice. Lack of agreement among experts is especially prevalent in social fields of enquiry because of the nature of the social sciences and of their application to practice. The social sciences are intrinsically value-laden ways of understanding. It is possible to adopt an explicitly value-oriented stance – positive or negative about the phenomenon being explored. It is equally possible to adopt a relatively impartial stance, but not one that is wholly neutral. Decisions on the focus for study reflect values about what is worth investigating in the first place. Carrying out a study will be implicitly and often explicitly underpinned by positive or negative values about the topic, about ideas informing which aspects of the topic should be attended to or ignored, and about the choice of methods of investigation. The practical use to which findings may be put through related policies is bound to reflect particular political values. Unsurprisingly, there is rarely consensus among academics or practitioners on the values informing their views. Nor is there any means of proving to everyone's satisfaction which values are the right ones to hold.

Therefore, learning to be critical as you engage in academic enquiry implies accepting a particular approach to your work. We are probably all familiar with being critical in the sense of not accepting things that happen in our family, social and working lives with which we disagree, whatever our cultural background. But for students who do not have a western university cultural background it may require a bigger cultural step to feel comfortable with being publicly critical, according to the implicit rules of academic enquiry and debate, than it will be for students who have been immersed in this tradition.

A place for being critical in academic enquiry

Postgraduate courses and research programmes leading to academic qualifications are an induction into the world of academic enquiry, writing and ways of thinking. Your participation in them offers you a form of academic apprenticeship. There are many opportunities to learn from experts by observing how they contribute to this process, whether by interacting with them face-to-face or through the medium of their writing. Even more important is the extended opportunity for you to learn-by-doing through trying out academic activities, including critically reviewing literature, presenting an argument at a seminar, applying an idea to see if it works in practice and receiving expert feedback.

Your own academic expertise will develop through this apprenticeship experience. Your habitual way of thinking about your area of study will probably become more sophisticated. You will find yourself gaining knowledge about the field including some which is at the leading-edge of what any expert knows, about topical areas of debate where experts disagree, about the limits of what is known, and about the extent to which prescriptions for practice derived from one context can be applied to another. You will also develop insights into the critical nature of the academic enquiry that produces this knowledge and its areas of controversy. You will become familiar with the ways in which academics holding very different views about the same phenomenon will put forward their own argument persuasively while seeking to counter or to refute the arguments of other academics who oppose their view.

One aspect of your thinking that you will surely notice changing is your ability to adopt a critical stance towards others' claims to knowledge about aspects of the area of study, and a self-critical stance towards your efforts to produce knowledge through your research and writing. The notion of 'being critical' tends to have a particular meaning in the academic world, reflecting values deriving from the western university cultural tradition. Here is our definition. Being critical in academic enquiry means:

▶ *adopting an attitude of scepticism* or reasoned doubt towards your own and others' knowledge in the field of enquiry (e.g. a theory, research findings or prescriptions for improving practice) and the processes of producing this knowledge (e.g. 'armchair' theorising, research investigations, reflecting on practice);
▶ habitually *questioning* the quality of your own and others' specific claims to knowledge about the field and the means by which these claims were generated;
▶ *scrutinising* claims to see how far they are convincing in the light of checking (e.g. whether the components of a theory are logically consistent, whether there is sufficient evidence to back a generalisation based on research findings, or whether the values underlying prescriptions for improving practice are acceptable);
▶ *respecting* others as people at all times – challenging others' work is acceptable, but challenging their worth as people is not;
▶ *being open-minded*, willing to be convinced if scrutiny removes your doubts, or to remain unconvinced if it does not;
▶ *being constructive* by putting your attitude of scepticism and your open-mindedness to work in attempting to achieve a worthwhile goal – challenging others' work to find a better way of doing things is acceptable, but indulging in destructive criticism of others' work just to demonstrate your intellectual prowess at their expense is not.

Easier said than done, of course. But the more you learn to be critical, the more you take responsibility for your academic learning activity and efforts to inform your own and others' practice (rather than being merely the passive receiver of others' wisdom, or the overactive promoter of your unjustified opinions that leave others unconvinced). Through engaging critically with the literature relating to your field of enquiry in a constructive way, you develop your capacity to understand and evaluate practice, research, theories and policies. You may also inform your efforts to conduct research and possibly to commission investigations, and to apply practical prescriptions derived from the literature.

Your ability to take responsibility for your academic learning rests on becoming a critical consumer of literature who is also a self-critical writer. In our view, it is essential that you apply to your own work the same critical approach that you are learning to apply to others' writing. For the academics who assess your work will be critical readers of what you have written. The assessment criteria will in all probability include the extent to which your work demonstrates your ability to be critical in engaging with the literature.

In Table 1.1 we have highlighted the link between elements of your endeavours in your academic apprenticeship as a critical reader and their application to your writing for assessment by other critical readers. Those entailed in critical reading will be discussed in the remainder of this chapter, and their reflection in self-critical writing will be considered in Chapter 2. For now, we wish to draw your attention to the way each element of critical reading has its counterpart in self-critical writing. Whatever you look for as a critical reader of literature, your assessors will also look for in your writing when judging the extent to which your account of what you have read meets the assessment criteria.

For instance, you may wish to know what the authors' purpose was in writing their account of, say, some research they have conducted. Knowing their purpose will help you to identify whatever argument they are developing and why they are developing it, and how they are attempting to support their argument through their claims to knowledge based on what they have found. You should similarly clarify and state your purpose in what you write as a self-critical writer reviewing this research. Your assessors will wish to know what your purpose was in writing your account to help them identify what argument you are developing and why you are developing it, and how you have attempted to support your argument through your critical evaluation of these researchers' work. Make it easy for your assessors to find out!

As you read down the list of elements of self-critical writing, you will see that they relate to meeting the needs of your readers so that they can grasp what you are trying to communicate. But just as important, they also maximise your chances of convincing your readers that whatever argument you are putting forward is compelling. Both meeting your readers' needs and convincing them will help to ensure that your account meets their assessment criteria. So it is vital to develop a strong sense of the audience for whom you are writing.

When reading the literature, it is worth making a habit of noticing what other writers do that helps or hinders your attempt to grasp whatever they are trying to communicate to you. Emulate the good and avoid the bad practices in your own writing, because your top priority is to communicate to your readers. The chapters in Parts 2 and 3 incorporate various techniques designed to assist readers, like dividing the text into a series of sections separated by subheadings (e.g. Chapter 3), or providing an indication in the introduction about what will be covered in the remaining sections of the chapter (see page 92). As you read these chapters, look out for techniques that give you clues about what their authors are trying to communicate to you. Build these techniques into your own writing.

Table 1.1 *Linking a critical approach to your reading with a self-critical approach to your writing*

As a critical reader of the literature, you:	As a self-critical writer of assessed work, you:
▶ consider the authors' purpose in writing the account	▶ state your purpose in what you write to make it clear to your readers
▶ examine the structure of the account to help you understand how the authors develop their argument	▶ create a logical structure for your account that assists you with developing your argument, and make it clear to your readers
▶ seek to identify the main claims the authors make in putting forward their argument	▶ state your own main claims clearly to help your readers understand your argument
▶ adopt a sceptical stance towards the authors' claims, checking whether they support convincingly what they assert	▶ assume that your readers adopt a sceptical stance to your work, so you must convince them by supporting your claims as far as possible
▶ question whether the authors have sufficient backing for the generalisations they make	▶ avoid making sweeping generalisations in your writing which you cannot justify to your readers
▶ check what the authors mean by key terms in the account and whether they use these terms consistently	▶ define the key terms you employ in your account so that your readers are clear what you mean and use these terms consistently
▶ consider whether and how any values guiding the authors' work may affect what they claim	▶ make explicit any values that guide what you write
▶ distinguish between respecting the authors as people and being sceptical about what they write	▶ avoid attacking authors as people but be sceptical about what they write
▶ keep an open mind, retaining a conditional willingness to be convinced	▶ assume that your readers are open-minded about your work and are willing to be convinced if you can adequately support your claims
▶ check that everything the authors have written is relevant to their purpose in writing the account and the argument they develop	▶ sustain your focus throughout your account, and avoid irrelevancies and digressions in what your write
▶ expect to be given the information that is needed for you to be in a position to check any other literature sources to which the authors refer	▶ ensure that your referencing in the text and the reference list is complete and accurate so that your readers are in a position to check your sources

Box 1.2
A sense of audience: profile of the typical academic who assesses your writing

Age	Anyone's guess.
Lifestyle	Busy – appreciates writing with a logical structure, clear focus and fluent writing style that communicates efficiently.
Attitudes	Fair and respectful – concerned solely with the quality of your writing. Sceptical – will not accept your argument unless you can prove your case. Open-minded – ready to be convinced.
Favourite subject	The area of study – knowledgeable about the area in general but not about detailed issues or about your professional experience, so welcomes a brief description but only insofar as it is relevant to your argument.
Likes	Books – so knows the literature well and expects you to have read the literature you write about and to report it accurately. Reading high-quality writing – carefully constructed, well-argued, balanced, meticulous on detail and reflective.
Pet hates	Waffle – ill-structured writing whose focus is diffuse and which leads nowhere. Avoidable errors – whether typographical, punctuation or grammatical, which careful proofreading could have picked up. Over-generalisation – wild claims that go far beyond any backing they may have. Poor referencing – failure to acknowledge authors, inaccurate or incomplete reference lists.
Most likely to say	'Answer the question set in your assignment!' 'Keys to writing success are a logical structure and a clear focus.' 'Take the criteria for assessment into account when planning your written work.' 'Your literature review should be critical, not just descriptive.'

A mental map for navigating your way around the literature

It will be helpful to develop a mental map to guide your thinking when engaging critically with literature in your area of study. The literature will probably represent unfamiliar and potentially confusing territory, especially when you are just starting out on your intellectual journey. A map enables you to find a route through the sheer quantity and complexity of the literature by working out what you need to know and then navigating your way towards the answer you seek. We will define a set of tools for thinking that form a key to this map, and then outline four of its most significant components. We will exemplify how these components contribute to people's ability to make sense of the social world and indicate how they interrelate. Together, these tools and components can be used like a map to guide you in making sense of what you read. You may refer back to them at any point to help you see what the authors of the literature are doing as they attempt to convince you through their writing. But you should also be aware that our attempt to provide you with a mental map has its own limitations. We have greatly simplified complex ideas that philosophers spend their lives critically thinking and arguing about, so you will need to consult other sources if you want to learn about such ideas in depth. (Our attempt at mental map-making is, of course, as open to critique as any other academic writing.)

Tools for thinking are necessary for understanding the social world, because your experience of it and your ability to communicate that experience does not rest solely on your senses. The social world is also interpreted through language – as we are doing here to communicate with you about engaging critically with the literature. The notion of 'education', for example, is a social construct: education is an idea employed by convention to refer to various experiences, activities and even the state of being of the educated person. But there is not a one-to-one correspondence between the social world out there and people's interpretation of it in their minds. In common experience, different people understand what may be the same social world in different ways using a variety of terms to interpret and evaluate their experience. One person's valuable educational activities (say, opportunities for children to learn through play) may be another person's deplorable waste of time (if opportunities for learning through play are interpreted as merely encouraging playing around, without learning).

We will consider how our set of tools for thinking – the key to the mental map – is incorporated in finding out about the social world through:

▶ two dimensions of variation among claims to knowledge;
▶ three kinds of knowledge generated by reflecting on, investigating and taking action in the social world;
▶ four types of literature whose authors are attempting to develop and convey different kinds of knowledge;
▶ five sorts of intellectual 'project' in which people engage who are working in a field of enquiry, leading to the creation of literature.

One set of tools for thinking...

These tools for thinking are embedded in the language through which people communicate by means of literature. They enable you to understand the social world and they have a hierarchical structure. But be warned: writers vary in what they mean by each of these tools for thinking, how they employ each tool and how they conceive the relationship between the tools. No idea, not even a tool for thinking, has an absolutely fixed and universally agreed meaning. Here is our version of what these tools are.

What are concepts?

Ideas like 'education' are *concepts*: terms used for classifying, interpreting, describing, explaining and evaluating aspects of the social world. The meaning of any concept may be defined using other concepts, so 'education' may be defined using concepts like 'instruction', 'creativity', 'training' or 'skill formation'. But there is no guarantee that everyone will define any concept in the same way. If no one has a monopoly on the possession of knowledge or prescriptions for practice, no one has a monopoly on the meaning of any concept either. Consequently, there is great potential for confusion and failure to communicate if the implicit definition of key concepts adopted by authors does not match their readers' implicit definition of these concepts. What authors can do, however, is to offer a 'stipulative definition' of concepts to indicate what they mean when using particular terms (e.g. pages 117–21). We, as authors, are giving a stipulative definition of concepts for making sense of the social world to provide you with your map. (But we cannot guarantee that all authors would define them according to our stipulation.) For clarity in communicating about ideas, it is important to consider what you and others mean by particular concepts. Otherwise you may find yourself unclear, as a reader, about what authors mean when they use undefined terms that are central to their argument. As a writer, you may confuse your readers unless you give a stipulative definition of the core concepts that you are employing.

Since the social world is infinitely complex, it is not humanly possible to focus on all aspects of social phenomena like education at the same time. Concepts may be grouped in various ways, and used as symbols where a concept (like the idea of a 'map' to guide your thinking) is used to represent something else (here, a multiplicity of concepts and ways of using them to structure thinking about aspects of the social world). Grouping concepts has the advantage of enabling you to attend closely to certain parts of the phenomenon you are studying. But to do so carries the inevitable disadvantage that you are likely to ignore other parts of the phenomenon that another group of concepts would have drawn to your attention. There seems to be no single best way of making sense of the social world. All ways entail compromises because no one is capable of attending to everything at once. Let us examine more closely how concepts are used in the creation of different sorts of knowledge that you will find represented in the literature.

What are perspectives?

Sets of concepts are often combined to form *perspectives*: selected facts, values and assumptions forming a screen for viewing social events and processes. A cultural perspective focuses on facts, values, assumptions and codes governing what can be thought and done connected with the central concept of culture (Firestone and Louis, 1999). People may pick out different features of the social world through different screens, but they cannot look through all possible screens simultaneously. Any perspective, such as the cultural orientation, forms a lens for interpreting phenomena in the social world (e.g. page 116). So a cultural perspective on education might constitute a screen, directing your attention to the way educational activities contribute to moulding the beliefs and values of those being educated. It incorporates a bundle of related concepts that draw attention to some aspects of the social world while downplaying others. Cultural concepts include the sharing of beliefs, values and 'norms' or rules of behaviour. An important concept within this perspective is the notion of ritual, where an activity symbolises something else. Degree ceremonies in higher education institutions are a celebratory ritual. The procession of academics and the award event symbolise how academics are publicly acknowledging the achievement of their students who have successfully completed their degree studies, and are now welcoming them into the ranks of graduates of the university or college. The degree certificate that each successful student receives is physically just a piece of paper with her or his name on it. Yet it also symbolises the student's achievement. This particular piece of paper can be acquired only by passing the assessment requirements for the award of the degree.

What are metaphors?

A *metaphor* is a way of describing one thing as something else that is perceived to be like it in some way. Where a screen for interpreting the social world is viewed as centring on a particular idea, key concept or image, this screen is often viewed as a metaphor for those aspects of a social phenomenon to which it draws our attention. The notion of a metaphor is a good example of an idea or concept whose meaning varies between writers. Some use the term metaphor interchangeably with the term perspective to highlight a central concept forming a particular screen, as where reference is made to the 'cultural metaphor'. Others implicitly define metaphor more narrowly, to capture in a single concept the image of some activity in the social world. Our image of tools for thinking as a key to a map for navigating your way around the literature is an example of such a metaphor. They do not literally provide you with a physical key, nor is there a physical map, but we hope that the image sums up for you what we are actually trying to offer.

A well-known metaphor in organisation theory is March and Olsen's (1976) image of a 'garbage can', created to sum up the process of decision-making in organisations. They wished to draw attention to a particular aspect of the phenomenon of organisational decision-making: the extent to which there may be ambiguity and unpredictability over why opportunities for making decisions arise, who participates in which decisions, and why they do or do not participate. The 'garbage can' metaphor captures the aspect of decision-making on which they wish to focus in a single image. Streams of different kinds of rubbish, representing opportunities for decision-making or organisation members who are entitled to participate, are thrown into a garbage can or dustbin. What eventually emerges from the mix is tipped out in the form of decisions. Notice that by drawing attention to ambiguity in decision-making, this metaphor draws attention away from other aspects of the phenomenon – not least the extent to which organisational decision-making may be orderly and predictable. As a critical reader, you will often find yourself engaging with an account where a particular perspective or metaphor has been adopted. It is important for you to reflect on which aspects of the social phenomenon being discussed are highlighted, and which underplayed or ignored altogether.

More than one perspective or metaphor may be used to interpret the social world in the same analysis. A common approach is to examine a phenomenon first from one perspective, then from another. Difficulties can arise when the two perspectives embody concepts that are not compatible with each other. If a cultural orientation emphasises how people share beliefs and values but, say, a political perspective emphasises how they use power to achieve their personal goals at others' expense, which explanation are you to accept? Another approach is to combine two or more perspectives by adopting stipulative definitions of the concepts from each perspective that are compatible with each other. A combined cultural and political perspective may use a stipulative definition of power that allows for power to achieve goals by working together as well as power to achieve goals through conflict. But employing combined perspectives becomes difficult because of the large number of concepts that may be involved. There is a limit to human capacity to keep a large number of ideas in mind at one time.

What are theories and models?

These terms refer to explanatory and often evaluative accounts of some aspect of the social world, incorporating a bundle of related concepts defined in a particular way. *Theories* are widely viewed as a coherent system of connected concepts, sometimes lying within one or more perspectives. They may be used to interpret, explain or, more normatively, to prescribe what should be done to improve an aspect of the social world, as in a 'progressive theory of education'. Such a theory may be couched within a psychological perspective on individual development embodying the metaphor or image of 'nurturing growth'. *Models* generally entail a small bundle of concepts and their relationship to each other (e.g. pages 144–6). They tend to refer to a specific aspect of a phenomenon, which may be incorporated as part of a broader theory. A model of progressive education may concern a specified sequence of activities designed to provide a progressive education in a particular setting. Theories and models may or may not be informed by research or practical experience.

What are assumptions and ideologies?

Any interpretation of the social world rests on certain *assumptions*: taken-for-granted beliefs of which a person making a claim about the social world may be unaware. A progressive theory of education, for example, may rest on the assumption that learning how to learn is more important as a preparation for adult life than learning lots of facts. The validity of any assumption may always be questioned, often by considering whether there is evidence to support or challenge it, or by checking whether the assumption is logically consistent with associated claims being made about the social world.

The term *ideology* implies a system of beliefs, attitudes and opinions about some aspect of the social world based on particular assumptions. An ideology guides action to realise particular interests or goals. This action may entail preventing others from realising their interests. The 'educational philosophy' espoused by many teachers and lecturers is an ideology comprising their system of beliefs, attitudes and opinions about education, as in the view that 'education is about developing a lifelong love of learning'. It will be intrinsically value-laden, because any view of the purposes, content and methods of education, and of the ideal balance of control between the different groups involved, entails considerations about what should and should not be done that reach beyond facts. As we illustrated above, people may disagree over the values governing their view of what makes for good education.

The notion of an ideology is sometimes employed neutrally, referring to any system of beliefs whether true or false. But it is sometimes used more critically to imply a false or distorted set of beliefs, belying a partisan interest or goal that is not being made fully explicit. Marxists suggest that the content of people's ideology is at least partly determined by economic conditions, and in a capitalist society this ideology reflects their position of advantage or disadvantage within a hierarchy of social classes. The educational philosophy that 'the purpose of formal education is to provide the skilled and compliant workforce necessary for our nation's economic competitiveness in a global economy' may be interpreted critically as protecting employers' position of advantage, in so far as members of today's and tomorrow's workforce come to accept this ideology and are deflected from acting to better their economic position in respect of employers. In your critical reading, it is important first to identify where writers' claims about the social world reflect their ideology, and then to question the assumptions and values that underlie the ideology itself.

Two dimensions of variation among knowledge claims...

Arguments assert conclusions about what does, should or should not happen in relation to some aspect of the social world (e.g. pages 229–30). These conclusions are drawn from one or more *claims to knowledge*, assertions that something is, or normatively should be, true. Such claims to knowledge are supported, in turn, by some form of evidence that warrants the conclusion being drawn. Knowledge claims are made with varying degrees of certainty, but note that it is a separate issue whether the degree of certainty is justified. The academic literature is not short of examples of highly speculative claims to knowledge of the social world made with enormous confidence that they are certain truths. Yet no knowledge of the social world can ever be beyond all doubt, as we discussed above. It is always appropriate for you critically to ask whether there is sufficient evidence to support the degree of certainty with which a claim is made.

Uncertainty whether claims are true is often made explicit when writers state that claims are tentative or cautious. A formal means of signalling tentativeness is through *hypotheses*. A hypothesis is a claim consisting of a proposition or statement that something is the case, but which is as yet unproven. An enquiry into an aspect of the social world might begin with a hypothesis whose validity is then tested to check whether evidence supports it or not. Alternatively an enquiry may produce hypotheses as outcomes, amounting to speculations that could be tested in future. However, many hypotheses in the study of the social world are so general that they are not amenable to straightforward testing. How, for example, could the hypothesis be convincingly tested that 'learning how to learn is a more effective preparation for adult life than learning lots of facts'? What would count as sufficient evidence to warrant the conclusion that the hypothesis was disproved or supported?

Claims are also made with varying degrees of *generalisation* from the context of practice or experience from which they were derived to the range of other contexts to which they are supposed to apply. For example, a claim about the effectiveness of progressive education might be made solely in relation to British primary schools, or alternatively in relation to all schools and other educational arrangements anywhere. Frequently, sweeping generalisations are not explicit about the range of contexts to which a claim applies. The extent of the claim is implied rather than stated, as in the assertion that 'learning how to learn is a more effective preparation for adult life than learning lots of facts'. Implicitly, this claim is asserted to have universal applicability – to all children everywhere, past, present or future. But note that generalisations are, in themselves, just assertions that something is known, not proof that it is known. Anyone can make generalisations – we have just done exactly that at the beginning of this sentence! It is another matter whether there is sufficient evidence that whatever is claimed really does apply to all the contexts to which the claim is explicitly or implicitly asserted to apply. So you may always, appropriately, ask the critical question whether there is sufficient evidence to support the degree of generalisation in the claim being made.

The broader the generalisation that some claim has *applicability* to a wider range of contexts, the more difficult it is to demonstrate that there is sufficient evidence from all these diverse contexts to support the claim. But generalisations also vary over their *level of abstraction* from the intricate details of any specific context. The broader the generalisation, the more likely it is to be at a high level of abstraction, glossing over details of individual contexts to make a claim about some quite abstract feature that is supposedly common to them all. The generalisation 'learning how to learn is a more effective preparation for adult life than learning lots of facts' glosses over the multiplicity of details that may vary between different contexts. They include:

▶ learning environments, whether a computer-equipped classroom or simply an open space;
▶ the characteristics of learners, whether adventurous or quietly reflective;
▶ the diversity of stakeholders involved in learning, whether students, parents or teachers;
▶ purposes for promoting learning, whether for its own sake or to contribute to society;
▶ values reflecting ideologies about what is learned, how it is learned and what learning is for;

- features of adult life, whether work is pleasurable or harsh, and leisure plentiful or scarce;
- the nature of facts, whether an ethnocentric series of historical dates or the arithmetical relationships used in calculating earnings and spending.

We have mapped these variations among claims to knowledge in Figure 1.1. Note that we are putting forward a model here, offering a diagrammatic representation of relationships between concepts that we have selected and whose meaning rests on our stipulative definitions. We suggest that the degree of certainty and the degree of generalisation are key dimensions of variation. The more certainty is asserted about a claim, the more vulnerable it is to the critical question whether there is sufficient evidence to support this degree of certainty. The broader the generalisation embodied in a claim, the more vulnerable it is to

Figure 1.1 *Dimensions of knowledge claims and their vulnerability to critical questioning.*

Degree of certainty

Degree of generalisation	Low *Tentative whether a claim is true*	High *Confident that a claim is true*
Low *Applicability to a specific context at a low level of abstraction*	Low vulnerability to critical questioning because the claim to knowledge is weak and generalisation to other contexts is minimal. **Critical question:** • **Is there sufficient evidence from the specific context to support any tentative claim?**	Moderate vulnerability to critical questioning because the claim to knowledge is strong but generalisation to other contexts is minimal. **Critical question:** • **Is there sufficient evidence from the specific context to support any confident claim?**
High *Applicability to all contexts at a high level of abstraction*	Moderate vulnerability to critical questioning because the claim to knowledge is weak but generalisation to other contexts is extensive. **Critical question:** • **Is there sufficient evidence from the specific context and other contexts to support any tentative claim entailing extensive generalisation?**	High vulnerability to critical questioning because the claim to knowledge is strong and generalisation to other contexts is extensive. **Critical question:** • **Is there sufficient evidence from the specific context and other contexts to support any confident claim entailing extensive generalisation?**

the critical question whether there is sufficient evidence to support this extensive degree of generalisation. The claims to watch are those particularly prevalent in literature about the social world embodying recommendations for improving practice. They tend to make the strongest claims to knowledge, often combining a high degree of certainty with implicitly or explicitly a high degree of generalisation, at a high level of abstraction (represented in the lower right-hand cell of the diagram). Conversely, least vulnerable to critical questioning are those that make the weakest claims to knowledge: tentative assertions about a specific context that avoid generalisation beyond this context (represented in the upper left-hand cell of the diagram).

As a critical reader, you will find it useful to identify the degree of certainty and degree of generalisation of the claims to knowledge you come across in the literature, giving you clues about the sorts of critical questions to ask before you are convinced. As a self-critical writer you will wish to protect your writing from the criticism of the critical readers who are assessing it. You should be cautious about asserting greater certainty over your claims to knowledge than you have evidence to support, and about making broad generalisations except perhaps at a high level of abstraction.

Three kinds of knowledge – theoretical, research and practice...

Tools for thinking are intrinsic to developing the different kinds of knowledge that you will find expressed in the literature, and to your capacity to be critical about them. We have summarised the relationship between the tools for thinking and our typology of three kinds of knowledge in Figure 1.2 (another model). The tools for thinking are employed in contrasting ways to generate and question the three kinds of knowledge we have distinguished.

What is theoretical knowledge?

Tools for thinking are most overtly implicated in *theoretical knowledge* – you cannot have a theory without a system of connected concepts. Theoretical knowledge implies a theory about some aspect of the social world based on particular claims about what is or should be the case, as in a progressive theory of education. Theoretical knowledge is, in other words, not just a theory but a theory about something. You can always critically question how the concepts in a theory are being implicitly or explicitly defined and whether the system of concepts in a theory is coherent.

Generating this kind of knowledge may involve variable linkage with the other kinds. At one extreme, 'armchair' theorising entails reflection on personal experience in an area of practice, sometimes supported by reflection on what has been read in the literature and so potentially drawing on others' theoretical, research or practice knowledge. Where the links with other kinds of knowledge are weak, armchair theorising can lead to interpretations, explanations or even prescriptions for practice that are not backed by evidence. Anyone can dream up a theory. But since there is not a direct correspondence

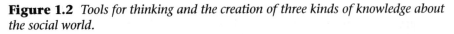

Figure 1.2 *Tools for thinking and the creation of three kinds of knowledge about the social world.*

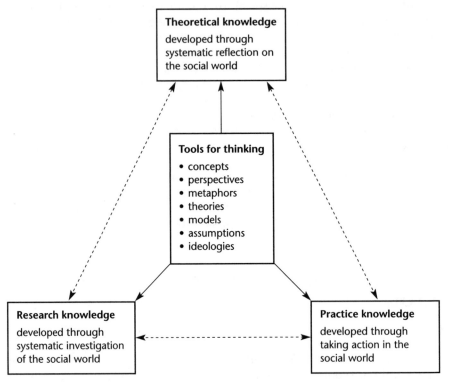

between the social world and interpretations of it, the strength of the claims made about the social world according to any theory can always be critically questioned by asking how far they are supported by evidence from research or practice. At the other extreme, as we shall see, theorising can be intimately linked to seeking evidence about what actually goes on out there.

What is research knowledge?

Research in the social world is a focused and systematic empirical investigation of an area of practice and experience to answer a central question about what happens and why, and sometimes also about how to generate improvement. *Research knowledge* consists of claims about what happens that are supported by evidence gathered through data collection and analysis in the course of an investigation. Research may be atheoretical, where it is not explicitly linked with any perspective, theory or model. But because research cannot be conducted without using tools for thinking, it is inevitable that particular concepts or groups of concepts will be employed. They may be undefined and employed unsystematically, but concepts will inform choices about what evidence to gather and how to interpret findings. Alternatively, one or more perspectives, theories or models may be used consciously to inform data collection and analysis (e.g. pages 92–3), whether in guiding decisions on what data to collect or in developing explanations of the findings.

The research approach may vary, from an investigation by professional researchers who do not attempt to intervene in the phenomenon they study, through an *intervention* where researchers work in partnership with those they study to help them improve their practice, to practitioners' action research where they investigate their own practice. The research process proceeds through the application of particular *methods* or techniques for focusing the investigation, collecting data as the basis of evidence, analysing it and reporting the results. These detailed methods tend to reflect a particular *methodology*, the researchers' philosophical assumptions about the nature of the social world (for example that social phenomena are or are not subject to universal laws). The results of an investigation embody researchers' claims about what happens and why, and possibly about how to make improvements. They are typically made public, commonly by publishing an account of the research in the literature. This account may be more or less descriptive, explanatory or evaluative, depending on what central question the researchers were attempting to answer.

The research reports in Part 2 of the book are all undertaken by professional researchers. They all employ tools for thinking, focus on an aspect of practice in the area of study, attempt explicitly or implicitly to answer a central question, and contribute to research knowledge by making claims about what happens on the basis of their findings. Some investigations are explicitly informed by a theory or a perspective, and some are concerned with improving practice according to the researchers' values.

What is practice knowledge?

You know a great deal about practice in your domain of the social world, but you may not be aware of just how much you know. Practice implies everyday activity. The practitioners involved interpret and evaluate their practice, guided knowingly or unknowingly by tools for thinking related – however loosely – to theoretical knowledge. Part of *practice knowledge* is tacit, the know-how entailed in skilful performance of practical tasks which practitioners use without necessarily being aware of how they do it. But some of this know-how can be raised to consciousness by reflecting on practice, possibly informed by theories, and by investigating and challenging habitual practice, as in some versions of action research. Knowledge of practice that is made explicit embodies claims about what does or should happen in the practical domain concerned. Some of this explicit practice knowledge is summarised in the literature, as when experienced practitioners write an account of their practice or where informed professionals, like inspectors, report on their work in evaluating practice (see Chapter 4). The basis of practice knowledge claims appearing in such literature is open to critical questioning for the same reasons as the other kinds of knowledge. Anyone can dream up an account of what she or he does and claim that it is good practice. But you can always question what meaning is being given to concepts used, whether the concepts are used coherently, and whether the account is supported by evidence.

Your motivation for studying may be to inform your attempts to improve your own and others' practice in your organisation. As you read this sentence you are actually using tools for thinking to raise your awareness of the nature of tools for thinking, and of how they relate to your and others' practice knowledge and the research and theoretical knowledge contained in the literature. Informing your practice through becoming a critical consumer of the literature involves engagement with the claims that you, other practitioners, theorists and researchers make in the literature about your practical domain.

Box 1.3
Practice makes perfect – or does it?

Which of these statements do you agree with, and why? Your answers will reflect your assumptions about the relationship between different kinds of knowledge and their ability to influence your own and others' practice.

1 'Research and theory merely tell practitioners what they know already, but perhaps hadn't thought about in that way.'
2 'Practitioners should do as they are told; policy-makers know best.'
3 'There's nothing so practical as a good theory!' (A favourite saying of the social psychologist Kurt Lewin)
4 'Research gets at the truth but practice is biased because it is driven by ideologies.'
5 'Great talkers are not necessarily effective practitioners; knowing what to do in theory is not the same as knowing how to do it in practice.'
6 'Good practice involves making choices about action; theory and research help to inform those choices.'
7 'Researchers simply identify patterns in practice so there's no need to inform research with theory.'
8 'You don't need to know any theory to be an effective practitioner.'
9 'Trainers have the solutions to practical problems so put their prescriptions faithfully into practice.'
10 'Theory is bunk – practitioners need to know what to do, not why they should do it.'

Four types of literature – theoretical, research, practice and policy...

Theoretical, research and practice knowledge that is written down and published, whether in paper or electronic form, constitutes much of the literature that you will read for your study. When you first come across a text, say a book or an article, it is worth identifying what type of literature it is. Different types of literature tend to emphasise claims to different kinds of knowledge. Each type of literature is also subject to particular limitations affecting the validity of the claims it embodies. The potential strengths or weaknesses of these claims are likely to depend on different factors. By identifying the type of literature at the outset you can alert yourself to what you should look for in the text to help you decide the extent to which any claims are convincing, including any generalisation about the extent of their applicability to different contexts.

Each kind of knowledge is commonly expressed through an associated type of literature, as summarised in Table 1.2. As you would expect, theoretical, research and practice knowledge are to be found in literature with the same name. The additional type is *policy* literature, which emphasises practice knowledge since policy-makers are essentially concerned with improving some domain of practice. They base their vision for improvement on their evaluation of the present situation according to the values and assumptions underlying their political ideology. Their evaluation of what is wrong with the present situation, and predictions about what will work better, may or may not be informed by the findings of research. For each type of literature, we have included an indicative list of limitations that may affect claims made. These potential limitations underline just how open to challenge and alternative interpretation knowledge of the social world may be. Becoming a critical reader entails developing the habit of questioning whether these sorts of limitations affect claims made in the literature you come across during your studies. Potential limitations such as these will be incorporated in guidance on developing a critical analysis of any literature text that we will be offering at the end of this chapter.

The distinctions we draw between types of literature are, of course, very crude. Most texts, whether an original study or a textbook summary, give greatest emphasis to one kind of knowledge. But many will reflect more than one, as in, say, a report of research which was informed by a particular theory, involved interviewing practitioners to gather their verbal accounts of their practice and culminated in recommendations for policy-makers that might indirectly lead to future improvement of that practice. Even here, we suggest that the authors' main purpose was to develop research knowledge. So we would categorise this report as research literature. You are sure to find a diversity of other texts relating to more than one kind of knowledge, such as:

▶ theoretical literature which draws on research findings about the practice of policy-making to develop a theory of the policy process;
▶ research literature based on data drawn from practice literature (e.g. research to determine the patterns, across a large number of inspection reports, of inspectors' judgements on particular domains of practice in individual organisations – see Chapter 4);
▶ research literature exploring the nature of the practice knowledge that practitioners are capable of making explicit (e.g. an investigation of practitioners' perceptions of good or bad practice in their experience – see Chapter 6);
▶ policy literature comprising a statement of policy-makers' vision for good practice that was developed in consultation with representatives of practitioners and with researchers.

Table 1.2 *Types of literature and indicative limitations of claims to knowledge expressed in them*

Type of literature	Common features	Some potential limitations of claims to knowledge
Theoretical (emphasises theoretical knowledge)	Academic theorists develop a system of related concepts and apply them to understand an aspect of the social world, and sometimes to advocate improvement in practice	▶ Key concepts may not be defined ▶ Concepts may not be mutually compatible ▶ Assumptions about the social world may be false ▶ Attention may be drawn away from important features of the social world ▶ A supposedly impartial theory may be affected by implicit values reflecting a particular ideology ▶ Explicit values underlying any advocated improvement may be unacceptable ▶ Evidence from the social world may not support the theory
Research (emphasises research knowledge)	Academic researchers or practitioners on advanced or undergraduate courses report on the conduct and outcomes of a systematic investigation into an aspect of the social world, and sometimes make recommendations for improving practice and policy	▶ The focus of the research may be diffuse ▶ The research may be atheoretical, yet employ theoretical ideas unsystematically ▶ Any conceptual framework may not be rigorously applied to inform data collection and analysis ▶ The design and methods may not be given in sufficient detail to check the rigour of the investigation ▶ The design and methods may be flawed ▶ Generalisations about the applicability of the findings to other contexts may lack sufficient supporting evidence ▶ The findings may contradict those of other research investigations ▶ Recommendations for improving practice and policy may not be adequately supported by the findings ▶ Values connected with an ideology about the aspect of the social world under investigation may affect the choice of topic for investigation and the findings
Practice (emphasises practice knowledge)	Academic tutors, informed professionals, trainers or experienced practitioners offer an account of lessons for good practice in an aspect of the social world, based on personal experience or on the evaluation of others' practice	▶ Significant factors affecting the capacity to improve practice may be ignored ▶ Criteria for judging the quality of practice may be implicit and unjustified ▶ Generalisations about the applicability of any advocated practice and means of improvement to other contexts may lack sufficient supporting evidence ▶ Values connected with an ideology about good practice and how most effectively to improve it may affect recommendations for practice and how to improve it ▶ The evidence base may be flimsy, narrow and impressionistic

| Policy (emphasises practice knowledge) | Policy-makers and their agents articulate a vision of improved practice in an aspect of the social world and the means of achieving their vision | ▶ Implicit or explicit assumptions about the need for improvement and the content of the vision may be based on values connected with a political ideology which is unacceptable
▶ Any analysis of the current situation, the vision and means of achieving it may be uninformed by research and may contradict research findings |

...and five sorts of intellectual project for studying that produce literature

The authors' purposes determine which kinds of knowledge they draw upon and generate in creating any type of literature. Many areas of study that relate closely to a professional practice, such as education, are *applied fields* of enquiry. These fields take concepts, models and theories from various *social science disciplines* including sociology, psychology, philosophy or economics. But academic study in applied fields is largely driven by a concern with improving practice, and so reflects whatever range of values those engaged in this study hold about practice and its improvement. A useful way of alerting yourself to the different purposes for producing literature is to consider the intellectual project undertaken by any author of a text. Drawing on the classification offered by Bolam (1999), we have distinguished between five intellectual projects for studying the social world (Table 1.3). They serve different purposes that affect the nature of the knowledge claims and associated literature that is produced. By a project here we mean a scheme of enquiry to generate the kinds of knowledge that will achieve specified purposes. The five intellectual projects are:

▶ *knowledge-for-understanding* – attempting to develop theoretical and research knowledge from a disinterested standpoint towards an aspect of the social world, in order to understand, rather than improve, practice and policy and their underlying ideologies;
▶ *knowledge-for-critical evaluation* – attempting to develop theoretical and research knowledge from an explicitly negative standpoint towards practice and policy, in order to criticise and expose the prevailing ideology underlying existing practice and policy and to argue why it should be rejected, and sometimes advocating improvement according to an alternative ideology;
▶ *knowledge-for-action* – attempting to develop theoretical and research knowledge with practical application from a positive standpoint towards practice and policy, in order to inform improvement efforts within the prevailing ideology;
▶ *instrumentalism* – attempting to impart practice knowledge and associated skills through training and consultancy from a positive standpoint towards practice and policy, in order directly to improve practice within the prevailing ideology;
▶ *reflexive action* – attempting to develop and share practitioners' own practice knowledge from a constructively self-critical standpoint towards their work, in order to improve their practice either within the prevailing ideology or according to an alternative ideology.

Table 1.3 *Five intellectual projects for studying aspects of the social world*

	Intellectual project for studying an aspect of the social world				
	Knowledge-for-understanding	**Knowledge-for-critical evaluation**	**Knowledge-for-action**	**Instrumentalism**	**Reflexive action**
Rationale	To understand policy and practice through theory and research	Critically to evaluate policy and practice through theory and research	To inform policy makers' efforts to improve practice through research and evaluation	To improve practitioners' practice through training and consultancy	To improve practitioners' own practice through evaluation and action for improvement
Typical mode of working	Social science-based basic research and theory	Social science-based basic research and theory	Applied research, evaluation and development activity	Designing and offering training and consultancy programmes	Action research, basing practice on evidence
Value stance towards an aspect of the social world	Disinterested towards policy and practice	Critical about policy and practice	Positive towards policy and the possibility of improving practice	Positive towards policy and the possibility of improving practice	Critical of practitioners' own practice and positive about the possibility of improving it
Typical question about the social world	What happens and why?	What is wrong with what happens and why?	How effective are interventions to improve practice?	How may this programme improve practice?	How effective is my practice and how may I improve it?
Place of theoretical knowledge in the study	Informed by and generates social science theory	Informed by and generates social science theory	Informed by and generates practical theory	Largely atheoretical, informed by a practical theory of training	Variably atheoretical and developing a practical theory
Common types of published literature produced	Academics' social science-based theory and research (reference may be made in associated policy literature)	Academics' critical social science-based theory and research	Informed professionals' practice and academics' applied research (reference may be made in associated policy literature)	Trainers' and consultants' practice literature (reference may be made in associated policy literature)	Practitioners' practice literature
Main target audience for published literature	Policy-makers, academics, practitioners on advanced education programmes	Policy makers, academics, practitioners on advanced education programmes	Policy-makers, academics, trainers, practitioners on advanced education programmes	Practitioners, other trainers, those practitioners on education and training programmes	Practitioners themselves

If you are a participant on an advanced education programme, such as a masters degree or professional doctorate, you will be engaged in your own intellectual projects as you study for your assessed work. The emphasis of such programmes tends to be on developing your capacity to undertake the *knowledge-for-understanding, knowledge-for-critical evaluation* and *knowledge-for-action* projects, where critical reviewing of literature plays a central part in supporting or challenging claims to knowledge.

As a critical reader of the literature, identifying which intellectual project authors have undertaken is an invaluable way of giving yourself an overview of what they are trying to do, why and how they are doing it, who they are trying to communicate with and how they are attempting to convince their projected audience. An insight into their intellectual project offers clues about potentially profitable directions for your critical questioning. The intellectual project pursued by any authors whose literature you review will display certain features:

▶ their *rationale for undertaking the study* – indicating how explicit or implicit values about some aspect of the social world, theorising, research methodology and methods may affect their focus and the nature of the knowledge claims they make;
▶ their *typical mode of working* – suggesting which kinds of knowledge they are attempting to develop and how they make use of different types of literature;
▶ their *value stance* towards the aspect of the social world they are studying – reflecting their attitude towards policy and practice and attempts to improve them;
▶ the *typical question* or questions they ask about the social world – determining which aspects they attend to or ignore and the focus of the answers they obtain;
▶ their *assumptions about the place of theoretical knowledge* in the study – guiding whether they employ any explicit definition of individual concepts or those grouped into a theory, and influencing the extent to which ideas are drawn from the social sciences or practice;
▶ the *types of literature they produce* – reflecting their rationale for studying, the kinds of knowledge they are attempting to create, and the audience with whom they are trying to communicate;
▶ the *target audience* being addressed – the people concerned with the aspect of the social world whose understanding or practice they wish to inform.

We have compared the five intellectual projects and their features in Table 1.3. When reading literature, you may identify the authors' intellectual project by considering each feature in turn to check which project it best fits. Bear in mind that these categories are crude and that intellectual projects are not always pursued separately in reality (e.g. pages 174–6). You may expect to come across authors whose activity spans more than one intellectual project, as where an account of social science-based research designed primarily to generate knowledge-for-understanding includes in the conclusion some recommendations for improving policy and practice (reflecting a knowledge-for-action agenda). However, even in such cases, we contend that you will be able to identify the main emphasis of a study as being connected with a single intellectual project.

We have now presented the key and components of your mental map for making sense of the literature you may be expected critically to read. Before considering how you may use this map to help you conduct a critical analysis of a particular text, you should be clear how your critical analysis of each individual text might contribute towards your review of a multiplicity of texts relating to the aspect of the social world you are studying. But what exactly is a literature review?

Reviewing the literature

A review of the literature is something personal. It is a product of the intellect of whoever took charge of their academic learning activity by deciding the focus, selecting texts for review, interpreting and engaging critically with them, ordering and synthesising what was found, and writing the final account. We define a literature review as:

> *a reviewer's critical account designed to convince a particular audience about what published (and possibly also unpublished) theory, research, practice or policy texts indicate is and is not known about one or more questions framed by the reviewer.*

Note what this definition excludes. We have all too often come across what students have called their literature review, but which consists of no more than an unfocused summary description of the content of diverse texts relating to some aspect of the social world, relying heavily on lengthy direct quotations. Such efforts would scarcely count as a literature review, according to our definition, because the students have not taken charge of their learning activity. Such attempts at a review are uncritical, merely restating what is in the texts; they are not built round the development of any argument; they are not obviously targeted at any identifiable audience; they fail to establish both the extent and the limits of what is known; and they are not demonstrably devoted to answering a specified question or issue. Avoid these pitfalls when you come to conduct a literature review!

Professionally conducted literature reviews that you are likely to read, like the one in Part 3, are written for publication. They are self-contained and designed to bring together knowledge that is dispersed within the literature on an aspect of the social world. Any literature review that you conduct for a course assignment, dissertation or thesis will be designed similarly to synthesise knowledge. But your review is a significant element of your academic apprenticeship, so it is also written for critical academic readers to assess. You have to communicate effectively, meet the assessment criteria and convince your assessors of the claims you make. For a dissertation or thesis, your review must function as an integral part of the development of your overall argument.

Whether written for publication or assessment, a literature review is integral to the knowledge-for-understanding, knowledge-for-critical evaluation and knowledge-for-action intellectual projects. It has several features. First, its *purpose* dictates its focus: an academic review relates to a review question or issue that may be:

- *substantive* (about some aspect of the social world – see page 216);
- *theoretical* (the concepts, theories or models informing the substantive question or issue);
- *methodological* (the approach to conducting the study).

The attempt to address this question or issue drives the reviewing process. It provides a criterion for selecting some texts for inclusion and rejecting others, the rationale for reading selectively within a text, the basis for a critical analysis of what has been read, and the focus for synthesising findings into a logically structured account putting forward a convincing argument. Second, the review synthesises claims to knowledge contained in a range of relevant texts in answering this question, attempting to demonstrate to the target *audience* the basis of reviewers' informed judgements about what is known, how strong the evidence is and what is not known from others' work relevant to the identified substantive, conceptual or methodological question. Third, it also enables reviewers to demonstrate the *significance* of their question and why an answer is worth seeking. The significance of a substantive question may be for the development of research or practice knowledge in the field of enquiry, that of a theoretical question may be for theory development, and that of a methodological question for justifying the choice of research methods. Finally, it enables reviewers to *locate their own work within the wider body of knowledge* in the area to which the substantive, conceptual or methodological questions are applied.

Producing a high-quality literature review is a challenging task. One secret of success is to clarify the guiding question or issue at the outset (we suggest that framing an issue as a question will help you to focus with precision on answering it) then sustain that focus right through to the conclusion (see also pages 178–9). Another secret is to remember always to be constructive when evaluating the literature, ensuring that your judgements are clearly backed by what you have found. If it turns out that what is known in relation to your question is not particularly robust or conceptually coherent, state this and justify your assertion. But then be prepared to suggest how, in your best, literature-informed, professional or academic judgement, the knowledge base could be enhanced, related practice improved or theory developed.

In our view, a high-quality literature review is likely to be:

- *focused* on an explicit substantive, conceptual or methodological question or issue;
- *structured* so as to address each question, perhaps broken down into sub-questions, in a logical sequence (see Chapter 10);
- *critical*, evaluating the extent to which any theoretical orientation is clear and coherent and any knowledge claims and the arguments they support are convincing (e.g. page 68);
- *accurately referenced*, so that each source can be followed up by readers of the review;
- *clearly expressed* to help your audience read the review easily;
- *reader-friendly*, introducing each question to be addressed;

▶ *informative*, providing synthesis through a strong conclusion which summarises a reviewer's answer to each question or sub-question according to the literature cited and its strengths and weaknesses, and arbitrating between any opposing positions reviewed;

▶ *balanced*, indicating that whatever range of viewpoints expressed in the literature about each question have been carefully weighed, and that the reviewer's judgements are demonstrably based on a careful assessment of the relevant strengths and limitations of that literature.

These characteristics of a high-quality literature review are worth applying self-critically to your own writing which results from your critical reading of the literature for your assessed work. For more detailed general guidance on reviewing the literature, we recommend that you consult the sources in the annotated list in Appendix 1.

Taking charge: developing a critical analysis of a text

Since a literature review is built up by synthesising material from different sources, a useful starting point is to do a critical analysis of each selected text as you read it. You may guide your reading and reflection by asking the ten critical questions and, as appropriate, their sub-questions set out in the critical analysis form reproduced here (see Figure 1.3). They relate to the mental map we offered for charting your way through the literature and to our advice on developing a high-quality literature review. Most questions or sub-questions are followed by examples of more detailed prompts (in brackets) that you could use in examining the text in search of your answers. The questions are grouped to form a sequence:

▶ Question 1 encourages you to think about why you have selected the text and how your critical analysis of it may contribute to your enquiry.
▶ Questions 2, 3, and 4 guide you in determining what the authors are attempting to do and in summarising whatever content of the text is of significance to you.
▶ Questions 5, 6, 7, 8 and 9 help you critically to analyse different aspects of this content to see how far it is convincing.
▶ Question 10 invites you to form a conclusion, in the light of your critical analysis, based on your informed judgement about the extent to which any claims relating to the focus of your enquiry are convincing, and why.

In Figure 1.3 we have introduced each question or group of questions in this sequence (in bold italics). We have given a brief commentary on each question (in italics) and have referred to relevant sections in the present chapter so that you may go back to them when working on the critical analysis of a text.

Figure 1.3 *Advice on making effective use of questions to ask as a critical reader of a text.*

Critical Analysis of a Text

Question 1 invites you to be self-critical by justifying to yourself why you are reading the text, and how your critical analysis of it is directed towards achieving a constructive purpose. Asking this question every time you examine a text helps you to avoid the pitfalls of reading material that is not relevant to your purpose, or of writing an unfocused description of everything you read rather than a critical literature review!

1. **What review question am I asking of this text?** (e.g. what is my central question? why select this text? does the critical analysis of this text fit into my investigation with a wider focus? what is my constructive purpose in undertaking a critical analysis of this text?)

It is crucial that you begin by identifying a question or issue that you wish to address through your critical analysis of one or more texts drawn from the relevant literature. This question or issue provides you with a rationale for selecting a particular text and a constructive purpose for reading it critically. Any text should potentially contribute to addressing the question or issue. (See the section on reviewing the literature.)

Questions 2, 3 and 4 help you to work out, in summary, what the authors of a text are trying to achieve and what they are attempting to communicate to their target audience. These questions also alert you to potentially fruitful lines of critical questioning.

2. **What type of literature is this?** (e.g. theoretical, research, practice, policy? are there links with other types of literature?)

Identifying the main type of literature that the text belongs to will help you to predict what its features are likely to be. The type of literature will indicate the main kind of knowledge embodied in any claim, enabling you to check whether potential limitations of this kind of knowledge apply. (See the section on types of literature, including Table 1.2.)

3. **What sort of intellectual project for study is being undertaken?**

Establishing the authors' intellectual project will clue you in to what they are trying to achieve, why and how. You will be aware of whom they are seeking to convince of their argument and associated claims to knowledge. You will then be in a good position to ask critical questions about what they have done. (See the section on different sorts of intellectual project, including Table 1.3.)

(a) *How clear is it which intellectual project the authors are undertaking?* (e.g. knowledge-for-understanding, knowledge-for-critical evaluation, knowledge-for-action, instrumentalism, reflexive action?)

(b) *How is the intellectual project reflected in the authors' mode of working?* (e.g. a social science or a practical orientation? choice of methodology and methods? an interest in understanding or in improving practice?)

(c) *What value stance is adopted towards the practice or policy investigated?* (e.g. disinterested, critical, positive, unclear? what assumptions are made about the possibility of improvement? whose practice or policy is the focus of interest?)

(d) *How does the sort of intellectual project being undertaken affect the research questions addressed?* (e.g. investigating what happens? what is wrong? how well does a particular policy or intervention work in practice?)

(e) *How does the sort of intellectual project being undertaken affect the place of theory?* (e.g. is the investigation informed by theory? generating theory? atheoretical? developing social science theory or a practical theory?)

(f) *How does the authors' target audience affect the reporting of research?* (e.g. do the authors assume academic knowledge of methods? criticise policy? offer recommendations for action?) ▶

▶ **4. What is being claimed?**

As a basis for considering whether what the authors have written is convincing, you will need to identify any argument that they are putting forward in the text and to clarify the main claims to particular kinds of knowledge that underlie it. Concentrate on identifying a small number of major ideas by summarising the content of the text. Try to avoid getting distracted by lots of minor details. (See the section on kinds of knowledge, including Figure 1.2.) As further preparation for critical consideration of the authors' claims, it is helpful to work out the degree of certainty with which any knowledge claim is asserted and the degree to which the authors generalise beyond the context from which the claim to knowledge was derived. (See the section on dimensions of variation among knowledge claims, including Figure 1.1.)

(a) *What are the main kinds of knowledge claim that the authors are making?* (e.g. theoretical knowledge, research knowledge, practice knowledge?)
(b) *What is the content of the main claims to knowledge and of the overall argument?* (e.g. what, in a sentence, is being argued? what are the three to five most significant claims that encompass much of the detail? are there key prescriptions for improving policy or practice?)
(c) *How clear are the authors' claims and overall argument?* (e.g. stated in an abstract, introduction or conclusion? unclear?)
(d) *With what degree of certainty do the authors make their claims?* (e.g. do they indicate tentativeness? qualify their claims by acknowledging limitations of their evidence? acknowledge others' counter-evidence? acknowledge that the situation may have changed since data collection?)
(e) *How generalised are the authors' claims – to what range of phenomena are they claimed to apply?* (e.g. the specific context from which the claims were derived? other similar contexts? a national system? a culture? universal? implicit? unspecified?)
(f) *How consistent are the authors' claims with each other?* (e.g. do all claims fit together in supporting an argument? do any claims contradict each other?)

Questions 5, 6, 7, 8 and 9 are complementary critical questions. Each helps you to focus on a different potential challenge to the claims to knowledge underlying any argument. Together, your answers to these questions provide a basis for your critical evaluation of the text as a whole and its contribution to answering your review question (Question 1 above) that guides your critical analysis as a contribution to your constructive purpose.

5. To what extent is there backing for claims?

It is important to check the extent to which the main claims to knowledge on which any argument rests are sufficiently well supported to convince you, whether through evidence provided by the authors or through other sources of backing. (See the section on dimensions of knowledge claims, including Figure 1.1, and the section on types of literature, including the potential limitations of claims to knowledge listed in Table 1.2.)

(a) *How transparent are any sources used to back the claims?* (e.g. is there any statement of the basis for assertions? are sources unspecified?)
(b) *What, if any, range of sources is used to back the claims?* (e.g. first-hand experience? the authors' own practice knowledge or research? literature about others' practice knowledge or research? literature about reviews of practice knowledge or research? literature about others' polemic?)
(c) *If claims are at least partly based on the authors' own research, how robust is the evidence?* (e.g. is the range of sources adequate? are there methodological limitations or flaws in the methods employed? do they include cross-checking or 'triangulation' of accounts? what is the sample size and is it large enough to support the claims being made? is there an adequately detailed account of data collection and analysis? is a summary given of all data reported?)
(d) *Are sources of backing for claims consistent with the degree of certainty and the degree of generalisation?* (e.g. is there sufficient evidence to support claims made with a high degree of certainty? is there sufficient evidence from other contexts to support claims entailing extensive generalisation?)

▶

▶ **6. How adequate is any theoretical orientation to back claims?**

Any text must employ certain concepts to make sense of whatever aspect of the social world is being discussed. Many texts will feature an explicit theoretical orientation as a framework for understanding and possibly as a basis for the authors' recommendations for improvement. You will need to decide whether the claims being made are clear and coherent, and whether you accept the assumptions on which they rest. To assist your critical reflection, check which concepts and other tools for thinking have been used, what they are taken to mean and how they frame the claims being made. (See the section on tools for thinking, the section on types of literature, including the potential limitations of claims to knowledge listed in Table 1.2, and the section on different sorts of intellectual project, including Table 1.3.)

(a) *How explicit are the authors about any theoretical orientation or conceptual framework?* (e.g. is there a conceptual framework guiding data collection? is a conceptual framework selected after data collection to guide analysis? is there a largely implicit theoretical orientation?)

(b) *What assumptions does any explicit or implicit theoretical orientation make that may affect the authors' claims?* (e.g. does a perspective focus attention on some aspects and underemphasise others? if more than one perspective is used, how coherently do the different perspectives relate to each other?)

(c) *What are the key concepts underpinning any explicit or implicit theoretical orientation?* (e.g. are they listed? are they stipulatively defined? are concepts mutually compatible? is use of concepts consistent? is the use of concepts congruent with others' use of the same concepts?)

7. To what extent does any value stance adopted affect claims?

Since no investigation of the social world can be completely value-free, all claims to knowledge will reflect the value stance adopted. So it is important to check what values have guided the authors of any text, how these values affect their claims and the extent to which the value stance makes the claims more or less convincing. (See the section on tools for thinking, the section on types of literature, including the potential limitations of claims to knowledge listed in Table 1.2, and the section on different sorts of intellectual project, including Table 1.3.)

(a) *How explicit are the authors about any value stance connected with the phenomena?* (e.g. a disinterested, critical or positive stance? is this stance informed by a particular ideology? is it adopted before or after data collection?)

(b) *How may any explicit or implicit value stance adopted by the authors affect their claims?* (e.g. have they pre-judged the phenomena discussed? are they biased? is it legitimate for the authors to adopt their particular value stance? have they overemphasised some aspects of the phenomenon while underemphasising others?)

8. To what extent are claims supported or challenged by others' work?

It is highly improbable that any study of an aspect of the social world will be unrelated to others' work. A valuable check is therefore to examine whether links are made with other studies, and the degree to which others' work supports the claims being made. You may wish to refer to other texts that address phenomena related to the text you are analysing.

(a) *Do the authors relate their claims to others' work?* (e.g. do the authors refer to others' published evidence, theoretical orientations or value stances to support their claims? do they acknowledge others' counter-evidence?)

(b) *How robust is any evidence from others' work used to support claims?* (e.g. see question 5(c))

(c) *How robust is any evidence from others' research and practice that challenges the authors' claims?* (e.g. see question 5(c))

9. To what extent are claims consistent with my experience?

Your own experience of the social world will probably not be identical to that being studied in the text, but it is still relevant. In considering how convincing the claims made in a text may be, it is worth checking whether these claims have significant similarities with your experience and also evaluating whether they sound feasible or unrealistic, given what you know from experience.

▶

▶ *Question 10 requires you to sum up what you have learned from the answers you have gained from all the previous questions and to come to an overall well-informed and balanced judgement about the convincingness of the claims being made. What you have learned contributes to addressing your review question (Question 1) that led you to select the text and develop your critical analysis of it, and ultimately towards achieving your underlying constructive purpose.*

10. What is my summary evaluation of the text in relation to my review question or issue?

In making a summary evaluation of the text, you need to support your own best literature-informed professional or academic judgement by seeking backing from the answers you have gained to the critical questions (5 to 9 above).

(a) *How convincing are the authors' claims, and why?*
(b) *How, if at all, could the authors have provided stronger backing for their claims?*

Both your summary evaluation and the more detailed answers to all the other questions (1-9 above) will now be available for you to draw upon selectively in writing your account of the text as you address the question or issue that has driven your critical reading activity.

There is a blank critical analysis form in Appendix 2. You may wish to photo-copy it and then complete one form for each text that you analyse in detail. If you have access to a computer, you may prefer to create a master file by typing in the content of the blank form and then use it as a template. You will be able to copy the master file for each text you critically analyse and fill in your answers to the questions. You may save each completed critical analysis form as a separate file on your computer or print it out as your record. Computerising the form in this way would offer you the flexibility to write as much as you like in response to each question.

We invite you to help yourself learn to be a more critical reader by review-ing any of the research reports in Part 2 or the literature review in Part 3. Completing the critical analysis form for each chapter you review and refer-ring back to topics discussed in this chapter as necessary will help you to form the habit of being critical when reading the literature. The form is designed to apply to most types of literature that you are likely to meet in the course of your studies, including material that you may download from the Internet. You could use the form to guide you in reviewing any other literature in any area of study connected with the social world. But do not forget that you must take charge of the review process. It is your responsibility to learn how to make creative and selective use of the guidance we have offered, according to the question or issue you wish to address. So it is for you to decide which critical analysis questions are most important for any individual text, what your answers are to them, and how to combine what you have found into an account which will stand up to the scrutiny of your assessors.

We have included a couple of critical literature review exercises that you may either use as they stand or adapt to suit review questions that you would like to answer. They are designed to help you make the transition from being a critical reader to a self-critical writer, and both are based on the critical analysis of individual texts. We suggest that you try them out on texts which are cen-tral to a review you wish to undertake, and that you take our earlier advice about focusing and either use the questions we have supplied if they are appropriate, or else devise your own.

Exercise 1 is a *single-text critical review* of a chapter or article reporting on research. Any of the chapters in Parts 2 or 3 would be suitable, or you may choose an article or chapter from other literature. You may wish to focus on answering the two review questions we have suggested or put forward your own. The suggested structure for the single-text review relates directly to the ten questions contained in the critical analysis form. So you may read your text, complete the critical analysis form, then write your review of this text based on your answers to the critical analysis questions.

Exercise 1
Single-text critical review of a chapter or article reporting on research

You are invited to review one of the chapters in Part 2 or 3, or to choose an article or chapter reporting on research from other literature. Your task is to write a critical review of the article or chapter, of up to 1,000 words, to answer these two review questions:

1 What does the literature reviewed suggest may be key factors promoting or inhibiting the effectiveness of (a particular aspect of practice that you have chosen in the field of enquiry)?
2 To what extent are the factors identified applicable to my professional context or one known to me?

The critical analysis questions to ask when reviewing a chapter or article are contained in the critical analysis form (Appendix 2). You are recommended to divide your written account into a sequence of sections and devise your own subheading for each section relating to the area of practice which is the focus for your critical review.

Suggested structure for your single-text critical review

Title
▶ Your choice of title should include the keywords that will indicate to the reader what you are doing (a critical review of a selected piece of literature) and the aspect of practice that forms your focus.

Introduction to the critical review (about 100 words)
▶ A statement of the purpose of your review – critically to review the selected text (give the names of the authors, the title of the chapter or article and the date of publication) as a contribution to answering the two review questions:
   1 'What does the selected literature reviewed suggest may be key factors promoting or inhibiting the effectiveness of (the particular aspect of practice in the field of enquiry you have chosen)?'
   2 'To what extent are the factors identified applicable to my professional context or one known to me?'

▶

Summary of the research design – what the investigators were trying to find out and what they did (about 200 words)
▶ A summary of the authors' purposes for the text and the kind of enquiry they engaged in, including an indication of the type of literature they produced (refer to your answer to critical analysis question 2) and their intellectual project (refer to your answer to critical analysis question 3).
▶ A brief indication of why this text is relevant to the review questions guiding your critical review (critical analysis question 1).
▶ A brief summary of how they went about their investigation (e.g. the research design, methodology, sample, methods of data collection and analysis).

The authors' main findings and any broader claims relating to the review questions for the critical review (about 200 words)
▶ A comparative summary of the main claims made by the authors of the text relevant to key factors promoting or inhibiting the effectiveness of the aspect of practice on which you have chosen to focus (refer to your answer to critical analysis question 4) – a synthesis of, say, up to five main points.
▶ An indication of the range of contexts to which the authors claim or appear to claim that their findings may apply (e.g. they imply that their claims about effectiveness apply to all contexts or do not specify any limits on the extent to which they may be universally applicable).

Evaluation of the authors' main findings and any broader claims relating to the review questions for the critical review (about 300 words)
▶ Your comparative evaluation of these findings and any broader claims, critically assessing how far they are convincing *for the context from which these claims were derived.* (Refer to your answers to critical analysis questions 5–9, possibly referring to additional literature to support your judgement in relation to critical analysis question 8.) In your critique, you may wish to refer back to your earlier account of the authors' purpose, intellectual project and how they went about their enquiry (e.g. you may wish to assert that the value stance of particular authors led to bias which affected their findings).
▶ Your comparative and critical assessment of how far the claims made by the authors of the text may be applicable to *your professional context or one known to you* (critical analysis questions 5–9, possibly referring to additional literature to support your judgement in relation to critical analysis question 8). In your critique you may wish to refer back to your earlier account of how the authors went about their enquiry (e.g. you may wish to assert that the findings from a particular intellectual project were derived from a context which is so different from yours that you consider the prescriptions for practice emerging from this work are unlikely to apply directly to your context).

Conclusion (about 200 words)
▶ Your brief overall evaluation of the text reviewed to assess its contribution to answering your review questions (refer to your answer to critical analysis question 10).
▶ The summary answer to the first review question offered by the text reviewed, including a statement of your judgement, with reasons, about

▶

how far the findings and any broader claims are convincing for the context from which they were derived.

▶ The summary answer to the second review question, including a statement of your judgement, with reasons, about how far the findings and
any broader claims are applicable (e.g. at how high a level of abstraction?) to your professional context or one known to you.

References

▶ Give the full reference for the chapter or article you have reviewed.

▶ If you refer to any additional literature, list the texts to which you have
referred, following the normal conventions for compiling a reference list.

Exercise 2 takes the review process a step further by inviting you to undertake
a *multiple-text review* of three or more texts reporting research which are relevant to the same aspect of practice in the field of enquiry. You will have to
group and synthesise your answers to critical analysis questions for each text
in writing your review. The suggested structure offers one way of doing so. As
with the first exercise, you may use one or more of the chapters in Parts 2 and
3, and other texts that you choose for yourself. Either focus on the review
questions we have suggested or formulate one or more alternatives. You may
read your chosen texts, complete the critical analysis form for each of them,
then write your review by synthesising your answers to particular critical
analysis questions across all these texts. Completing this exercise will result in
an in-depth account whose length will be roughly equivalent to that of many
assignments for masters courses.

Exercise 2
Multiple-text critical review on reports of research

You are invited to review three or more chapters from Part 2 or 3, or to
choose one or more articles, chapters or books reporting on research from
other literature. Your task is to write a critical review of these texts together,
referring to other literature as appropriate, of up to 4,000 words. The review
is designed to answer these two review questions:

1 What does the literature reviewed suggest may be key factors promoting
or inhibiting the effectiveness of (a particular aspect of practice that you
have chosen in the field of enquiry)?

2 To what extent are the factors identified applicable to my professional
context or one known to me?

Whatever texts you choose, they should all focus on the same aspect of
practice in the field of enquiry. The critical analysis questions to ask when

▶

reviewing a chapter or article are contained in the critical analysis form (Appendix 2). You are recommended to divide your written account into a sequence of sections and devise your own subheading for each section relating to the area of practice which is the focus for your critical review.

Suggested structure for your multiple-text critical review

Title
▶ Your choice of title should include the keywords that will indicate to the reader what you are doing (a critical literature review) and the aspect of practice that forms your focus.

Introduction to the critical review (250–750 words)
▶ A statement of the purpose of your review – critically to review the selected texts in depth as a contribution to answering the two review questions:
  1 'What does the selected literature reviewed suggest may be key factors promoting or inhibiting the effectiveness of (the particular aspect of practice in the field of enquiry you have chosen)?'
  2 'To what extent are the factors identified applicable to my professional context or one known to me?'
▶ Your justification for selecting this area of practice (e.g. its significance for improving the aspect of practice), perhaps referring to other literature to support your argument.
▶ Your acknowledgement of the scope of your critical review (e.g. an indication of the texts you will analyse in depth, giving the names of the authors, title and date of publication for each, and the reasons why you selected them for critical review).
▶ Your acknowledgement of the limitations of your critical review (e.g. that your focus is confined to these few texts and there are likely to be others relating to this aspect of practice which you will not be examining in depth).
▶ An indication of the topics to be covered in each of the remaining sections of your review so that the reader can see how you will develop your argument.

Introduction to the texts being critically reviewed (250–750 words)
▶ A summary of the authors' purposes for each of the three or more texts and of the kind or kinds of enquiry they engaged in, including an indication of the type or types of literature they produced (refer to your answers to critical analysis question 2) and their intellectual projects (refer to your answers to critical analysis question 3).
▶ A brief indication of why these texts are relevant to the questions guiding your critical review (critical analysis question 1).
▶ A brief summary of how they went about their investigation, for example:
  – for a research report, the research design, sample, methods of data collection and analysis;
  – for a research synthesis, the sequence of topics addressed and range of sources employed;

- for a theoretical work, the main theoretical ideas, the sequence of topics and any use of evidence;
- for a practical handbook, the sequence of topics addressed and any use of evidence.

The authors' main claims relating to the questions for the critical review (500–1,000 words)

▶ A comparative summary of the main claims made by the authors of each text relevant to key factors promoting or inhibiting the effectiveness of the aspect of practice on which you have chosen to focus (refer to your answers to critical analysis question 4) – a synthesis of, say, up to five main points for each text reviewed, indicating the extent to which there is overlap between texts in the claims made.

▶ An indication of the range of contexts to which the authors claim or appear to claim that their findings may apply (e.g. they imply that their claims about effectiveness apply to all contexts or do not specify any limits on the extent to which they may be universally applicable).

Evaluation of the authors' main claims relating to the review questions for the critical review (1,500–2,000 words)

▶ Your comparative evaluation of these claims, critically assessing how far claims made by the authors of each text are convincing *for the context from which these claims were derived.* (Refer to your answers to critical analysis questions 5–9, possibly referring to additional literature to support your judgement in relation to critical analysis question 8). In your critique, you may wish to refer back to your earlier account of the authors' purpose, intellectual project and how they went about their enquiry (e.g. you may wish to assert that the value stance of particular authors led to bias which affected their findings).

▶ Your comparative and critical assessment of the extent to which the claims made by the authors of each text may be applicable to *your professional context or one known to you* (critical analysis questions 5–9, possibly referring to additional literature to support your judgement in relation to critical analysis question 8). In your critique you may wish to refer back to your earlier account of the authors' purpose, intellectual project and how they went about their enquiry (e.g. you may wish to assert that the findings from a particular intellectual project were derived from a context which is so different from yours that you consider the prescriptions for practice emerging from this work are unlikely to apply directly to your context).

Conclusion (250–750 words)

▶ Your brief overall evaluation of each of the three or more texts reviewed to assess their combined contribution to answering your review questions (refer to your answer to critical analysis question 10).

▶ The summary answer to the first review question offered by all the texts reviewed, including a statement of your judgement, with reasons, about how far the claims across all three or more texts are convincing for the contexts from which they were derived.

▶ The summary answer to the second review question, including a statement of your judgement, with reasons, about how far the claims across all three or more texts are applicable (e.g. at how high a level of abstraction?) to your professional context or one known to you.

▶ Reasons why you think, in the light of your critical review, that it may be difficult to determine the effectiveness of this aspect of practice and to apply generalisations about it between contexts.

References

▶ The list of texts to which you have referred, including those you have analysed in depth, following the normal conventions for compiling a reference list.

In the next chapter we will consider the process and reporting of a small-scale research investigation that is to be assessed. Both the literature review and your other references to it, whether to inform the study or interpret the findings, will be crucial components of your dissertation or thesis. Your ability to be self-critical as a writer will help you to ensure that you demonstrate to the critical readers who assess your work that you have engaged critically with the literature and have developed a convincing argument of your own.

References

Bolam, R. (1999) 'Educational administration, leadership and management: towards a research agenda', in T. Bush, L. Bell, R. Bolam, R. Glatter and P. Ribbins (eds), *Educational Management: Redefining Theory, Policy and Practice*. London: Paul Chapman.

Firestone, W. and Louis, K. S. (1999) 'Schools as cultures', in J. Murphy and K. S. Louis (eds), *Handbook of Research on Educational Administration*, 2nd edn. San Francisco: Jossey-Bass.

March, J. and Olsen, P. (1976) *Ambiguity and Choice in Organisations*. Bergen: Universitetsforlaget.

Chapter 2

Designing and writing about research: developing a critical frame of mind

Louise Poulson and Mike Wallace

We have examined the process of becoming a critical reader of literature, highlighting the connection with applying that knowledge in a self-critical way to designing and writing a research study. It is important that you come to think of yourself as part of a community of critical readers and writers of research. If you are participating in a postgraduate course or research programme, this community experience is a significant part of your induction into the world of academic enquiry. Being critical is partly a frame of mind, but it is also a self-checking mechanism for your work on a research enquiry. It enables you to question your ideas and your writing, and to read it with an awareness of how others may do so.

The purpose of this chapter is to examine the nature of small-scale research, looking at what is possible within such work, and considering what it might contribute to a field of enquiry. First, we discuss challenges that small-scale researchers face, indicating the key components that contribute to high-quality empirically based studies. Second, we put forward a model of the logic of the research process, distinguishing what you do from the account you write, and then discuss how researching and writing drafts of your account may be integrated as you go along. We consider some of the compromises that researchers have to make, especially when undertaking studies of modest scope. The emphasis is on applying a critical frame of mind to the dual process of conducting a small-scale research investigation and writing about it. A crucial outcome of your research will be communicating your ideas to other critical readers in the research community. You may be working on a dissertation or a thesis, a crucial part of your academic apprenticeship. Here you learn what researching is about by doing it for yourself and attempting to produce a convincing account of what you have found out. One key critical reader for your writing will be your supervisor and others will be your eventual examiners. Finally, we offer one way of structuring such a written account, consistent with our model and discussion of the research process.

Plenty of books are now available which offer detailed practical advice on the whole research process or on particular aspects of it. If you are undertaking small-scale research, we strongly recommend that you refer to such texts throughout your study. The annotated list in Appendix 1 contains several texts that you could use to supplement our general guidance.

Making the most of small-scale reseach

While much small-scale research is undertaken for dissertations and theses, many experienced professional researchers periodically engage in studies of similar scope. Sometimes their purpose is to explore a new idea or topic to find out whether it is feasible for a research enquiry, or to pilot a particular approach or instrument prior to undertaking a larger study. At other times small-scale research might be part of a major investigation, as where a case study is conducted of a specific aspect of the wider phenomenon being explored. Large studies often combine different components, each of which may vary widely in scope. The research reports in Part 2 offer examples of such small-scale research and also individual components of larger studies, some of which are more ambitious than you could realistically attempt for a dissertation or thesis. However, while the context in which such studies were done may be different from that of an individual completing a research investigation for a dissertation or thesis, many principles and procedures are similar. In the physical and natural sciences, doctoral theses may be written about an aspect of a much larger study when students work with their supervisor as part of a team in a laboratory. But in the humanities and the social sciences it is more likely that as a student you will work alone, perhaps researching a problem or an issue arising from your professional context.

A key question for all small-scale researchers is: how much is it possible to achieve in work of modest scope? Even if small in scale, a tightly focused study that is well designed and executed can contribute to the delineation of an issue or problem in the field of enquiry. It may open up a new avenue for investigation, illuminate and exemplify a substantive topic already identified within the field, or approach a familiar substantive issue from a different theoretical perspective. Less commonly, it might even develop a new methodological approach to a topic.

For a dissertation or thesis, one of the first things to do is to clarify the focus and define the parameters of the research. In short, you should identify your intellectual project: consider what you will concentrate on, and what is practicable for a lone researcher with limited resources and a tight time-scale. A challenge facing you is to design a study that is both practicable and of sufficient scope and significance to yield worthwhile data. Be wary of pre-judging what you will find (see Chapter 7)

Someone may be interested in an example of national policy change and how it impacts on practice in organisations affected. Obviously, a wide-ranging empirical investigation of the national context of policy implementation in a representative sample of organisations would be beyond the scope of most individual dissertations or theses. But an individual researcher could reasonably undertake a clearly delineated study of implementation in a locality, or even a single institution within a bounded time-scale. While the scope of such a study might be limited, if it were carefully thought out and conceptualised, it would still have the potential to make a contribution to understanding of the phenomenon. To do so, it would have to be narrowly focused, with a clear specification of what was being undertaken and an explanation of how it would be done. The specific problem or topic being studied would have to be linked to the wider context of the field of enquiry, indicating why it was a significant problem to study. In the example above, this linkage might be to the wider policy context, and perhaps to changing notions of practice in the organisations to implement the change.

A further means of strengthening the significance of a small-scale study is by making clear links between the work being conducted and existing literature in the field and, if appropriate, related fields. These links can be made in relation to three aspects of your enquiry (paralleling the focus for an academic literature review outlined in Chapter 1):

1 the *substantive* focus of the study – the particular topic or issue that constitutes the substance of the investigation within a field of enquiry;
2 the *theoretical* issues – how particular concepts, or theoretical perspectives, may guide and inform the study, and what the strengths and limitations of such perspectives are;
3 *methodological* approaches – in a particular field a methodology might be accepted as standard practice. You may use this approach in your study, or turn to a different methodology, perhaps by attempting to gain in-depth knowledge of a phenomenon in a particular context.

If the investigation makes strong substantive, theoretical and methodological connections with other studies within the field, its potential value will be enhanced. In relation to a dissertation or thesis, you might ask:

▶ How is my study similar to other work in substance, theory or methodology?
▶ In what ways does it build upon or extend previous work and is there other research that confirms the direction of my findings?
▶ What does my study do that has not been done before?

It is important to remember that small-scale research need not always generate its own data. The collection of *primary data* direct from the subjects of your research is often the most time-consuming, expensive and difficult part of an investigation. There are numerous statistical databases and other archive materials now accessible through the Internet which could be used as the basis for a study (see Chapter 4). Gorard (2001) exemplifies how he undertook a piece of small-scale research using *secondary data*: statistical information that had already been collected and was easily available through the Internet from government sources. He explains that he started by questioning the assertion made in research literature that schools in Wales did not perform as well as their counterparts in England. He then set out to test this assertion by using existing statistical data to reanalyse the comparative results of equivalent schools in both countries. Gorard outlines how using secondary data sources enabled him to tackle an important topic that would have been impossible had he attempted to collect the data himself:

The findings of this simple value-added analysis ran contrary to the schooled for failure hypothesis (about schools in Welsh LEAs). They defended children, teachers and schools in Wales, and met with considerable local media and some political interest... The complete study, including data collection, transcription and analysis took me one afternoon at an additional cost of less than £10 for photocopying and access to census figures. I would have been very happy to conduct this study for my masters' dissertation instead of traipsing round schools conducting yet another survey (which is what I actually did). I would have saved time, money and produced more interesting results for my discussion section.

(Gorard, 2001: 48)

Note that Gorard had a clearly focused idea for a study. It led to the formulation of a clearly specified hypothesis, firmly grounded within existing research literature. He then tested this hypothesis, not by attempting to collect new evidence himself, but by careful analysis of existing data. The outcome was an example of small-scale research that had wider significance and impact. It also showed how a key to successful small-scale research is achieving a balance between a tightly focused topic embodying a practicable design and making connections with the wider context in which the problem has arisen.

What makes for a high-quality final written account of a small-scale study? Here are the top ten components we, as critical readers, would look for:

1 a clearly-focused substantive topic, with the focus sustained throughout, incorporating a well defined broad central question leading to detailed research questions or hypotheses;
2 a critical review of literature in the field, and clear connections drawn between existing knowledge and the small-scale study (in terms of the substantive topic, theories and concepts, and methodology);
3 an appropriate methodological approach and detailed methods for answering the research questions or testing the hypotheses;
4 a well-structured and explicit design for the study whose methods are fit for their purpose;
5 data that is analysed thoroughly, with the processes of data preparation, summary and analysis clearly set out;
6 discussion of the analysis or findings that relates back to the original research questions or hypotheses, and to the critical review of literature;
7 a reflective summary of what the study has achieved, its strengths and weaknesses, any problematic issues that arose, and any implications for future research (and policy or practice if appropriate);
8 accurate referencing, both in the text and in the reference list, so that, in principle, any reference may be followed-up;
9 clear expression with attention to writing style, punctuation, spelling and grammar, so that the account may be easily understood;
10 the development of a logical argument from the title to the end of the account, providing as much backing as possible for the claims being made.

Make the most of your small-scale research by bearing these components in mind, together with the principles of self-critical writing outlined in Table 1.1 in the previous chapter, when planning the structure and presentation of your dissertation or thesis. It is also advisable to refer from the outset to the statement of criteria used in assessing your work that is likely to be included in the students' handbook for the programme. Ensure that your written account meets each of these criteria.

Box 2.1
Ten pitfalls to be avoided in a small-scale study

1 Too diffuse a focus for the study or attempting to collect too much data to analyse.
2 A descriptive or uncritical review of the literature ('X said this; Y said that').
3 Lack of linkage between the research questions and the review of literature.
4 No connection made between the research questions and the methodology and detailed methods of data collection chosen for the study.
5 Failure to make explicit how the study was designed: its time-scale, how the research subjects or sites sampled were chosen, how research instruments were designed and tested, or how the data were analysed.
6 Data not analysed in sufficient detail or depth to provide an answer to the research questions.
7 Inadequate description or explanation of what the data showed.
8 Lack of discussion of the findings and their significance, how they answered the research questions, tested the research hypotheses, or illuminated the issues studied.
9 Weak conclusions, and failure to return to the original questions or hypotheses and say what the study has achieved, what problems were encountered, and what issues arose from the work.
10 Over-ambitious or over-generalised recommendations for policy or practice that are not backed by evidence from the study.

Experiencing the reality of the research process

There is bound to be a difference between your experience while you are working through the research process and the final written account of it that you eventually produce at the end of your investigation. Early on, it is not uncommon to feel quite confused. Clarification comes with time because you are learning as the enquiry unfolds. At first, the focus may be diffuse, perhaps based on a hunch that some social practice needs improving. As you start on your literature review and each source leads you to further sources, the amount you feel you should read may seem to be ever expanding. Later on, the research methods you adopt may turn out to produce a mass of data that seems impossible to analyse. Even when writing up your findings you may be unclear how one section fits in with your other sections. Your fullest understanding about what you are doing comes only when you complete the final written account, because you have been learning throughout your research experience.

Yet this account of what you have done and what you have learned must be focused and logical, progressively developing and providing backing for the argument you are putting forward. Everything you have written should be linked to this focus. In our experience as supervisors, the more carefully planned and focused a research enquiry is from the outset, the easier students find it to conduct the research while writing draft sections of their account as they proceed, always working towards a defensible final written account that will stand up to the critical scrutiny of examiners. It is crucial to begin drafting your account from the outset of your study, amending and adding to it as your understanding of what you are doing and knowledge of the field increases. Expect to revise the draft of your introductory chapter several times as you gain clarity about your focus, but to revise the draft conclusion chapter only once.

One possible structure for organising the content of what you write in your dissertation or thesis will be offered at the end of the chapter. But first, we will guide you through a structured approach to the research process, where focusing and writing draft sections of your account are integral parts of your work from beginning to end.

Identifying a practicable topic and focusing your research

Most students begin work for a dissertation or thesis with a general idea of the area they are interested in researching or a particular issue that they want to address. It is likely that you will begin by identifying a substantive topic. Sources might include:

- your personal or professional experience;
- your current situation;
- your reading of literature in the field;
- a policy context or initiative;
- pilot or exploratory work;
- your supervisor's advice.

You can sharpen up what may start out as a vague idea for a topic by reformulating it as a *central question*, still expressed in general terms, that your investigation will make some contribution towards answering (e.g. page 195). If, say, you are interested in improving some area of practice in a particular organisation, you might pose this central question in such terms as: how effective is the area of practice in these kinds of organisation, and how may it be improved? Note that the central question is not specific to practice in any particular organisation. It may even help to adopt the central question as your title for your dissertation or thesis as a way of focusing your effort and indicating to your eventual readers the focus of your enquiry.

It is a good idea at this early stage to ask yourself *why* you are interested in the particular topic, and *from where* the idea has come. You might be intrigued by a topic or concerned about a problem that has arisen from your professional practice. It might be a more theoretical issue that you have come across in your reading which you want to explore in a practical setting. You might want to examine an aspect of policy or the relationship between policy and practice.

Working out three more specific *aims* for your research will help you further to sharpen your thinking about how you will address this topic and make a contribution to answering the central question:

▶ your *substantive* aim focuses on exactly what you intend to find out about the substantive topic (e.g. to determine factors affecting the effectiveness of some aspect of a policy or practice in a specific context);
▶ your *theoretical* aim focuses on what concepts and, perhaps, overarching theory you intend to employ to realise your substantive aim (e.g. to employ a particular set of concepts as a framework for investigating your chosen aspect of the policy or practice in this specific context);
▶ your *methodological* aim focuses on how you are going to find out what you will be seeking to realise your substantive aim (e.g. to employ a particular methodology, research design and methods of data collection and analysis to address your central question by investigating the aspect of the policy or practice in this context).

Once you have identified why you are interested in the topic, a further question is: why is this topic important or worth addressing as a piece of small-scale research? Its significance might relate to your intellectual project, depending on whether you are concerned with understanding the nature of policy and practice, developing a critique, improving practice by informing policy-makers, developing guidance for practitioners or informing your own practice. Initially, it may not be easy to identify your intellectual project, but as you begin to define and refine your research topic and central question, referring back to our classification of intellectual projects (Table 1.3 in Chapter 1) will help you to clarify the purpose of your study.

In attempting to fulfil your three aims, you will need to think through how you will address related *issues or problems* to which your effort will give rise. Fulfilling your substantive aim will entail deciding exactly which aspects of your substantive topic you will be investigating in detail in the specific context for your investigation. Fulfilling your theoretical aim will entail considering the strengths and limitations of the theory or set of concepts you will be employing to help you focus on particular aspects of the substantive topic. Fulfilling your methodological aim will entail reflecting on the strengths and limitations of the methodological approach to understanding the social world and the methods you will employ to investigate the substantive topic.

The next stage in your thinking is to try expressing the specific aspects of the substantive topic that interest you as initial ideas for more detailed and specific *research questions or hypotheses* that link with your broader central question (e.g. page 137). Suppose it is a policy, or the relationship between a policy and practice. Which particular aspect of that policy are you interested in? Over what period of time? In relation to whom or what? While you may identify research questions early on, you will probably continue clarifying your focus as you read and review the relevant literature, refining your research questions or hypotheses as you proceed.

It is important to make explicit your own *value stance* towards the substantive topic that will affect your intellectual project in undertaking your investigation, as we highlighted in the first chapter. Surfacing your value stance is not always easy. People are not always aware of their own beliefs, values and assumptions because they are frequently held as part of a world-view, or ideology, within which particular practices or beliefs are taken to be normal or natural. However, part of becoming a critical reader and self-critical writer is to raise your awareness of the implicit beliefs, values and assumptions that you hold, and how they might be different from those of others. Your value stance will affect the nature of your central question and so the content and outcomes of your enquiry.

Framing your ideas as a central question and perhaps initial ideas for more detailed research questions is an important step in clarifying what you are aiming to do, and in assessing whether you have identified a practicable study. The gradual process of identifying, refining and answering research questions connected with a more general central question will drive the research process and the associated structure for writing it up, as outlined in Figure 2.1. The logic of the process is first to ask worthwhile focusing questions and then to answer them through your enquiry.

Potentially insightful research questions are characteristically:

▶ capable of being stated clearly and concisely;
▶ answerable because they are specific enough to be investigated convincingly;
▶ new, not having been asked by others already;
▶ practicable, so that they can be answered within the time, resources and methodologies available;
▶ linked to theory, policy or practice.

When starting to frame your thoughts about the central question as specific research questions, you can ask yourself of each one: am I asking a research question that I can feasibly answer within the limits of small-scale research? If the question does not seem possible to answer, then you might ask how you could modify it so that it becomes answerable. Experiment with the formulation of your research questions until they are clear, succinct and focused. You will probably find that your initial ideas for research questions are soon revised. As you begin to review the literature or undertake pilot work (a preliminary investigation), the research questions may become more specific, or subsidiary questions may be generated. Sometimes the focus of these research questions may shift as you learn more about the topic. Whatever your approach, it is worth reviewing your research questions regularly, and considering whether they should be

Figure 2.1 *The logic of the research process as reflected in the written account.*

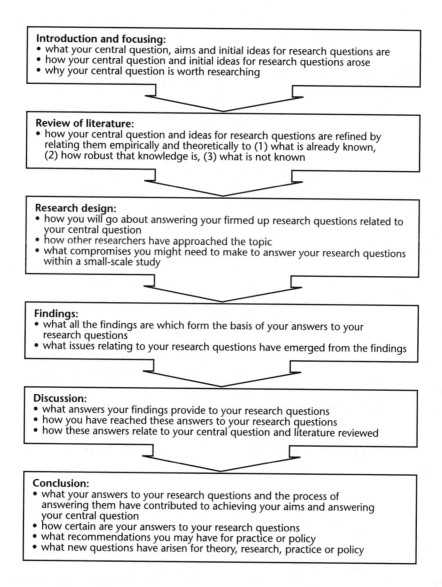

Introduction and focusing:
- what your central question, aims and initial ideas for research questions are
- how your central question and initial ideas for research questions arose
- why your central question is worth researching

Review of literature:
- how your central question and ideas for research questions are refined by relating them empirically and theoretically to (1) what is already known, (2) how robust that knowledge is, (3) what is not known

Research design:
- how you will go about answering your firmed up research questions related to your central question
- how other researchers have approached the topic
- what compromises you might need to make to answer your research questions within a small-scale study

Findings:
- what all the findings are which form the basis of your answers to your research questions
- what issues relating to your research questions have emerged from the findings

Discussion:
- what answers your findings provide to your research questions
- how you have reached these answers to your research questions
- how these answers relate to your central question and literature reviewed

Conclusion:
- what your answers to your research questions and the process of answering them have contributed to achieving your aims and answering your central question
- how certain are your answers to your research questions
- what recommendations you may have for practice or policy
- what new questions have arisen for theory, research, practice or policy

revised in the light of what you have done or learned. Through doing so, you avoid a situation where you have done interesting work, but the outcome bears little relationship to the original questions with which you started. As you work on identifying a set of research questions, it will be helpful to remind yourself how your questions reflect your intellectual project (Table 1.3).

Defining a topic, a central question, a set of research aims and research questions contributes to developing a critical frame of mind. Examining ideas and possible research questions critically and reflexively will help you to clarify what you want to do, and to justify why your topic and research questions are important and worth studying. This initial thinking provides the basis for writing the first draft of the introductory chapter, where you outline what you are doing and why. In explaining your focus and its justification to your readers, you will also need to provide a background to the topic and the central question. So if you are writing about practice in a particular organisation, you will need to describe what it is, how it operates and the context in which it is located. You may also explain how it is similar or different from other comparable organisations. If you are examining an aspect of policy you will need to outline briefly the purpose of the policy and the context of implementation. Alternatively, if you are examining an aspect of policy in a particular national context then you will also need to provide relevant information about it. But the watchwords here are *brevity* and *relevance*. Consider the question: what is the minimum of information that readers require to make sense of my work? Always bear in mind the readers for whom you are writing, and the conventions and expectations of the cultural context in which it will be read.

As a self-critical writer, constantly bear in mind the question: what do the readers need to know next? Provide them with clear signposts to enable them to make connections between one section or chapter and whatever follows (e.g. pages 114–5, 121). There is an old saying: 'First, tell them what you are going to tell them. Then tell them. Finally, tell them what you have told them!' You can provide signposts at the end of your introductory chapter and the beginning and end of each chapter that follows. At the end of the introduction and the end of each subsequent chapter, offer a brief summary of what has been discussed or presented, and (except for the last chapter) an indication of what will come in the next chapter. At the beginning of each chapter after the introduction, give an outline stating what topics will be covered in that chapter.

Applying critical reading to your own ideas for research questions

As you identify a practicable topic and define the parameters of a possible study, you will need to find out what is already known about the topic, and whether similar research questions to yours have been asked before. This is where your skill as a critical reader will be applied in reviewing existing research literature. An important part of the process will involve the development of a mental map to guide you through what initially may appear to be a complex, diverse and even contradictory body of work. The mental map outlined in Chapter 1 consisted of:

- one set of tools for thinking;
- two dimensions of variation in claims to knowledge;
- three kinds of knowledge generated;
- four types of literature;
- five sorts of intellectual project.

You will be applying the tools for thinking to ask review questions about the chapters, books and articles you read. These review questions will be related to your research questions. You are likely to ask the same review question of a group of relevant texts, as with Exercise 2 in Chapter 1. There, the two review questions we suggested you seek to answer in each exercise were concerned with the substantive focus of a study, concentrating on the factors promoting or inhibiting the effectiveness of a particular aspect of practice in the field of enquiry. Your central question and initial research questions will enable you to identify your own review questions to inform the substantive focus of your enquiry.

A part of the literature review that many students find difficult is that which concerns the theoretical or conceptual focus of a study. The theoretical orientation for your investigation consists of the tools for thinking embodied in theoretical knowledge that others have used to analyse substantive issues, and that you might wish to consider for framing your own analysis. You might generate a review question about the theoretical orientations of authors who have done research relevant to your substantive focus. Review questions and sub-questions that you might ask of a group of texts could include:

▶ What are the main *concepts* that different authors are using or developing in this group of texts?
  - Do they offer a clear stipulative definition of the key ideas?
  - If they do not do so, are there any implicit definitions?
  - Do different authors within the field differ in their stipulative definition of key concepts?
  - How do these concepts relate to my research questions – are some more helpful than others?
▶ What are the main *perspectives* evident in work in this field of enquiry?
  - Are any perspectives associated with particular disciplines (e.g. social psychology, sociology) and so likely to make particular assumptions about the social world?
  - Which perspectives appear to fit best with my research questions?
  - How do the perspectives relate to my intellectual project and to my values?
▶ Are any *metaphors* used to interpret or represent the social world?
  - What do these metaphors indicate about their users' assumptions about the social world?
  - How accurately do these metaphors reflect the aspect of the social world that they are used to interpret?
▶ What *theories or models* are used?
  - Are these theories and models made explicit?
  - Are they descriptive or normative, and if the latter, do I share their authors' values?
▶ What *assumptions or ideologies* can be detected within the group of texts (and these are often the least explicit aspects of authors' theoretical or conceptual orientation)?
  - What is the value-stance of the authors?
  - How does the value-stance of these authors relate to my values?

You will also need to evaluate the claims to theoretical, research or practice knowledge made in groups of related texts, and to identify what kind of knowledge is being claimed. These claims may be made with varying degrees of certainty and assertions about their generalisability to many contexts. Remember that the greater the degree of certainty and the higher the claim to generalisability, then the stronger the evidence will have to be for such assertions to be convincing.

While reviewing the literature in a field, you will probably read a large amount of material. The mental map will help you to make sense of what may appear at first to be a diverse and sometimes contradictory body of work. Throughout, keep in mind that a review of literature is connected to the rest of the study. It is not a discrete section of a thesis or dissertation, but has a vital function within the study as a whole. The main purposes for a critical literature review are to:

▶ locate your own central question and research questions in relation to existing work;
▶ assist you in developing an argument about the substantive topic;
▶ frame your research theoretically, including the choice of concepts as tools for thinking about the substantive topic;
▶ justify your choice of methodology and methods, while acknowledging their limitations.

Once you have begun to familiarise yourself with the literature in the relevant field, you will use your understanding to inform the construction of your own study. An important part of learning to read critically involves evaluating the literature in terms of its relevance to your research questions. You may find that someone has already asked similar questions, but their research was undertaken with a different population or from a different perspective. They might also have highlighted areas that need further work, gaps in what is known or limits to current methodologies. Such work can help you to refine your research questions, locate your study theoretically and conceptually, and make some claim to an original contribution within a field.

A further stage in the process is that of synthesising critical reading of many texts from the literature into a persuasive argument within your own written account (see Chapter 10). Here you are not merely identifying who said what and when about a topic, but rather guiding your writing by asking yourself, and answering, review questions that summarise what you have learned from the literature in relation to your central question, including the following:

1 What is known about the topic I am researching, and from what types of literature?
2 What are the most important 'landmark' works within the field?
3 Which areas of this work are centrally relevant to my topic and research questions?
4 How robust is the claim to knowledge in particular texts and across groups of texts?
5 What range of positions and approaches exist in relation to this topic?

6 What are the major relevant debates and disagreements among researchers within the field?

7 What have been the main approaches and methodologies used in researching relevant problems in this field?

8 What is my own position in relation to the way relevant problems in the field have been researched, and my justification for taking it?

9 Where are the relevant gaps and weaknesses within the field (substantive, theoretical and methodological)?

10 How will answering my research questions make a contribution to the literature in this field of enquiry?

The review of literature should lead smoothly into the next chapter of a dissertation or thesis, which is an explanation and justification of the methodology, research design and methods of data collection and analysis you have adopted.

Methodology and research design

You will probably begin writing in draft about your research design long before you implement it. Here we will concentrate on what should go into the final written account, and so, by implication, what you should have thought through before actually collecting your primary or secondary data. Communicating your research to others will involve stating how you did it, how you arrived at particular conclusions, and on what basis you are making any claim to knowledge. For any empirical study, it is necessary to make clear the process by which you conducted the research and to justify why you took your approach. Decisions about methodology and methods of data collection and analysis are not made in a vacuum. A justification of methodology needs to be made in relation to the firmed up research questions, to the kind of knowledge to which you are seeking to contribute, to your values and philosophical assumptions about the nature of the social world, and to accepted or established ways of conducting research within your field of enquiry. The theoretical framework of a study also informs the way in which that work will best be conducted (e.g. pages 195–202).

Among common weaknesses in discussions of methodology in dissertations or theses are three particularly to avoid. First, there is a tendency to rehearse 'paradigm war' debates. Such discussions describe the key features of different methodologies used in educational research and their underlying ontological and epistemological assumptions, but only discuss the strengths and weaknesses of different approaches in very generalised terms. Second, many discussions outline possible methodological approaches, but then assume that there is an obvious approach to take for a particular topic without justifying why it is the accepted way of proceeding. They offer little discussion of any alternative approaches that might have been taken. Third, sometimes the discussion of methodology is largely unconnected to the substantive research questions addressed by the investigation, to a theoretical framework, to existing work within the field, or to the researcher's philosophical assumptions about the nature of the social world. As we stated earlier, there should be explicit links between each section of any research report. As each section, or chapter, is drafted and revised, try to keep in mind a clear sense of its purpose in the overall text.

A brief review of relevant literature relating to the methodological issues or problems arising from your attempt to find an answer to your research questions will help you justify what you are doing by reference to others' approaches. Following from the discussion of methodology, a good research report will make explicit the overall design of the empirical investigation, and how the design relates to the firmed up research questions. In effect the research design is how you operationalise those questions. Whether researchers follow a largely quantitative or qualitative methodology, readers need to know how the investigation was conducted and the structure that guided it. Ideally, the account should give readers enough information for them to be in a position to do the same or similar research. It is sometimes suggested that in studies which are largely qualitative and interpretative, research design is either unnecessary or less important: researchers do not set out with any pre-specified questions, but wait to see what emerges from the research setting, and then interpret what they have experienced. In exploratory studies the research design is often more flexible, allowing for the inclusion of elements at a later stage of the research process, but this is not the same as having no design! Miles and Huberman (1994: 16–17) raise exactly this issue, cautioning against the problems arising from under-designed qualitative projects, especially for inexperienced researchers:

> Contrary to what you might have heard, qualitative research designs do exist. Some are more deliberate than others…Any researcher, no matter how unstructured, comes to fieldwork with some orientating ideas…Highly inductive, loosely designed studies make good sense when experienced researchers have plenty of time and are exploring exotic cultures, understudied phenomena, or very complex social phenomena. But if you are new to qualitative studies and are looking at a better understood phenomenon…a loose inductive design may be a waste of time…Tighter designs also provide clarity and focus for beginning researchers worried about diffuseness and overload.

All researchers set out with some idea of what they are aiming to do, why, where, how and with whom. It is questions relating to the what, where, how and with whom aspects of a study that guide the research design. For relatively inexperienced researchers, it is important both to create a well-structured research design and to represent this design as clearly and succinctly as possible in the final written account of the work. The research design offers readers a map of your investigation. It enables them to see how all the elements of the study fit together, over what period of time the study was conducted, what instruments or methods were used to collect data and at what intervals, who the research subjects or informants were, and why and how they were chosen.

In small-scale research it is crucial to have considered at the design stage what you could feasibly do, and what compromises you should make to ensure that a project was practicable but also rigorous. Such compromises might relate to the design of the study, the range of data collected and the population or sites sampled. A small number of research sites or respondents might be chosen, particularly if it were a labour-intensive qualitative or mixed-method study. Here the trade-off is likely to be between depth and breadth. The number of sites or people would need to be chosen carefully to ensure that the research questions could be adequately answered from the data gathered and the potential for generalisation from them made clear. However, a strong study can still be undertaken with a limited number of sites. While there are many examples of experimental studies being undertaken for theses and dissertations (especially in psychology) with a limited number of research subjects, the potential is limited for a single researcher to undertake larger-scale experimental or quasi-experimental designs, such as intervention studies or evaluations.

It is important in writing about the research design to give an account of particular choices or compromises made, and the reasons for so doing (e.g. pages 183–5). Explaining such decisions, discussing the problems encountered and indicating how you have attempted to address them all help your readers to understand the rationale for your design. You also demonstrate to them that you are capable of reflecting self-critically on your work and evaluating the strengths and limitations of particular choices. The strongest dissertations or theses are not necessarily ones in which no difficulty was experienced. They may be ones where challenges are discussed, how they were met is explained, and a reflective account is offered on what was learned in addressing them. It is another aspect of the process of becoming a critical reader and self-critical writer of research (see Chapter 7).

Once the overall design of the research has been set out succinctly, you are in a position to explain in more detail the methods and instruments used in the study. They will include methods or instruments used to gather and analyse the data, an account of how you chose the population or sites that formed your sample, and how any ethical issues were addressed (such as permission to access research sites, protecting the identity of informants, or any issues related to working with children or other research subjects). Self-critical writers of research make their choices and procedures as transparent as possible, reflecting on the strengths and limitations of a particular method, instrument or approach to sampling. Here are some self-critical questions to ask as you approach writing about the conduct of your research:

1 Why were the methods or instruments used the most effective in the circumstances for generating data to answer the research questions?
2 How were the instruments designed and constructed (e.g. questionnaires, attitude scales, observation or interview schedules)?
3 How were the instruments checked to ensure that they worked as they were intended to do, or represented what they were intended to represent (e.g. whether questionnaire questions made sense to respondents, or whether items on an attitude scale adequately represented concepts being investigated and measured adequately what they were intended to measure)?
4 What steps were taken to ensure that the instruments or procedures worked reliably, and were applied consistently across all contexts in which they were used?
5 How were any methods or instruments tested or piloted and what modifications were made as a result of any piloting?
6 What was the population studied (e.g. where the research was conducted, who the informants were, how and why they were chosen, and how access was gained to them)?
7 What were the strengths and limitations of choosing to investigate the particular research population?

8 What events or processes were studied within each site, and how frequently were they sampled (e.g. how they were selected, and the extent to which they represented the full range that could have been studied)?

9 What documents were sampled from research sites (e.g. how they were accessed, from where the documents originated and who authored them)?

10 Overall, what data was collected?

Once you have explained how, where and when you collected data, your next task is to outline the process by which you checked, summarised and analysed it. This part of the research process is easily overlooked in writing up a study, but is crucial in a dissertation or thesis to inform your examiners how you prepared the data for analysis and carried out the analysis itself (e.g. pages 204–5). How the analysis was done tends not to feature in published accounts of research because they are generally subject to strict word limits. We refer you to any of the many research methodology textbooks, including those in our annotated list in Appendix 1, which deal with checking and cleaning data sets and how to code and summarise them.

The critical readers of your work will expect you to make explicit the procedures used for checking, summarising and analysing data because they need to be convinced that the claims you make on the basis of your analysis are well grounded in the procedures you adopted. If the data set is quantitative, or rather has quantifiable variables, then you will need to explain what statistical procedures and tests were conducted and why, from the most basic, such as analysis of frequencies, to the more complex. It is inadequate merely to state that the data set was analysed using a computer software package. Such packages are tools to help organise data and do operations speedily, but it is you, the researcher, who decides what forms of analysis will be done and in what order. Equally, there are several computer software packages that will help you analyse qualitative data, but they do not make the decisions for you about how a data set will be analysed. Procedures for coding and analysing qualitative data are less standardised than for quantitative data, adding to the importance of making them explicit in a dissertation or thesis. Underpinning such explanations, as ever, should be an awareness of the audience for your writing: a good account of your analytic procedure should enable your examiners to follow exactly how the procedure was carried out. It should leave them, in principle, in a position to replicate the analysis and reach similar conclusions.

A concluding reflective consideration of the strengths and limitations of your design, in the light of your review of the relevant methodological literature, rounds off the discussion of how you did the empirical work. Let your readers know where your account is taking them next by signposting them towards the account of what you found when you implemented your design.

Presentation of findings

This part of your account is central: it sets out the evidence on which your argument will rest. As with the research design, you can help yourself by thinking through before you collect data how you are going to structure and present the written account of what you find and your analysis of the findings. The purpose of the research design is to explain how that evidence was gathered, synthesised and tested or interpreted. The account of findings should show the outcome of the research: how the research questions were answered, or the results of any hypothesis testing. The research questions, or hypotheses, will then provide the basis for structuring your presentation of your findings. Provide a signpost for your readers by explaining in an introductory section for this part of your report how the presentation of findings will be organised, what each section will address and how these sections link to relevant previous chapters or sections (especially to the key section containing the specification of your research questions).

A key decision is how you will present and display the findings. Presentation of the findings should be guided by the research questions you have asked. The type of data you have collected largely determines how you display your findings, and how you will have analysed them. If you have done a study involving variables analysed quantitatively, then the presentation will involve text, graphs, tables and charts. There are conventional ways of presenting statistical analysis of data in tabular form, to which you should adhere (see Chapters 3, 4, 7 and 9). A simple but important step is to check that you have included all the information in the table that is necessary for your readers to interpret it. Whatever the conventions of presenting numerical data, any tables, charts or graphs need to be labelled, making clear what they represent. In the text there should be an explanation of what the table shows. To a certain extent, the content of tables, graphs or charts may be self-evident, but it is part of your academic apprenticeship to learn how to explain them accurately and succinctly.

With data that consists largely of text, any themes or patterns found in the data will be presented, together with your interpretation of them, explaining how the evidence answers the research questions (e.g. pages 139–43). A problematic issue for many qualitative researchers is how much textual data, such as quotations from informants, to include in presenting findings. There are no hard and fast rules about this, but readers should be provided with enough evidence to see how an interpretation was reached. One tactic is to include a range of short quotations from informants that highlight a particular phenomenon or pattern of meaning and, if there are any, quotations from informants that do not fit the pattern. Another is to indicate what was the most common finding within the overall range, backed by illustrative quotations for the most common finding and the extremes of the range. Researchers presenting qualitative data need to be particularly careful not to appear to have chosen data selectively to support their pre-judged interpretation: developing an argument first, and selecting and presenting examples of data that support it later.

Some questions to ask of any textual data presented in a research account are as follows:

▶ How and why was this example chosen?
▶ How typical is it of other events, or of comments or responses on this issue?
▶ Were there any other examples which could have been selected that might suggest a different interpretation?

Miles and Huberman (1994) argue that presentation of qualitative data in summarised forms, such as matrices or charts, can help to make clear the overall patterns. Ultimately, it depends on you, the researcher – and the questions you have asked – whether you present qualitative analysis of data in this form, or present only segments from texts of interviews, documents or obser- vations. The key point is that you should be explicit about selecting particular data presented in a chapter on findings.

The final section of the chapter presenting findings in a thesis or dissertation should be a summary of the key findings and any issues arising. You are, in effect, reminding your readers what you have done in the chapter. It is here also that you will signal to them where these issues will be taken up subsequently.

Discussion of findings and conclusion

The chapters or sections containing the discussion of findings and conclusions often present a considerable challenge to students. Avoid the temptation to move straight from setting out the findings to conclusions and recommendations. If you find this part of the research process difficult, one possible reason is that that you will have become very familiar with your work, and assume that what you know is obvious to your readers. Another issue is that researchers often attempt to discuss the implications of findings within a section as they are presented. There is a cer- tain logic to this approach, especially with qualitative data. However, it is also necessary to discuss the *overall* significance of findings and their relationship to the wider issues connected with your substantive topic. Relating findings to the wider substantive, theoretical and methodological issues identified in the review of literature can easily be neglected by attempting to present findings and discuss their implications at the same time. The key to this part of the dissertation or thesis is *critical reflection*. After the findings have been presented, the discussion of them is an opportunity to take a step back from the work and exercise the critical frame of mind that you have been developing (e.g. pages 160–3). In summary, the discussion section in a research report or chapter in a thesis is where you:

▶ highlight what was particularly important or significant about the findings in relation to your central question;
▶ comment on any unexpected or unusual findings (depending on the extent to which the study was exploratory and open-ended);
▶ return to discuss the substantive, theoretical and methodological issues identi- fied earlier, and link key findings from your work with the literature reviewed.

In other words, the discussion section or chapter is where you establish the links between your findings and the wider field of enquiry: the contribution that your research makes to this field. Establishing such links is particularly important for small-scale research. While your study, in itself, may make only a modest contribution to the field, it might also add to the accumulation of knowledge and understanding of relevant social phenomena and practices. The wider field in which your study is located might also lend confirmatory strength to your findings (see pages 84–7). Remember to indicate how you will draw conclusions about the implications of your findings for your research questions and, in turn, your more general central question.

In the conclusion of your account, you pull all aspects of the work together, consider with what degree of certainty the study answered your research questions, and highlight what it implies for your central question. You also have an opportunity to:

- evaluate the extent to which you achieved your substantive, theoretical and methodological aims;
- evaluate the overall theoretical framework, methodology and research design;
- reflect on the work as a whole;
- identify and discuss what has been learned;
- consider what you might have done differently if you conducted the research again with the experience and knowledge you now have;
- outline any implications for future research, and set out a possible research programme;
- suggest any implications or make any recommendations for improving policy or practice.

You may well discover that your research has generated as many further questions as the ones it has answered, and you may be able to suggest wider implications for future research (e.g. pages 128–130) or identify a research programme to be undertaken in the future. There may be implications for policy or practice, and it is essential that you connect any recommendations for improvement with evidence from your research. Otherwise why should your sceptical readers be convinced to accept your recommendations? It is unwise to over-generalise from your findings, for example advocating that a national policy should be reformed on the basis of one small-scale study. Here it is worth returning to Figure 1.1 in Chapter 1 and using the critical questions about claims to knowledge to help you reflect self-critically on your work and evaluate the extent to which you can generalise in making recommendations from your small-scale investigation.

Box 2.2
The 'linkage tracker test' for accounts of a research enquiry

Every part of a defensible account of research should link logically together, from the title, with its keywords indicating the focus of the study, through the central question being addressed, the literature review, the research questions, the research design, the data collection instruments, the summary of the findings, the analysis and discussion of the findings, the conclusions and any recommendations, to the reference list and any appendices.

How well do all the parts of your written account of your research link together? As critical readers of your work, dissertation and thesis supervisors and examiners are likely to look out for any digressions and for any claims or arguments that have not been adequately backed up. Ensure that your dissertation or thesis is defensible by constructing a logical account of your research, and then applying the linkage tracker test to it.

▶

▶

The linkage tracker test for self-critical writers

First select any piece of the text, including a table, figure, reference or appendix. Then ask yourself two questions:

1 Why is this material here?
2 How does this material relate to the stated focus of the research?

It should be clear why anything is included in your account, and how it relates to the stated focus of the research.

Second, try tracking the logical links between parts of your account, going forwards in the direction of the conclusions and any recommendations, and backwards towards the introduction and the title. There should be a logical sequence from title to recommendations or from recommendations to title. Anything that is not directly or indirectly linked might be irrelevant to answering your research questions. If so, do you think it should it be removed?

The linkage tracker test for critical readers

The linkage tracker test may be applied to any written account of research. Your supervisor or examiner may apply it to your work. But as a critical reader yourself, you will find it instructive to apply the linkage tracker test to others' work. You might try applying it to any of the research report chapters in this book.

Once you have drafted the conclusion, you have reached a point that probably seemed impossible when you were starting out on the work for your dissertation or thesis. But while a full draft of the manuscript has been completed, there is further work to be done. Check through the logic of your account, from title to final recommendation, and be prepared to revise earlier sections where you were not as clear about what you were doing as you have become as you near the end of the process. Pay careful attention to the presentation of your work. Countless manuscripts submitted for masters and doctoral degrees, and to the editorial boards of journals, contain errors that could easily have been corrected by the writer. Sloppy presentation, inaccuracies, poor bibliographic referencing and inattention to detail can undermine a potentially impressive piece of work. Again, remember to put your critical frame of mind to work: apply self-critically to your own writing the critical reading strategies that you have developed in relation to other texts.

Structuring the written account of the research

There are various ways to structure the final written account that constitutes your dissertation or thesis itself. Figure 2.2 summarises the sort of structure that is commonly employed in the humanities and social sciences for a study involving empirical research. You might wish to use it as a starting point for thinking through the structure of your account, and possibly as a checklist to ensure that you include all the necessary components. Our framework reflects the logic of the research process we have discussed. (Each chapter in the framework covers the logical ground of the ideas in the parallel arrow box in Figure 2.1.) The suggested structure contains more detail of the components of your account that might be included in a particular chapter. You may wish to adapt this structure to suit the logic of your enquiry. One issue for you may be over how much ground to cover in each chapter. You may want to separate out parts of the literature review or the findings into more than one chapter, or to combine the presentation of findings with their discussion in the same chapter. Whichever way you structure the account, the components should all be there, in a clear and logical progression that together develop and provide backing for your argument. Never lose sight of your priority to ensure that the claims you make in your written account are sufficiently backed by evidence to convince the critical readers who will evaluate your work – your examiners.

Figure 2.2 *A possible structure for your dissertation or thesis.*

COMPONENTS OF A DISSERTATION OR THESIS: A CHECKLIST

Title

▶ Containing keywords that reflect the central question you are seeking to answer, expressed in general terms.

Abstract

▶ A brief summary (say, around 200 words) of the purpose of the study, any empirical work and your main conclusions.

Acknowledgements

▶ Any acknowledgement you wish to make of the support of individuals (e.g. your supervisor, your family) and of the cooperation of informants

Chapter 1   Introduction

▶ A statement of purpose – to contribute to answering a central question expressed in general terms, usually about a substantive topic in your field of enquiry.
▶ A summary of the more specific aims of your research:
  - *substantive* (e.g. to determine factors affecting the effectiveness of some aspect of policy or practice in a specific context);
  - *theoretical* (e.g. to employ a specified set of concepts as a framework for investigating the effectiveness of this aspect of a policy or practice in this context);
  - *methodological* (e.g. to employ a particular methodology and research design and methods of data collection and analysis to address the central question by investigating the aspect of a policy or practice in this context).
▶ A justification of the significance of the substantive topic (e.g. its importance for policy or practice).
▶ A statement of your value position in relation to this topic that shapes the focus of your enquiry.
▶ A statement of the broad issues or problems linked to the specific aims of your research to be investigated in addressing the central question:

▶

▶
- *substantive* (indicating which aspects of the substantive topic identified in the central question you will be investigating in detail);
- *theoretical* (considering the strengths and limitations of the theory or set of concepts you are using to help you understand and analyse the substantive topic relating to the central question);
- *methodological* (considering the strengths and limitations of the methodological paradigm and methods you are using to investigate the substantive topic in addressing the central question).
▶ A brief description of the context of your enquiry. If you are investigating practice in a country other than the one in which you are studying for your dissertation or thesis, you may wish to insert a section outlining the national context relevant to your central question.
▶ An outline of the rest of the study – offering signposts to the content of the remaining chapters and how they develop your argument.

Chapter 2   Review of literature

▶ An introduction which offers signposts to what will be covered in each section.
▶ A *critical* and *focused* review of the literature guided by review questions relating to your substantive and theoretical issues or problems in turn. It is likely that most of the emphasis will be placed on the substantive area, then theoretical.
▶ A brief summary of your position concerning your substantive and theoretical issues or problems in the light of your review.
▶ The identification of one or more detailed research questions related to the central question.
▶ An indication of how the research design chapter will take forward your work in relation to the substantive and theoretical areas and your research questions.

Chapter 3   Research design

▶ An introduction setting out what you are going to cover in each section.
▶ Your research questions and/or hypotheses focusing on detailed aspects of the substantive topic that relate to the central question.
▶ The theoretical framework you are using to help you understand and analyse the substantive topic relating to the central question.
▶ A brief critical and focused review of the literature relating to your methodological issues or problems, indicating how other researchers have approached them and have investigated similar substantive topics.
▶ A brief summary of your position concerning your methodological issues or problems in the light of your review.
▶ Your methodology and methods:
- a justification for the methodological paradigm within which you are working;
- detailed methods of data collection you are using and your justification for using them
- specification of the sample of informants and your rationale for selecting them from the wider population;
- a summary description of your data collection instruments indicating how research questions and/or hypotheses about the substantive topic are addressed and your rationale for using the instruments chosen;
- a summary of the data collection effort (e.g. piloting, the number of interviews or the number of individuals surveyed);
- a summary of how data are to be analysed (e.g. statistical methods, use of matrices for qualitative data);
- ethical factors (e.g. confidentiality of interviews);
- the timetable for the research process (e.g. timing of first and second rounds of interviews).
▶ A concluding reflective consideration of the strengths and limitations of your design (e.g. reliability, internal and external validity, sample size relative to population size) and an indication that you will evaluate the design in the concluding chapter.
▶ An indication of how the presentation of findings chapter will present the results of implementing this design to answer your research questions and/or test your hypotheses.

Chapter 4   Presentation of findings

▶ An introduction where you set out the ground to be covered in each section.
▶ A summary of all the findings broken down into topics relating to the research questions and/or hypotheses, possibly supported by tables and matrices, diagrams and quotations from informants.
▶ A concluding summary of key findings and emerging issues you have identified.
▶ An indication of where they will be taken up in the discussion chapter.

Chapter 5   Discussion of findings

▶ An introduction where you set out the ground to be covered in each section.
▶ A discussion of topics identified earlier relating to the substantive, theoretical and methodological broad issues or problems, linking your key findings with your research questions and the literature you have reviewed.
▶ A concluding summary of how the key findings together provide a response to your substantive, theoretical and methodological issues or problems.
▶ An indication of where you will draw conclusions about the contribution of your findings to answering your central question in the conclusion and recommendations chapter.

Chapter 6   Conclusion and recommendations

▶ An introduction where you set out the ground to be covered in each section.
▶ Your conclusions relating to your substantive, theoretical and methodological aims, including an evaluation of your research design and the certainty of your answers to your research questions, in the light of the findings and experience of using your theoretical framework and methods.
▶ Implications of your findings overall for answering the central question expressed in general terms.
▶ Any recommendations for different audiences (e.g. policy-makers, researchers, trainers) with reference to their backing from the evidence you have gathered.
▶ Any new questions that arise from your study for theory, research, practice or policy.
▶ A final concluding statement which includes your summary contribution to answering the central question posed in the introduction and related to the title.

Reference list

▶ Containing all works to which reference is made in the text, but not background material to which you have not made direct reference.
▶ In alphabetical author order, and in the required format.

Appendices

▶ For example, research instruments, letters to informants, examples of raw data.

In this chapter we have indicated how the principles and procedures for becoming a critical reader of research can be developed and applied to the design and writing of a small-scale research study. We have offered one model of the process of designing and writing of a project that might be used to guide a dissertation, thesis or other small-scale investigation. It is not a definitive model, but rather a pragmatic one, based on experience of doing small-scale research and supervising masters and doctoral projects.

Part 2 contains a selection of reports on small-scale research and components of larger studies by established researchers in the field of enquiry covered in this book. They include work from a range perspectives and national contexts. Each chapter has an editorial introduction. In their research report, authors indicate how they addressed various issues connected with their research design and methods. Part 3 is the literature review chapter which exemplifies how a review may be structured. The chapters are briefer than masters dissertations or doctoral theses. Since they were written for publication rather than examination they will not be structured in precisely the same way as a dissertation or thesis, nor will they necessarily include every component in our checklist. What you will be unable to see (but you can rest assured that it did happen) is the careful drafting and redrafting that lies behind the final accounts presented. Nevertheless, there is much you can learn from the authors' account of how they approached the research process and from the structure and content of their final written report for critical readers like yourself.

References

Gorard, S. (2001) *Quantitative Methods in Educational Research*. London: Continuum.
Miles, M. and Huberman, M. (1994) *Qualitative Data Analysis*. New York: Sage.

Part 2

Meeting the challenge of reporting research

Chapter 3

Local school management: does it make a difference?

Bill Mulford, Lawrie Kendall and Diana Kendall

The substantive focus of this chapter is the move to local school management (LSM) in the state of Tasmania, Australia. The authors begin by locating the substantive topic within the wider context of reform in Australia, and highlight similarities between policy developments there and elsewhere in the world. They indicate why a study of reform in one state is of more than local interest and relevance, and address the underlying aims of LSM in relation to current thinking about decision-making in schools. They examine the constraints to developing devolved management in schools in terms of individual, institutional and cultural factors. Drawing on relevant literature, they link the study with wider issues in the field of school leadership, management and governance. A key question identified by the researchers was the extent to which LSM and other forms of devolved decision-making involved only superficial change, and might also compound resistance to radical reform. In their critical review of the field, the authors pinpoint the limitations of existing knowledge, concluding that evidence to support the success of LSM was not strong, and that more detailed investigation was needed. They clarify where their central question came from, why their own study was worth doing and what it aimed to contribute to the wider field of enquiry.

In relation to research design and methodology, the authors explain that the questionnaire was part of a larger project, and was designed to investigate the responses of different populations to various aspects of LMS. They indicate why they used Likert-type scales in the questionnaire, and the strengths and limitations of the analytic method (chi-square tests). The authors also consider the overall strengths and weaknesses of the research design. In the findings section, data are presented clearly and systematically in tables and charts, and explained verbally, followed by a discussion of findings. Here, the authors summarise the salient points arising from the data and explain how the research questions were answered. The implications of findings are discussed in relation to the wider research literature and policy context. This section is important because it establishes not only what this study found, but also the degree of consistency with other studies and its contribution to understanding the impact of LSM. The chapter concludes by returning to the central research questions and making some cautious recommendations about LSM.

Introduction: LSM in Australia

As part of wider public sector reform, the structure of school governance in Australia has been undergoing dramatic changes. Since the late 1980s, decentralisation has emerged as a key organising principle. Changes have included a decisive move to local school management (LSM), an increased devolution of responsibility and accountability for the implementation of centrally determined policies and priorities from centralised bureaucracies to individual schools and their communities.

Changes in school governance were far from cosmetic and were introduced with high hopes, largely inspired by similar initiatives in the United States (Murphy and Beck, 1995), New Zealand (Sullivan, 1994) and the United Kingdom (Russ, 1995). It was hoped that broader participation in the governance of a school would ensure that decisions were made which accurately reflect local as well as state and national objectives. Devolution of responsibility and wider participation in decision-making would ensure that schools are places where people are prepared for, and participate in, making decisions as part of the democratic process. In addition, school-based management, through greater local control over the use of resources and the setting of educational policy, would produce more effective educational outcomes.

By the beginning of the 1990s every Australian State and Territory had adopted some form of LSM. Ten years later governments continue to convey an urgent need for radical reform of schooling through decentralisation. In this chapter data from one of the states foremost among these developments, Tasmania, is examined to help answer the question: 'Does LSM make a difference?' However, the chapter will first examine research in the area and the major limitations of that research.

Research on LSM

Reforms in, and of, schools, no matter how well conceptualised, powerfully sponsored, brilliantly structured or closely audited, are likely to fail in the face of cultural resistance from those in schools (Harris and Hopkins, 1999). By their action, or inaction, teachers (Berends, 2000), middle managers (Dinham and Scott, 1999) and principals (Leithwood and Duke, 1999) help determine the fate of what happens in schools.

With increasing decentralisation to the school level, pressures have grown for those in schools to work more closely together. However, research suggests that only a small proportion of schools can effectively generate collective initiatives (Joyce et al., 1999). One explanation for this failure is that collective decision-making conflicts with the autonomous, privatistic culture of schools (Hargreaves and Hopkins, 1991). There is also a hint in the research that some teachers (Logan et al., 1996; Peters et al., 1996; Hamilton and Richardson, 1995) and principals (Dimmock and Hattie, 1994) prefer the relatively safe environment of congeniality that superficial structural and procedural change can bring, allowing teachers to let the administrators 'get on with it' while teachers retreat to the solitude of their classrooms.

LSM may therefore involve superficial change or, at worst, serve only to compound the difficulties that might be experienced when individuals in a school resist reform. Research concerning school leadership teams confirms the difficulties involved. It has been found that such teams first have to attend to many adult issues (Dibbon, 2000). They begin by developing the skills needed to function as a group, then to solve problems with colleagues – or, as Mulford (1994: 32) calls it, 'losing time to gain time'. They have to learn how to craft forms of shared leadership, including sharing leadership with the principal and middle managers, and how to collect and use data. It is only as members of leadership teams learn to work together and make and implement decisions that they begin genuinely to address student matters (Chrispeels et al., 2000).

Another explanation for the failure to effect collective action in schools may be the faith some place in principals as the major vehicle for implementing reforms, including LSM (Caldwell and Hayward, 1998). It may be that when principals become strong advocates for change in teachers' practice they risk undermining the consensual nature of shared decision-making (Bishop and Mulford, 1995). In fact, other research has shown that teachers' allegiance to LSM cools over time, especially as the demands of LSM pile up and divert them from their classroom responsibilities (ACT, 1994; Grady et al., 1994; Wallace, 1999; Weiss and Cambone, 1994). The process by which teachers come to trust the authenticity of power sharing is a slow one. What has been found to be important is the goal emphasis of principals *and* goal consensus among staff (Goldring and Pasternack, 1994; Leithwood et al., 1994; Short et al., 1994). The New Zealand experience of LSM (Sullivan, 1994) has demonstrated that the exclusion and marginalisation of teachers from reforms has a counter-productive effect where there was a move from a high-trust collegial to a low-trust hierarchical management system. School bureaucracies only become communities when governance regimes are perceived as legitimate by teachers and that legitimisation of governance comes mainly from teachers being actively involved in decision-making (Vergugo et al., 1997; Robertson and Briggs, 1998).

Unfortunately, the picture that emerges is of administrative, rather than professional or community, outcomes and control (Leithwood and Menzies, 1998; Thomas, 1996). Decision-making may have been moved closer to the 'front lines', but the decisions are of little importance or significance for those in the 'trenches'. This situation is unfortunate because it is likely to result in minimal impact on schools (Leithwood and Menzies, 1998; Seashore Louis, Kruse and Associates, 1995).

All in all, we can conclude that evidence for the success of LSM is not abundant. This conclusion poses a dilemma when we compare it with the rapidly growing evidence of what is required for successful school reform: collective as well as individual teacher efficacy (Murphy and Beck, 1995; Silins et al. 1999, 2000; Silins and Mulford, 2002). Clearly more detailed evidence is required about

LSM and its introduction. We need to understand better issues such as: the degree and areas of adoption, especially administrative and teaching and learning; its benefits and costs and whether participants believe on balance its introduction is a good thing; the demands it places on participants; and its effects, especially on the relationships between teachers and principals and on professional authority. The Tasmania research reported later builds these details into its research design. Before turning to that research, however, some limitations of previous LSM research are outlined.

Limitations of previous research

The existing research on LSM is limited in various ways, including: not differentiating between primary and secondary schools (Dinham and Scott, 1996; Dimmock and Hattie, 1994; Dempster, 2000); not differentiating between levels in schools such as principal, teachers, parents (Stoll and McBeath, 1997) and subject departments (Bennett and Harris, 1999); relying upon data gathered exclusively from principals (Caldwell and Hayward, 1998; Reid, 1998; Stoll and MacBeath, 1997; Wohlstetter et al., 1997); and relying on data about only one point in time (Wildy, 1996; Wildy and Wallace, 1994). The Tasmania research takes account of most of these limitations by including both primary and secondary (or high) schools and teacher and principal responses. It also frames its questions to take account of the time taken to introduce LSM.

LSM in Tasmania: the SGEO Project

During 1996, a team of researchers began a systematic evaluation of the transformation of school governance in the Australian state of Tasmania. They closely examined the different ways in which LSM operates and the outcomes of the changes in the structure of school governance for schools, principals, teachers, students, school communities and civil society more generally.

A systematic and thorough approach was needed because the research on devolution in other states of Australia had, in the main, relied on small samples of schools and teachers. None had incorporated individual level student and parent data, and none had attempted to model statistically the relationship between school governance and various measures of educational production at the school level. Another weakness of some of the earlier studies was that the research was carried out by the same people who had been responsible for the development and implementation of a particular model of devolution.

The School Governance and Educational Outcomes Project (SGEOP) sought to remedy this situation by developing a unique, comprehensive, state-wide database that was distinctive in its scope (a 100 per cent state-wide sample) and its depth (linking ecological, school and individual level data) that permitted the systematic mapping and modelling of school governance, educational production (including student attainment), social demography and political culture. SGEOP was also carried out by researchers who were independent of the development and implementation of the devolution process.

Research design and methods

In the first phase of the project, SGEOP distributed a series of questionnaires to all the principals, teachers and members of school councils across Tasmania. Overall, the response rates to our questionnaires varied. For principals it was 56.7 per cent (N = 122) and teachers 21.4 per cent (N = 833). However the distribution of teacher responses across schools represented coverage of 77.2 per cent (N = 170) of government schools in the state. There was little variation in response rate across the different levels of schooling (primary, secondary or high).

When comparisons were made between the responses of these respective groups it was decided that percentages would provide a more meaningful mode of comparison than disparate groups of frequencies. The scaling of questions in the surveys was a variation of Likert scales, for example: 'To a significant extent, To a moderate extent, To some extent and Not at all'; 'Improved, Not changed and Diminished'; 'No increase, Some increase and A large increase'. One advantage of Likert scales is that the data generated can be manipulated at nominal, ordinal and/or interval levels of measurement. A mean score has been included in the tables presented (with a score of 1 being given to the 'significant' or 'large' end of the scale) to allow an indication of a measure of central location (average) of the item represented, at the interval level of measurement, which also provides another comparison between responses aside from that covered by the percentages.

The statistical testing of significance of the data presented in the tables has been completed with the use of chi-square k samples. There are three criteria for such a test: first, that a 'difference' hypothesis is being tested; second, that there are more than two populations to be tested; and third, that independent sampling procedures have been used. The nominal level of measurement has been utilised for the statistical test of significance, as the assumptions underlying this level of measurement are not as stringent as those underlying both the ordinal and interval levels of measurement, making the inferences undertaken more appropriate for data drawn from surveys (Kendall, 1996).

In addition to Likert scales, there were a number of open-ended questions that provided for multiple responses. Patterns of responses were examined and wherever possible categories most appropriate to a particular pattern of responses were identified and the percentage of responses in each category recorded.

Generally, the methodological approach used in this study has been referred to as a 'causal/comparative design' as the data is collected after the events of interest have occurred. The research seeks out causes, relationships or meaning by searching back through the data. The major weakness of a causal/comparative design is that there is a lack of control over independent variables. The major strength is that the conclusions drawn about the effects of events are made under normal conditions.

Results

The results are presented under six broad headings, covering: extent of adoption of LSM; changes to management functions, in particular and overall; changes in role, time demands, duties and responsibilities and relationships; alterations to professional authority of principals and teachers; effects of LSM on promotion and appraisal of teachers; and effects of implementation of LSM.

1. Extent of adoption of local school management

Teachers and principals were asked to indicate to what extent they believed their school had adopted LSM. Table 3.1 illustrates the responses given by primary and secondary (or high) school teachers and principals. A chi-square value of 52.3 indicated that there were statistically significant differences between teachers and principals about the extent of adoption of LSM. The majority of primary school principals (65.8 per cent) felt that LSM had been adopted to a 'significant extent', whereas only 44.4 per cent of high school principals and 48.9 per cent of primary school teachers indicated that they felt there had been a 'significant extent' of adoption. High school teachers differed from primary school principals, primary school teachers and high school principals, in that their perceptions of the extent of adoption were approximately 30.0 per cent of the scales, that is 29.8 per cent to a 'significant extent', 35.9 per cent to a 'moderate extent' and 31.3 per cent to 'some extent'.

When respondents were asked in what ways has LSM been adopted, 43.3 per cent of teachers and principals responded to this open-ended question with a total of 404 comments. These responses were registered in answer to an open-ended question with more than one response being able to be recorded by any particular respondent. Only comments that made up 10 or more per cent of the total comments, and represented the first three rankings, are reported in Table 3.2.

Table 3.1 *To what extent has LSM been adopted by your school?*

	To a significant extent %	To a moderate extent %	To some extent %	Not at all %	X̄ score
Primary school principal	65.8	26.6	7.6	0.0	1.42
High school principal	44.4	50.0	5.6	0.0	1.61
Primary school teacher	48.9	33.9	16.5	7.0	1.69
High school teacher	29.8	35.9	31.3	3.0	2.08
Total	45.3	34.0	19.4	1.3	1.77

λ square = 52.3. *statistically significant at 0.05 level.

Table 3.2 *In what ways has LSM been adopted?*

	Percentage
Budget decisions, prioritising needs	19.0
Curriculum planning, reviewing programmes	11.0
Whole school involvement in policy-making	10.0

2. Changes to management functions, in particular and overall

Principals (not teachers) were asked whether or not, in their view, LSM had improved, changed or diminished certain features of their schools. Results are shown in Table 3.3. The majority of principals felt that financial management (87.9 per cent), the use of resources (82.0 per cent), community involvement in decision-making (78.9 per cent) and school community relations (70.8 per cent) had improved. Principals were less certain about improvements to the quality of teaching (50.0 per cent 'not changed') or quality of student learning (51.9 per cent 'not changed'), student discipline and behaviour (61.2 per cent 'not changed') and student engagement in school life (53.6 per cent 'not changed'). It is interesting to note that features which principals predominantly considered not to be changed concerned teaching and students.

Table 3.3 *In your (principals') view have the changes in LSM improved, not changed or diminished the following features of your school?*

	Improved %	Not changed %	Diminished %	$\bar{X}$ score
Financial management	87.9	6.6	5.5	1.18
The use of resources	82.0	16.9	1.1	1.19
Community involvement in decision-making	78.9	18.9	2.2	1.23
School-community relations	70.8	27.0	2.2	1.30
Quality of teaching	45.0	50.0	5.0	1.50
Student engagement in school life	44.0	53.6	2.4	1.58
Quality of student learning	44.3	51.9	3.8	1.60
Student discipline and behaviour	35.3	61.2	3.5	1.68
Total	61.0	35.8	3.2	1.41

Agreement as to whether or not LSM had been good for the school is illustrated in Table 3.4. Principals were very positive in their responses to this item, with primary school principals indicating 83.1 per cent agreement and high school principals indicating 88.2 per cent agreement. More than 50.0 per cent of primary school teachers (50.4 per cent 'unsure') and high school teachers (58.3 per cent 'unsure') were uncertain about the value of LSM. A calculated chi-square value indicates a statistically significant difference between the respondents. Whereas primary and high school principals exhibit no statistically significant differences in their responses, they differ from both primary and high school teachers. The responses of primary school teachers show a statistically significant difference from the responses of high school teachers.

Opinion regarding the benefits of LSM outweighing costs, or matching costs, or costs outweighing benefits is displayed in Table 3.5. Principals (60.3 per cent, primary and 70.6 per cent, high) felt that the benefits of LSM outweigh the costs, whereas primary teachers felt that benefits outweighed or matched costs (36.3 per cent and 41.3 per cent respectively). Opinion from high school teachers was less clear, with responses that benefits outweigh costs, 29.0 per cent, match costs, 35.8 per cent and costs outweigh benefits, 35.2 per cent. A calculated chi-square of 36.59 shows there is a statistically significant difference between the responses of principals and teachers. Primary school teachers (X = 1.86) and primary principals (X = 1.52) differ significantly in their responses as do high school teachers (X = 2.06) and high school principals (X = 1.41). High school teachers differ significantly in their responses to both primary principals and high school principals.

Table 3.4 *To what extent would you agree with the view that LSM has been a good thing for your school?*

	Agree %	Unsure %	Disagree %	$\bar{X}$ score
High school principal	88.2	11.8	0.0	1.12
Primary school principal	83.1	13.0	3.9	1.21
Primary school teacher	41.3	50.4	8.3	1.67
High school teacher	26.2	58.3	15.5	1.89
Total	43.1	47.3	9.6	1.67

λ square = 83.82. *statistically significant at 0.05 level.

Table 3.5 *Has the effort in pursuing LSM been worth it?*

	Benefits outweigh costs %	Benefits match costs %	Costs outweigh benefits %	X̄ score
High school principal	70.6	17.6	11.8	1.41
Primary school principal	60.3	27.4	12.3	1.52
Primary school teacher	36.3	41.3	22.4	1.86
High school teacher	29.0	35.8	35.2	2.06
Total	49.1	30.5	20.4	1.86

λ square = 36.59. *statistically significant at 0.05 level.

The main benefits and costs of LSM, as perceived by the combined sample of teachers and principals, are reported in Tables 3.6 and 3.7 respectively. These responses were registered in answer to an open-ended question, any particular respondent being able to record more than one response, with the total number of responses for main benefits being 449 and for main costs 498. Only comments that made up more than 8 per cent of the total comments, and represented the top five rankings, are reported in Tables 3.6 and 3.7. The main benefit of LSM was seen to be that teachers felt that they took more part in democratic decision-making and the main cost was seen to be diminished time for, and quality of, teaching.

Table 3.6 *What do you see as the main benefits of LSM?*

	Percentage
Teachers feel part of more democratic decision-making	28.9
School has control over own resources	11.4
There is a feeling of ownership	10.2
School able to develop environment to suit students	10.0
Community and parents more involved in school	8.5

* total response = 449

Table 3.7 *What do you see as the main costs of LSM?*

	Percentage
Time for, and quality of, teaching diminished	48.8
Extra duties incurred were not trained for	11.8
Lack of resources and funds	10.4
Teacher morale lowered	9.0

* total response = 498

3. Changes in role, time demands, duties and responsibilities and relationships

Teachers and principals were asked to what extent did they believe that their roles had changed as a result of the move to LSM, as shown in Table 3.8. Primary (60.0 per cent) and high (69.2 per cent) school principals indicate their role has changed to a 'large extent', whereas primary (55.8 per cent) and high (53.1 per cent) school teachers report that their roles have changed to 'some extent'. There is a statistically significant difference between the perception of teachers and principals with regard to the extent of their change in role.

Teachers and principals were asked if their role had changed and, if so, in what way. Their responses are recorded in Table 3.9 and confirm greater involvement in management but, possibly, at the expense of time for teaching. These responses were registered in answer to an open-ended question, with any particular respondent being able to record more than one response, the total number of responses being 423. Only comments that made up more than 8 per cent of the total comments and represented the top five rankings are reported in Table 3.9.

Table 3.8 *To what extent has your role changed as a result of the move to LSM?*

	To a large extent %	To some extent %	Not at all %	X̄ score
High school principal	69.2	23.1	7.7	1.40
Primary school principal	60.0	31.7	8.3	1.48
Primary school teacher	21.1	55.8	23.1	2.02
High school teacher	17.0	53.1	29.9	2.14
Total	41.8	40.9	17.3	1.76

λ square = 62.79. * statistically significant at 0.05 level.

Table 3.9 *In what ways has your role been altered?*

	Percentage
Less time for teaching: now a dual management role	23.6
More able to be part of policy development process	14.8
More committees and meetings to attend	13.7
More whole school responsibility	9.1
More responsible for financial planning, resource allocation	8.4

* total response = 423

LSM brought with its implementation some increases in demands on the time of principals and teachers. Table 3.10 illustrates the perception of the respondents to demands on their time. Primary and high school principals thought that the demands on their time had increased to a 'large extent': 87.6 per cent and 82.4 per cent respectively. Responses from teachers were less decisive with nearly half of primary and high school teachers reporting some increase (46.3 per cent primary and 45.5 per cent high) and nearly half of the teachers reporting a large increase (46.3 per cent primary and 42.4 per cent high). A calculated chi-square of 59.49 indicated that the difference in the perceptions of teachers and principals concerning the demands on their time was statistically significant at the 0.05 level.

Teachers and principals reported the extent to which they felt that there had been an increase in their duties and responsibilities as a result of LSM, as shown in Table 3.11. Most principals (primary 88.0 per cent and high 94.1 per cent) indicated that there had been a 'large increase' in their duties and responsibilities. Most teachers perceived an increase in their duties and responsibilities, but the degree of increase shows division of opinion, with primary teachers reporting 'some increase' (45.6 per cent) and a 'large increase' (42.6 per cent), and high school teachers registering 'some increase' (47.3 per cent) and a 'large increase' (34.4 per cent). There is a statistically significant difference between the perceptions of principals and teachers concerning increases in their duties and responsibilities.

Table 3.10 *With the move to LSM, to what extent has there been an increase in the demands on your time?*

	No increase %	Some increase %	Large increase %	$\bar{X}$ score
Primary school principal	1.8	10.6	87.6	2.87
High school principal	0.0	17.6	82.4	2.82
Primary school teacher	7.4	46.3	46.3	2.39
High school teacher	12.1	45.5	42.4	2.30
Total	5.3	30.0	64.7	2.43

λ square = 59.49. * statistically significant at 0.05 level.

Table 3.11 *With the move to LSM, to what extent has there been an increase in your duties and responsibilities?*

	No increase %	Some increase %	Large increase %	X– score
High school principal	0.0	5.9	94.1	2.94
Primary school principal	1.3	10.7	88.0	2.87
Primary school teacher	11.8	45.6	42.6	2.30
High school teacher	18.3	47.3	34.4	2.16
Total	12.1	41.2	46.7	2.35

λ square = 83.82. * statistically significant at 0.05 level.

Teachers were asked what additional functions they had acquired as a result of LSM. These responses were registered in answer to an open-ended question with any particular respondent being able to record more than one response, the total number of responses being 1,171. Only comments that made up more than 10 per cent of the total comments are reported in Table 3.12. Teachers and principals are reported together as, regarding this question, there was very little difference in the type and frequency of their comments. Table 3.12 illustrates the percentage of the total responses represented by the first three ranked responses to this open-ended question.

A majority of primary (67.6 per cent) and high (50 per cent) school respondents felt that LSM had improved relationships between teachers and principals. High school principals and primary teachers were divided in their responses with 50 per cent 'improved' and 50 per cent 'unchanged', and 46.5 per cent 'improved' and 40 per cent 'unchanged', respectively. Approximately half of the high school teachers (50.3 per cent) reported that relationships were 'unchanged', with the remaining half divided between 'improved' 25.4 per cent and 'diminished' 24.3 per cent. The responses of high school teachers were statistically significantly different from those of primary teachers and principals and high school principals (chi-square = 50.1). Results are shown in Table 3.13.

Table 3.12 *What additional functions do you have as a result of LSM?*

	Percentage
Numerous committees and meetings	17.2
Budgeting	14.9
Management and coordination of programmes	10.5

*1,171 responses from 87 principals and 400 teachers

Table 3.13 *Have LSM practices had an effect on the quality of relationships between teachers and principals?*

	Improved relationships %	Unchanged relationships%	Diminished relationships%	$\bar{X}$ score
Primary school principal	67.6	29.7	2.7	1.35
High school principal	50.0	50.0	0.0	1.50
Primary school teacher	46.5	40.0	13.5	1.67
High school teacher	25.4	50.3	24.3	1.99
Total	43.1	42.0	14.9	1.63

λ square = 50.01. * statistically significant at 0.05 level.

4. Alterations to the professional authority of principals and teachers

Teachers and principals were asked to what extent the move to LSM had affected the professional authority of the principal. A chi-square value of 5.41 indicates that there is no statistically significant difference between the responses of teachers and principals. At least two-thirds of principals and teachers considered that the professional authority of the principal has been noticeably altered either to a moderate extent or to a significant extent (columns 1 and 2 = 76.5 per cent, 67.5 per cent, 68.3 per cent and 65.9 per cent respectively). These results are illustrated in Table 3.14.

A majority of high school principals, primary principals and primary teachers consider that the professional authority of teachers has altered to a moderate extent or to a significant extent (columns 1 and 2 = 64.8 per cent, 58.4 per cent 57.3 per cent respectively), whereas over 50 per cent of high school teachers indicate that the extent of alteration of authority ranges from to 'some extent' to 'not at all' (columns 3 and 4 = 58.5 per cent). A statistically significant difference exists between the responses of high school teachers and the other respondents, exhibited by a calculated chi-square value of 24.62. Results are shown in Table 3.15.

Table 3.14 *In your assessment to what extent has the move to local school management altered the professional authority of the principal?*

	Significantly %	Moderately	Some extent %	Not at al %	X̄ score
High school principal	41.2	35.3	5.9	17.6	1.89
Primary school principal	31.1	36.4	19.5	13.0	2.09
Primary school teacher	30.4	37.9	13.7	18.0	2.19
High school teacher	30.3	35.6	18.1	16.0	2.20
Total	30.7	37.0	15.4	16.9	2.17

λ square = 5.41.

Table 3.15 *In your assessment to what extent has the move to LSM altered the professional authority of teachers in your school?*

	Significantly %	Moderately %	Some extent %	Not at all %	X̄ score
High school principal	29.5	35.3	17.6	17.6	2.11
Primary school principal	23.3	35.1	20.8	20.8	2.33
Primary school teacher	15.6	41.7	21.2	21.5	2.49
High school teacher	8.5	33.0	23.9	34.6	2.85
Total	14.9	38.3	21.8	25.0	2.56

λ square = 24.62. * statistically significant at 0.05 level.

5. Effects of LSM on promotion and appraisal of teachers

Over fifty per cent of primary teachers and primary and high school principals indicated that selection or promotion of teachers had not been altered by LSM (73.3 per cent, 66.7 per cent and 58.8 per cent respectively). High school teachers were evenly divided in their responses at 50 per cent and 50 per cent. Teachers differed significantly (chi-square = 26.02 with a probability of 0.000) when responding 'yes' to this item. Results are shown in Table 3.16. An open-ended question, asking those who reported that the selection and promotion of teachers had changed, followed up from the item recorded in this table. Seventy-eight responses were received from primary teachers of whom 35 per cent (27) reported that they considered selection was unfair, whereby people were appointed by patronage rather than merit. Of the 69 high school teachers responding to the open-ended question, 43 per cent (30) responded in a similar fashion to the primary school teachers.

Table 3.16 *Has LSM altered the selection or promotion of teachers in your school?*

	Yes %	No %
High school teacher	50.0	50.0
High school principal	41.2	58.8
Primary school principal	33.3	66.7
Primary school teacher	26.7	73.3
Total	34.4	65.6

λ square = 26.02. * statistically significant at 0.05 level.

Table 3.17 illustrates the responses of principals and teachers as to whether LSM had affected staff appraisal in their school. There appears to be a high level of agreement ranging from 74.2 per cent to 87.5 per cent that LSM had not affected staff appraisal.

Table 3.17 *Has LSM affected the process of staff appraisal in your school?*

	Yes %	No %
High school principal	12.5	87.5
Primary school principal	18.9	81.1
Primary school teacher	24.7	75.3
High school teacher	25.8	74.2
Total	23.9	76.1

λ square = 2.57

6. The effects of implementation of local school management

Table 3.18 illustrates the items referring to the perceived effects of the implementation of LSM on the schools. The responses of teachers and principals are listed by percentages (agree, unsure, disagree), mean scores – agree = 1, unsure = 2, disagree = 3 – and a calculated chi-square with an indication of significance at the 0.05 level.

Table 3.18 *Principals and teachers: Do you agree or disagree with the following statements about the effects of LSM?*

		Agree %	Unsure %	Disagree %	$\bar{X}$	λ^2
1. It has promoted more effective management of the school	Principals	86.6	12.4	1.0	1.14	27.90*
	Teachers	59.9	20.7	19.4	1.59	
2. It has improved decision-making	Principals	81.4	15.5	3.1	1.22	22.97*
	Teachers	58.1	19.7	22.2	1.64	
3. It has significantly increased community involvement in school decision-making	Principals	68.0	18.6	13.4	1.45	15.13*
	Teachers	46.3	27.1	26.6	1.80	
4. It has promoted greater equity in resource allocation	Principals	61.9	21.6	16.5	1.55	11.59*
	Teachers	43.2	27.5	29.3	1.86	
5. It has significantly improved equity in student outcomes	Principals	30.9	51.5	17.6	1.87	7.21*
	Teachers	26.4	42.3	31.3	2.05	
6. Greater equity in learning available to different groups of students	Principals	53.6	33.0	13.4	1.59	8.23*
	Teachers	47.7	26.8	27.5	1.79	
7. It has promoted more effective teaching	Principals	46.4	44.3	9.3	1.63	22.54*
	Teachers	39.5	31.3	29.2	1.93	
8. It has promoted a more effective learning community	Principals	70.1	24.7	5.2	1.35	20.40*
	Teachers	47.3	30.8	21.9	1.74	
9. It has significantly improved the quality of student learning	Principals	37.1	44.3	18.6	1.81	11.59*
	Teachers	28.6	34.7	36.7	2.08	
10. It has significantly improved student engagement in school life	Principals	39.2	43.3	17.5	1.78	10.13*
	Teachers	30.1	35.8	34.1	2.04	
11. It has significantly improved student discipline and behaviour	Principals	26.8	36.1	37.1	2.10	5.54*
	Teachers	23.4	26.6	50.0	2.27	
12. It has significantly improved school–community relations	Principal	61.9	29.9	8.2	1.46	18.0*
	Teachers	39.8	37.4	22.8	1.83	
13. Diversion of school's effort away from tasks of teaching and learning	Principals	45.4	13.4	41.2	1.96	1.98
	Teachers	44.0	19.3	36.7	1.93	
14. Diversion of my own efforts away from tasks of teaching and learning	Principals	57.7	9.3	33.0	1.75	7.86*
	Teachers	42.0	14.2	43.8	2.02	

* a statistically significant difference at the 0.05 level.

Both teachers and principals responded positively to items (1, 2 and 3) concerning the effects of LSM on 'promotion of more effective management' (Item 1: principals, 86.6 per cent agree; teachers, 59.9 per cent agree) and 'improved decision-making' (Item 2: principals, 81.4 per cent agree; teachers, 58.1 per cent agree). Principals responded more positively (68.0 per cent, agree) to 'increased community involvement in school decision-making' than did teachers (46.3 per cent, agree, 27.1 per cent unsure).

The opinions of teachers and principals also differed on the equity effects of LSM. Principals (61.9 per cent agree) felt that 'greater equity in resource allocation had been promoted', whereas teachers appeared to be less certain with 43.2 per cent agreeing, 27.5 per cent unsure and 29.3 per cent disagreeing. Teachers' responses (26.3 per cent agree with 42.3 per cent unsure) exhibited almost the same lack of certainty about 'improved equity in student outcomes', as did principals (51.5 per cent unsure). Item 6, dealing with 'greater equity in learning available to different groups', elicited a slightly more positive outcome (53.6 per cent agree) from principals in contrast to a less certain response (47.7 per cent agree, 26.8 per cent unsure, 27.5 per cent disagree) from teachers.

Questions (Items 7, 8 and 9) concerned the effectiveness of LSM regarding teaching and learning. The promotion of 'more effective teaching' as a result of LSM generated an inconclusive result as far as teachers (39.5 per cent agree and 31.3 per cent unsure) and principals (46.4 per cent agree and 44.3 per cent unsure) were concerned. Uncertainty about 'significant improvement in the quality of student learning' was evident among both teachers (28.6 per cent agree and 34.7 per cent unsure) and principals (37.1 per cent agree and 44.3 per cent unsure). Principals considered that LSM had 'promoted a more effective learning community' (70.1 per cent agree) in contrast to a mixed response from teachers (47.3 per cent agree, 30.8 per cent unsure and 21.9 per cent disagree).

Principals (39.2 agree and 43.3 per cent unsure) and teachers (30.1 agree and 35.9 per cent unsure) indicated uncertainty concerning (Item 10) 'improving students' engagement in school life'. Principals (61.9 per cent agree) felt that there had been an 'improvement in school–community relations' (Item 12), whereas teachers' responses appeared to be inconclusive, with 39.8 per cent agree 37.3 per cent unsure and 22.8 per cent disagree. Fifty per cent of teachers felt that 'student discipline and behaviour had not improved' (Item 11) and principals recorded mixed responses (26.8 per cent agree, 36.1 per cent unsure and 37.1 per cent disagree).

Response to items concerning the diversion of effort, both the school's effort (Item 13) and self-effort (Item 14), 'away from tasks of teaching and learning' saw both principals (45.4 per cent agree and 41.2 per cent disagree) and teachers (44 per cent agree and 36.7 per cent disagree) registering mixed opinions. Principals agreed (57.7 per cent) that their own efforts had been diverted away from teaching and learning, and teachers indicated mixed perceptions (42.0 per cent agree and 43.8 per cent disagree).

The mean scores for each of the 14 items are illustrated in Figure 3.1. There is a clear gap between the upper line representing the mean scores of the teachers and the lower line representing mean scores for the principals, except for item 13: diversion of the school's effort away from the tasks of teaching and learning. As shown in the chi-square column of Table 3.18 and illustrated in Figure 3.1, this gap indicates a statistically significant difference between principals' and teachers' responses on 13 of the 14 questionnaire items. More than 50 per cent of principals have a positive attitude to LSM effect on school management, decision-making, school–community relations and equity in learning opportunities, whereas more than 50 per cent of teachers see positive effects on only school management and decision-making.

The responses of high and primary school teachers to items dealing with the effects of LSM on schools are listed in Table 3.19. Primary school teachers' perceptions of the effects on LSM on their schools, in some areas, are more positive than the perceptions of high school teachers on the same matter. On items 1, 2 and 3, those related to administration, a majority of primary school teachers agree that 'more effective management has been promoted' (72.4 per cent agree), 'decision-making has improved' (69.3 per cent agree) and 'involvement in decision-making has increased' (57.7 per cent agree). High school teachers are less conclusive than primary school teachers on these items with 'more effective management', 'improved decision-making' and 'increased community involvement in school decision-making' registering 46.9 per cent, 46.4 per cent and 34.5 per cent agreement respectively. Primary school teachers (48.5 per cent agree, 27.2 per cent unsure and 24.3 per cent disagree) and high school teachers (37.6 per cent agree, 27.8 per cent unsure and 34.6 per cent disagree) responded, with some uncertainty, to the idea that LSM had 'promoted greater equity in resource allocation'.

When the question (Item 5) of 'improved equity in student outcomes' is addressed both primary teachers (43.1 per cent) and high school teachers (41.5 per cent) respond in a similar fashion in the unsure category. High school teachers show much less agreement (16.4 per cent) with this item than do primary school teachers (36.1 per cent agree). More than 50 per cent of primary school teachers indicate agreement to 'greater equity in learning opportunities are available to different groups of students', whereas high school teachers are less certain with a 39.6 per cent agree, 25.3 per cent unsure and 35.1 per cent disagree response.

Figure 3.1 *Perceived effects of the implementation of LSM on schools: mean scores.*

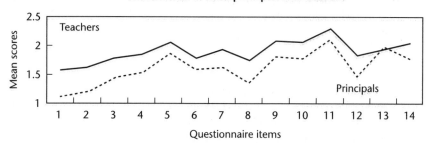

Table 3.19 *High and primary school teachers: Do you agree or disagree with the following statements about the effects of local school management?*

		Agree %	Unsure %	Disagree %	X̄	λ²
1. It has promoted more effective management of the school	Primary High	72.4 46.9	16.3 25.3	11.3 27.8	1.39 1.81	28.59*
2. It has improved decision–making	Primary High	69.3 46.4	16.8 22.7	13.9 30.9	1.45 1.85	23.63*
3. Significantly increased community involvement in school decision-making	Primary High	57.7 34.5	26.9 27.3	15.4 38.2	1.58 2.04	30.63*
4. It has promoted greater equity in resource allocation	Primary High	48.5 37.6	27.2 27.8	24.3 34.6	1.76 1.97	6.29*
5. It has significantly improved equity in student outcomes	Primary High	36.1 16.4	43.1 41.5	20.8 42.1	1.85 2.26	29.01*
6. Greater equity in learning available to different groups of students	Primary High	55.5 39.6	25.2 25.3	19.3 35.1	1.64 1.95	14.23*
7. It has promoted more effective teaching	Primary High	54.2 24.1	25.4 30.9	20.4 45.0	1.66 2.21	41.91*
8. It has promoted a more effective learning community	Primary High	63.7 30.4	27.3 34.5	9.0 35.1	1.45 2.05	55.60*
9. It has significantly improved the quality of student learning	Primary High	38.3 18.6	38.8 30.4	22.9 51.0	1.85 2.33	36.77*
10. It has significantly improved student engagement in school life	Primary High	43.1 16.5	35.1 36.6	21.8 46.9	1.79 2.04	41.64*
11. It has significantly improved student discipline and behaviour	Primary High	32.8 13.5	31.8 21.2	35.4 65.3	2.03 2.52	37.64*
12. It has significantly improved school–community relations	Primary High	50.7 28.5	35.8 38.9	13.5 32.6	1.63 2.04	28.38*
13. Diversion of school's effort away from from tasks of teaching and learning	Primary High	38.9 49.2	18.2 20.5	42.9 30.3	2.04 1.81	6.98*
14. Diversion of my own efforts away from from tasks of teaching and learning	Primary High	39.3 44.8	14.4 13.9	46.3 41.3	2.07 1.96	1.31

* a statistically significant difference at the 0.05 level.

Concerns about teaching and learning were addressed. Primary and high school teachers displayed difference in opinion (Item 7) to 'promotion of more effective teaching' (primary 54.2 per cent agree, high 24.1 per cent agree), (Item 8) 'promotion of a more effective learning community' (primary 63.7 per cent agree, high 30.4 per cent agree) and (Item 9) 'improvement in the quality of student learning' (primary teachers 38.3 per cent agree, high school teachers 18.6 per cent agree).

Both primary and high school teachers' responses were inconclusive concerning 'improved student engagement in school life' (Item 10). Primary teachers agreed (43.1 per cent) while 35.1 per cent were unsure. On the other hand, 46.9 per cent of high school teachers disagreed and 36.6 per cent were unsure. 'Improvement in student discipline' was seen negatively (65.3 per cent disagree) by high school teachers with primary teachers displaying uncertainty (approximately 30 per cent agree, unsure and disagree). Only 50.7 per cent of primary school teachers agreed that 'school–community relations' had improved and high school teachers registered a high response of unsure 38.9 per cent, with agree 28.5 per cent and disagree 32.6 per cent.

Diversion of the school's efforts (Item 13) and self-efforts (Item 14) away from the 'tasks of teaching and learning' received mixed responses from teachers. Agreement by primary and high school teachers that the 'school's effort' had been diverted was 38.9 per cent and 49.2 per cent respectively, and disagreement 42.9 per cent and 30.3 per cent respectively. Diversion of 'my own efforts' followed a similar pattern with primary teachers indicating 39.3 per cent agree and 46.3 per cent disagree and high school teachers showing 44.8 per cent agree and 41.3 per cent disagree.

The mean scores for each of the 14 items in Table 3.19 are illustrated in Figure 3.2. There is a clear gap between the upper line representing the mean scores of the high school teachers and the lower line of the primary school teachers except for item 14: diversion of the my own efforts away from the tasks of teaching and learning. As shown in the chi-square column of Table 3.19 and illustrated in Figure 3.2, this gap indicates a statistically significant difference between primary school teachers' and high school teachers' responses on 13 of the 14 questionnaire items. More than 50 per cent of primary school teachers have a positive attitude to LSM's effect on school management, decision-making, the school as a learning community, involvement in decision-making, equity in learning opportunities for different groups of students, effective teaching and school–community relations, with mean responses ranging from 1.39 to 1.66. In no case did any item responded to by high school teachers indicate 50 per cent or more agreement.

Figure 3.2 *Perceived effects of the implementation of LSM on schools: mean scores.*

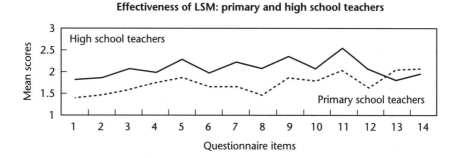

Effectiveness of LSM: primary and high school teachers

Discussion

LSM was introduced in Tasmania, as elsewhere, with high hopes that it would make schools more relevant and effective. Not only would wide participation in decision-making at the school level result in being better prepared for involvement in the democratic process but also in better educational outcomes. What do our results tell us about whether these expectations have been achieved? In brief, we have found greater involvement but not necessarily in democratic processes or in a transfer to better educational outcomes.

Consistent with the trends elsewhere, the expectations for the role of those in Tasmanian schools have clearly changed. Decision-making has moved strongly away from central agencies to individual schools. LSM is seen to have been adopted to a significant or moderate extent by almost 80 per cent of our sample. And in contrast to Dimmock and Hattie (1994), principals in Tasmania see this shift as a good thing (83 per cent primary – 88 per cent high) and that the benefits either outweigh or match the costs (88 per cent for primary and high school principals). These positive principal responses are despite their belief that their role has been changed to a large extent (60 per cent primary – 70 per cent high) with a large increase in the demands on their time (88 per cent primary – 82 per cent high) and in their duties and responsibilities (88 per cent primary – 94 per cent high). But also consistent with trends in Australia (Logan et al., 1996) and overseas (Vergugo et al., 1997), it is not clear that the shift of power is moving either beyond the principal to the staff and community or beyond the administrative to the educational.

First, is there evidence that there has been a shift of power beyond the principal to the staff and community? While the data is not completely consistent on this question, the answer must be that these shifts are not yet occurring in any significant way, especially in high schools. Only 41 per cent of primary and 26 per cent of high school teachers see LSM as a good thing or that it has changed to a large extent their role (21 percent primary – 18 per cent high) or duties and responsibilities (43 per cent primary – 34 per cent high). As well, 23 per cent of primary and 30 per cent of high school teachers say their role has not at all been affected by the move to LSM and 54 per cent of primary and 75 per cent of high school teachers perceive an unchanged or diminished relationships between teachers and their principal.

As was found by Logan et al. (1996), other worrying signs can be detected in the different responses of principals and teachers. On the whole principals believe they have adopted LSM in a form that involves others in a collaborative and cooperative way. They believe LSM has promoted effective school management and decision-making and has improved relationships in the schools. They see LSM as a good thing with potential further to improve Tasmanian schooling. In contrast, teachers do not see themselves involved in decision-making to the same extent as principals (46 per cent of teachers compared to 68 per cent of principals) and do not perceive as high a level of collaboration and cooperation (primary teachers 47 per cent – primary principals 68 per cent and high school teachers 25 per cent – high school principals 50 per cent), improved decision-making (58 per cent teachers – 81 per cent principals), or promotion of an effective learning community (47 of teachers – 70 per cent of principals).

There is a risk here of Tasmania following the decentralisation path laid in New Zealand where it was found that the 'principals' role changed from one of principal as team leader in spirit to one of manager in reality' (Sullivan, 1994: 14). This situation poses an interesting dilemma for school principals. Decentralisation that involves only administrative change can still increase principal power and prestige. But in so doing it may decrease the status of teachers as well as having detrimental affects on teaching and learning. As Sullivan (1994: 15) also concluded: 'Principals can take on roles that increase their status but at the same time remove them from the partnership that existed in schools, while decreasing the status of the classroom teacher.'

Teachers themselves may be partly to 'blame' for this situation. Preferring the relatively safe environment of congeniality that superficial structural and procedural change can bring, teachers may be happy to let the administrators 'get on with it' while they retreat to their classrooms. As the ATC (1994) research found, teachers are yet to be convinced that activities outside the classroom such as whole-school planning and school councils are important to their 'core business' of teaching and learning.

Also, teachers may well believe that 'an elephantine amount' of decentralisation talk has only 'brought forth a small "mouse" of results' (Weiss and Cambone, 1994: 291). If this is the case then it is unsurprising that teachers are not more enthusiastic about decentralisation. Whatever the reason, our results suggest that not only are Tasmania principals not investing in all their people but that their teachers are yet to make LSM their own. Despite this gloomy conclusion, we believe a 'window of opportunity' remains open. A culture of resistance has not yet formed. Rather than rejecting LSM outright, teachers seem to be saying that they have yet to make up their minds (for example, over 50 per cent of teachers are unsure whether LSM has been 'a good thing' for their school and over 65 per cent say that the benefits of pursuing LSM either outweigh or match the costs).

Silins and Mulford (2002) identified three major and aligned elements in successful school reform. The first element related to how people are treated, the second to a professional community and the third to the presence of a capacity for learning. We believe our results confirm that an important early key to the successful introduction of LSM is how people are treated, especially in achieving personalised relationships and being actively involved in decision-making in areas of relevance and importance. We agree with Silins and Mulford (2002) that unless this first element is satisfactorily achieved it is unlikely that the other two elements will be relevant, let alone accomplished (see also Seashore Louis et al., 1995). Our results make it clear that more time needs to be spent by those in schools on first improving how people are treated. Empowerment (Vergugo et al., 1997) through broad-based leadership opportunities still has some way to go, especially in Tasmanian high schools.

Second, is there evidence that decentralisation has moved beyond the administrative to the educational? Along with previous Australian research findings (Grady et al., 1994; ATC, 1994; Logan et al., 1996; Thomas, 1996) and other (Leithwood and Menzies, 1998) research findings, our results indicate that there is a belief that LSM leads to increased control at the school level. But this is more likely to be achieved in administrative rather than educational areas and to be accompanied by a massive increase in workloads. While three-quarters of principals believe that LSM has improved financial management, use of resources, school–community relations and involvement in decision-making, over half believe that LSM has not changed the quality of teaching and learning. Close to half of all respondents believed the main cost of the introduction of LSM to be that the time for, and quality of, teaching had been diminished. Some 69 per cent of principals and 74 per cent of teachers disagree that LSM has significantly improved equity in student outcomes, quality of student learning (63 per cent of principals – 71 per cent of teachers) and student engagement in school life (61 per cent of principals – 70 per cent of teachers), or resulted in more effective teaching (54 per cent of principals – 61 per cent of teachers).

It might be, as was found by Weiss and Cambone (1994), that teachers' allegiance to LSM has cooled over time. This would especially be the case where administrative demands of LSM have built up and diverted teachers from what they see as their core classroom responsibilities. Consistent with Logan et al.'s (1996) results, there is some suggestion in our data that such disenchantment has happened. Well over half of Tasmanian principals and teachers believe that LSM has actually diverted their own as well as their school's efforts away from teaching and learning.

Yet Berliner and Biddle's (1995: 339) warning that 'the need to make site-based decisions about trivial matters may interfere with education' is a salutary one. While teachers may prefer congeniality over collegiality, an ongoing challenge for leaders of schools involved in effective educational reform will be 'to develop learning communities which value differences and support critical reflection and encourage members to question, challenge and debate teaching and learning issues and dilemmas' (Peters et al., 1996: 63). However, as Weiss and Cambone (1994: 292) point out, educational leaders need to remember that 'the process by which teachers come to trust the authenticity of power sharing...and gain confidence in their own ability to provide direction and implement plans' to improve educational provision is slow.

On the whole, and consistent with previous findings (Reid, 1998), LSM has had the greatest acceptance and the most effect on educational matters in Tasmanian primary schools. Discrepancies between principals and teachers were greatest in high schools suggesting (as has been found elsewhere, see Stoll and MacBeath, 1997; Dempster, 2000), that teachers in secondary (high) schools view decentralised management very critically. These high school results should be of concern given other research (Harris and Hopkins, 1999; Berends, 2000; Dinham and Scott, 1999; Leithwood and Duke, 1999) clearly demonstrating that reform will fail in the face of resistance from teachers.

To reiterate an earlier point (Dibbon, 2000; Mulford, 1994) those in secondary schools are reluctant to find the time to attend to many of the adult issues that need to first be resolved to work effectively together in the interests of a continual improving provision of education. Our results may be reflecting the particularly privatistic culture of high schools (Hargreaves and Hopkins, 1991), especially where it is further cocooned within subject departments (Bennett and Harris, 1999) that are not well linked together. Yet being left alone to get on with one's teaching may no longer be the appropriate response.

Evidence is accumulating (e.g. Peters et al., 1996) on the importance of learning communities for continually improved educational outcomes. Such communities value differences, support critical reflection and encourage mem-

bers to question, challenge and debate teaching and learning issues. Put succinctly, the emphasis for effective educational outcomes is shifting from
individual to collective teacher efficacy.

Conclusion

LSM is making a difference but not yet the 'right' difference. Tasmanian principals are strong advocates of decentralisation but it is not yet resulting in
widespread improvement in teaching and learning. Principals can be strong
advocates for change but they will also need to move beyond being 'one
person bands'. They not only have to get the administration of their schools
'right', including the establishment of a school educational vision, but also
involve others in that administration including developing and implementing
that vision. In doing so they need to move beyond the administrative to the
educational through consensus building, meaningful collaboration and shared
leadership. In turn, this means moving teachers beyond comfortable congeniality and conformity to collegiality and a constructively critical, professional
learning community. Such fundamental change will take time and needs
greater support than is currently in evidence.

In conclusion, we can do no better than repeat Murphy and Beck's (1995:
241–2) plea:

> It is not our intention here to suggest that stakeholders in the educational community
> should abandon efforts at shared decision-making at the school level. At the same
> time, it is clear to us that, unless [LSM] is refocussed, it will never approximate the
> expectations of its advocates ... [It requires] two fundamental changes. First, politics
> will need to be directed to the task of creating an educational community. Second,
> organization and management will need to be formed in response to the needs of the
> learning environment, rather than vice versa.

References

ATC (1994) *The Council*. Newsletter of the Australian Teaching Council, Issue 3, November.
Bennett, N. and Harris, A. (1999) 'Truth from power? Organisational theory, school effectiveness
and school improvement', *School Effectiveness and School Improvement*, 10 (4): 533–50.
Berends, M. (2000) 'Teacher-reported effects of New American School design: exploring
relationships to teacher background and school context', *Educational Evaluation and Policy
Analysis*, 22 (1): 65–82.
Berliner, D. and Biddle, B. (1995) *The Manufactured Crisis: Myths, Fraud, and the Attacks on
America's Public Schools*. New York: Addison-Wesley.
Bishop, P. and Mulford, B. (1996) 'Empowerment in four primary schools: they don't really
care', *International Journal of Educational Reform*, 5 (2): 193–204.
Caldwell, B. and Hayward, D. (1998) *The Future of Schools: Lessons from the Reform of Public
Education*. London: Falmer.
Chrispeels, J., Brown, J. and Castillo, S. (2000) 'School leadership teams: factors that
influence their development and effectiveness', in K. Leithwood (ed.), *Understanding
Schools as Intelligent Systems*. Stamford, CT: JAI Press.

Dempster, N. (2000) 'Guilty or not: the impact and effects of site-based management on schools', *Journal of Educational Administration*, 38 (1): 47–63.

Dibbon, D. (2000) 'Diagnosing the extent of organisational learning capacity in schools', in K. Leithwood (ed.), *Understanding Schools as Intelligent Systems*. Stamford, CT: JAI Press.

Dimmock, C. and Hattie, J. (1994) 'Principals' and teachers' reactions to school restructuring', *Australian Journal of Education*, 38 (1): 36–55.

Dinham, S. and Scott, C. (1996) 'The teacher 2000 project: a study of teacher satisfaction, motivation and health'. Unpublished report, University of Western Sydney, Nepean.

Dinham, S. and Scott, C. (1999) *The relationship between context, type of school and position held in school and occupational satisfaction, and mental stress*, paper presented to the Australian College of Education/Australian Council for Educational Administration National Conference, Darwin.

Goldring, E. and Pasternack, R. (1994) 'Principals' co-ordinating strategies and school effectiveness', *School Effectiveness and School Improvement*, 5 (3): 239–53.

Grady, N., Macpherson R., Mulford, W. and Williamson, J. (1994) *Australian School Principals: Profile 1994*. Adelaide: Australian Principals Associations Professional Development Council.

Hamilton, M. and Richardson, V. (1995) 'Effects of the culture in two schools on the process and outcomes of staff development', *Elementary School Journal*, 95 (4): 367–85.

Hargreaves, D. and Hopkins, D. (1991) *The Empowered School*. London: Cassell.

Harris, A. and Hopkins, D. (1999) 'Teaching and learning and the challenge of educational reform', *School Effectiveness and School Improvement*, 10 (2): 257–67.

Joyce, B., Calhoun, E. and Hopkins, D. (1999) *The New Structure of School Improvement: Inquiring Schools and Achieving Students*. Buckingham: Open University Press.

Kendall, L. (1996) *Choice Criteria for Statistical Tests*. Canberra: University of Canberra, at http://www.ssrl.@utas.edu.au

Leithwood, K. and Duke, D. (1999) 'A century's quest to understand school leadership', in J. Murphy and K. Seashore Louis (eds), *Handbook of Research on Educational Administration*. Washington, DC: American Educational Research Association.

Leithwood, K. and Menzies, T. (1998) 'A review of research concerning the implementation of site-based management', *School Effectiveness and School Improvement*, 9 (3): 233–85.

Leithwood, K., Jantzi, D. and Fernandez, A. (1994) 'Transformational leadership and teachers' commitment to change', in J. Murphy and K. Seashore Louis (eds), *Reshaping the Principalship: Insights from Transformational Reform Efforts*. Thousand Oaks, CA: Corwin.

Logan, L., Sachs, J. and Dempster, N. (eds) (1996) *Planning for Better Primary Schools*. Canberra: ACE.

Mulford, B. (1994) *Shaping Tomorrow's Schools*. Melbourne, Victoria: Australian Council for Educational Administration Monograph No. 15.

Murphy, J. and Beck. L. (1995) *School-Based Management as School Reform*. Thousand Oaks, CA: Corwin.

Peters, J., Dobbins, D. and Johnston, B. (1996) *Restructuring and Organisational Culture*. Ryde, New South Wales: National Schools Network.

Reid, A. (1998) 'Regulating the education market: the effects on public education workers', in A. Reid (ed.), *Going Public: Education Policy and Public Education in Australia. Australian Curriculum Studies Association*. Deakin West, ACT: Author. pp. 57–66.

Robertson, P. and Briggs, K. (1998), 'Improving schools through school-based management: an examination of the process of change', *School Effectiveness and School Improvement*, 9 (1): 28–57.

Russ, J. (1995) 'Collaborative management and school improvement: research findings from "improving schools" in England', *International Studies in Educational Administration*, 23 (2): 3–9.

Seashore Louis, K., Kruse, S. and Associates (1995) *Professionalism and Community: Perspectives on Reforming Urban High Schools*. Thousand Oaks, CA: Corwin.

Seashore Louis, K., Marks, H. and Kruse, S. (1995) 'Teachers' professional community in restructuring schools', *American Journal of Education*, 104, (2): 103–47.

Short, P., Greer, J. and Melvin, W. (1994) 'Creating empowered schools: lessons in change', *Journal of Educational Administration*, 32 (4): 38–52.

Silins, H. and Mulford, B. (2002) 'Leadership and school results', in K. Leithwood, P. Hallinger, G. Furman, P. Gronn, J. MacBeath, B. Mulford and K. Riley, *International Handbook of Educational Leadership and Administration*, 2nd edn. Dordrecht: Kluwer.

Silins, H., Mulford, B. and Zarins, S. (1999) *Leadership for learning and student outcomes, the LOLSO Project'*, paper presented to the annual meeting of the American Education Educational Research Association, Montreal.

Silins, H., Mulford, B., Zarins, S. and Bishop, P. (2000) 'Leadership for organizational learning in Australian secondary schools', in K. Leithwood (ed.), *Understanding Schools as Intelligent Systems*. Stamford, CT: JAI Press.

Stoll, L. and MacBeath, J. (1997) *Changing perspectives on changing schools*, paper presented at the annual meeting of the American Educational Research Association, Chicago.

Sullivan, K. (1994) 'The impact of educational reform on teachers' professional ideologies', *New Zealand Journal of Educational Studies*, 29 (1): 3–20.

Thomas, F. (1996) *A Three-Year Report Card: Co-operative Research Project Leading Victoria's Schools of the Future*. Melbourne, Victoria: State of Victoria Department of Education.

Vergugo, R., Greenberg, N., Henderson, R., Uribe O. and Schneider, J. (1997) 'School governance regimes and teachers' job satisfaction: bureaucracy, legitimacy, and community', *Educational Administration Quarterly*, 33 (1): 38–66.

Wallace, J. (1999) 'Professional school cultures: coping with the chaos of teacher collaboration', *Australian Educational Researcher*, 26 (2): 67–86.

Weiss, C. and Cambone, J. (1994) 'Principals, shared decision-making, and school reform', *Educational Evaluation and Policy Analysis*, 16 (3): 287–301.

Wildy, H. (1996) *Principals' conceptions of their changing power relations in a devolving school system*, paper presented at the 8th Regional Conference of the Commonwealth Council for Educational Administration, Kuala Lumpur, Malaysia

Wildy, H. and Wallace, J. (1994) *Devolving power in schools: resolving the dilemma of strong and shared leadership*, paper presented at the annual meeting of the American Educational Research Association, New Orleans.

Wohlstetter, P., Van Kirk, A., Robertson, P. and Mohrman, S. (1997) *Successful School-Based Management*. Virginia: Association for Supervision and Curriculum Development.

Chapter 4

Investigating effective resource management in secondary schools: the evidence of inspection reports

Derek Glover and Rosalind Levačić

The substantive focus of this chapter is the shift to local management of schools in England. Initiatives for local school management were also the substantive topic of the chapter by Mulford et al., although the context was different. The two research reports also differ in emphasis, approach and methodology. A particularly interesting aspect of the research reported by Glover and Levačić is that it made use of existing sources of data – something we highlighted in Chapter 2 as worth consideration in a small-scale project such as a thesis or dissertation. In this case, the study used school inspection reports completed by the Office for Standards in Education in England. These documents are publicly available and accessible through the Internet. Glover and Levačić outline how the inspection reports provided a useful source of data for examining the extent to which schools were implementing a 'rational-technicist' model of resource management, and the association between adoption of this model and the educational effectiveness of schools. Using the inspection reports also enabled them to conduct a much more ambitious study than otherwise would have been possible with the resources and time available. A strength of the reports was that they were based upon an established framework for inspection and a consistent process of reporting which required inspectors to back judgements with evidence. However, as Glover and Levačić point out, there are differences in approach between processes of data collection for the purpose of compiling inspection reports and those employed in social science research.

A particularly interesting dimension of the study was that a framework was developed for analysing the content of the reports both qualitatively and quantitatively. The authors highlight that some kinds of data can be analysed both ways, rather than there being different types of data. Another important issue raised by Glover and Levačić is the need for caution in interpreting an association between variables: that association does not necessarily imply causation – in this case a positive association between 'rational' school and departmental planning and educational quality. The authors explore a number of possible interpretations for the positive association between the two variables and are cautious in reaching their conclusions. The problem of identifying appropriate methods to explore causal relationships between variables is discussed further in the chapter by Leithwood and Jantzi in this part of the book.

The rationale for the research

This chapter reports on research into resource management in secondary schools in England, using judgements made in school inspection reports as the data source. We are concerned here with the way in which documentary evidence can be accessed, analysed, recorded and then used as the basis for hypothesis generation and further investigation. The policy background for our work stems from interest in the extent to which governors and staff in schools practise effective and efficient resource management. This became an important issue with the introduction of national policies to devolve more managerial decision-making to school level, known as the 'local management of schools' initiative. At the same time, a quasi-market allowing parents to express a preference for a school was established and a national curriculum and assessment framework introduced. These changes were fundamental to the 1988 Education Reform Act in England and Wales and its attempt to raise educational standards.

A key element of government policy towards schools has been the expectation of greater economic rationality in school management: 'The purpose of local management of schools is to enhance the quality of education by enabling more informed and effective use to be made of the resources available for teaching and learning' (DFE, 1994: para. 5).

Alongside the devolution of financial autonomy to the governing bodies for schools has been the development of a national system of school inspection operated by the Office for Standards in Education (OFSTED). The 1992 Education Act, which established OFSTED, stipulated that schools should not only be judged on their standards and quality of education but also on the efficiency of the school's leadership and management. To this end a nationwide, unified system of inspection was developed and a national training and registration scheme for inspectors put in place. Guidance on the content and process of inspection was circulated to the staff and governors of schools, and the local education authorities (LEAs) responsible for most state school provision. The training and framework documents specified objective criteria by which teaching and learning was to be judged. Consideration of aspects of leadership and management was also included with efficient and effective resource management as a new element in school inspections.

Advocates of these reforms postulated a direct relationship between school effectiveness and school-based resource management conducted in a rational manner in which means are purposefully related to educational ends. This advocacy is evident in the official model of good management practice recommended amongst others by the Department for Education (1994), the Audit Commission (1993) and the National Audit Office (1994). (The latter two organisations are concerned with auditing and assessing the value for money of, respectively, local and central government services.) This official model of good practice is both rational and technicist. It is rational in allocating resources so as best to deliver organisational objectives and technicist in requiring a complex and analytical decision-making process. Our aims in undertaking the research were broadly to see how far headteachers and governors of schools were aware of and had adopted this 'rational-technicist' model and hence whether there was a relationship between educational effectiveness and the espousal of such a model of resource management.

The research questions we sought to address were:

1 To what extent was the rational-technicist model being adopted in schools?
2 Was there an association between the educational effectiveness of a school and the adoption of the rational-technicist model?
3 How did staff in schools that were judged to be educationally effective manage their resources?

In this chapter we examine briefly the theoretical framework of the research, which is derived from the literature; explain the research design focusing on the use of documentary evidence from inspection reports; discuss the use of this evidence; comment on the analytical framework developed for the contents analysis of the reports and how it was applied; and summarise the main findings derived from the content analysis undertaken. The detailed findings and the evolution of connected research are published elsewhere (Levačić and Glover, 1998; Glover et al., 1996a, 1996b; Glover et al., 1997). Here we concentrate on how the documentary evidence was created from which the research findings were obtained.

The theoretical framework

The 'classical' model of rational decision-making (Scott, 1987; Tarter and Hoy, 1998) has a long history in economics and management. It consists of three sequential steps:

1 determining a unique set of objectives or goals for the organisation;
2 obtaining all available information on the alternative means for achieving the desired ends or objectives of the organisation;
3 selecting the alternative which best achieves organisational objectives.

A rational decision-making process will secure organisational efficiency, defined as the achievement of maximum output for a given cost of resources. The unrealistic assumptions of the classical model have been modified for the application of rational approaches to organisations by Simon (1957), who replaced maximisation with 'satisficing'. Managers, faced with limited information and restricted capacities for making sense of what information they have, aim to obtain satisfactory rather than optimal results.

A further modification of classical rationality is the literature on management decision-making in the face of uncertainty from the external environment. Mintzberg's (1994) critique of the inability of companies successfully to pursue deliberate long-term plans and his advocacy of emergent strategy as a more realistic endeavour are now widely accepted. The view that effective school leadership involves flexible planning when schools are dependent on their relationship with a complex and demanding external environment is now well developed (see Fidler, 1996; Scheerens, 1997; Wallace, 1991). In this approach a school staff has a clear sense of direction and aims that are reflected in the creation of plans. These act as guides to action which are modified in the light of changed threats and opportunities. The rationality lies in having articulated school aims and a clear sense of direction, which guide decision-making.

The implementation of local management of schools, by which responsibility for financial management was delegated to the headteacher and governors of schools, was accompanied by increasing advocacy of an official model of good management practice in these institutions. This is highly rational in conception (Audit Commission, 1993; Audit Commission and OFSTED, 1993; DES, 1988; DFE, 1994; National Audit Office, 1994; National Audit Office, 1997; OFSTED, 1993).

The guidance places considerable emphasis on good practice requiring tight coupling between the financial plan as expressed in the school's annual budget and educational objectives, which should be prioritised and implemented through a 'school development plan'. This process is sequential. Objectives are agreed, and then information is obtained on the alternative means by which the objectives might be attained. The selection of the most appropriate course of action then depends upon knowledge of its projected costs balanced against expected benefits. Thus ends and means are clearly linked. The budgetary planning process, because it identifies costs and relates them to anticipated benefits, is an essential part of rational planning. The establishment of cyclic systems of audit, planning, prioritising, implementing and evaluating are advocated by the Audit Commission (1993) and the National Audit Office (1996). For example, The Audit Commission (1993: 2.2) states that:

> *The school should have a medium term educational and budget plan (covering at least three years) indicating the intended use of resources in achieving its educational goals. Even though the funding available to each school will change annually, the school development plan should outline which areas are the priority for spending, and why.*

The official model of good resource management was made more explicit in the inspection framework (OFSTED, 1993, 1995a, 1995b), which stated that the efficiency of the school should be judged in terms of:

1 the standard of financial planning and management;
2 the efficiency and effectiveness with which staff, learning resources and accommodation are deployed to attain the school's aims and objectives and to match its priorities;
3 the effectiveness of financial control procedures;
4 any steps taken by the school to evaluate its cost-effectiveness.

Hence the inspection reports for schools provided a ready source of documentary evidence for addressing our research questions.

OFSTED reports and the use of documents as research evidence

Although 'official' in the sense that the OFSTED reports are published by a government agency, they are an example of social research and as such open to the problems inherent in this (Hammersley, 1993). The data extracted from the documents depend upon the perceptions of the people who wrote the reports and the understanding and interpretation skills of the reader. Documentary evidence offers context and understanding and provides a relatively easy way of obtaining other people's views of a situation or process (Hopkins, 1985). Problems of access, sample size, time and recording are overcome by using documents as the next best thing to personal involvement. Blaxter et al. (1996) have shown how such evidence can be used to provide background and to offer secondary data to support or question evidence collected in other ways. However, in the research reported here the documents were used as our main source of data.

Our concern was to gather as much relevant information as possible from the inspection reports. Since 1993, this large and valuable public record resource has become available to all users. This library of reports on school inspections is held on the OFSTED website at http//www.OFSTED.gov.uk. By using the search facility it is possible to access the reports prepared for the first and second round of inspections in England and Wales, to download them for later reading or printing, and then to use them as the basis of analysis. While these reports can be considered as a primary source classified as either an administrative report or a formal study, it has to be remembered that they are a distillation of a great deal of information made available to the inspectors either from official sources like the Department for Education and Skills 'Panda' (benchmarking) reports and statistics from examination boards, or from the completion of structured forms prior to the visit, for example the headteacher's report, or from the evidence put forward by subject leaders in the documentation underpinning teaching and learning within their area of responsibility.

The problem inherent in this type of distillation is that what reaches the final report is dependent upon the writer's interpretation of the raw data – some selection of evidence has to be made before the report is written. The inspection procedures allow school governors and staff to question items of detail in the draft report but only the inspectors can make changes to the draft document. The impressions gathered during the inspection and collated by the registered (lead) inspector stand as the final report. So while the report documents should be consistent in content and judgement because they are based on a set framework for inspection, there is evidence that different inspectors would have seen things in a different way. These issues are outlined at length by Wilcox and Gray (1996) and Cullingford (1999).

For those considering the use of OFSTED, or other, inspection reports as a source for longitudinal work in the future it has to be recognised that changes over time exacerbate this divergence of viewpoint and content. In England and Wales most schools have now been inspected at least twice and although the reports do provide evidence of change over a period of time they are not strictly comparable. Personnel, policies and procedures change within schools – indeed the whole purpose of the inspection system is to enhance effectiveness through necessary change. The structure of guidance given to the inspectorate has also changed in response to criticism of the processes by teachers and governors from the schools involved. Change has also grown from reflection on the approach within the inspectorate, resulting in an attempt to reduce the tension caused by the process of inspection. In part this has been through more open relationships between inspectors and the school staff but there has also been a shift from an attempt to assess every element of school life to one that concentrates on the strengths and weaknesses and the contribution to school improvement evident in schools during the second four-yearly round of inspection visits.

For our purposes the requirement that assertions made in official inspection reports should be backed by some evidence, however brief that might be, enabled us to feel confident that we could use them as a source of information and for comparative purposes. In so doing we used the criteria put forward by Scott (1990) who suggests that in using documents of this sort there should be prior evaluation of their authenticity, credibility and representativeness. These documents were authentic because of the structure of their compilation, credible in so far as they had been written following a degree of consensus within the inspection team, and representative of the school in question because of the detail given for each component of the inspection and the breadth of the summary report. Additionally, Scott argues that readers will need to be aware of the *meaning* of a document. May (2001) sees this need in terms both of clarity and of comprehensibility. Our reading of the reports had to be conditioned by our ability to interpret what was actually stated. We could not stray into the realms of what was being hinted at through understatement or hidden messages intended to indicate problems to those who had been involved in the inspection process.

Documents are rarely analysed at the time of their compilation – rather they are subject to interpretation during a later period when social, cultural and economic frameworks may have changed. Between 1989 and 1994 schools were becoming responsible for most financial decision-making as part of what was then called 'local financial management' (e.g. Downes, 1988). Within a short time, however, usage shifted from one of focus on financial management to a more general local management of schools stressing the interdependence of resource management with management of the curriculum and appropriate human resource development (e.g. Levačić, 1995). The reports that we were using were compiled during this time of change and we were aware that as the first tranche of inspection reports became available they were being eagerly read by senior managers within other schools who were quick to learn from the critical comment of inspectors. In this respect change was being driven by central government through the inspectorate as well as within schools. It was essential, therefore, that we attempted to gather reports written as nearly as possible within the same administrative and policy context.

Just how reliable and comparable are the documents? It was argued by the politicians responsible for the development of assessment following the 1988 Education Reform Act that OFSTED is objective in its approach. It is based upon a published Framework for Inspection and Guidance to the staff of schools and inspectors. It is tightly structured with a detailed procedure for every aspect of the inspection to ensure comparability between schools, and to allow for the aggregation of types of data from the reports so that judgements may be made about national standards and changes over time. The guidance to inspectors is based on a classification of observed evidence collected over a three- to five-day period within the school. This evidence is then judged according to set criteria and classified according to the grouping into which it falls. For example, the teaching observed within a lesson is recorded in the *Record of Evidence* for the inspection, then classified according to a seven-point scale varying from 'excellent' to 'very poor'. This judgement forms the basis of the overall classification of the quality of teaching within the school. In short, the subjective, by virtue of the process of systematisation, is converted to what is claimed to be objective data.

We recognised that our investigation would be affected by some degree of subjectivity because of the compilation of reports by different people over a period of time. It was clear, however, that the conceptual framework within which we were analysing evidence of how school staffs were working was not subject to change over the three-year period during which the reports we used had been prepared.

Designing the empirical investigation

Our initial investigation was into the way in which schools were managing their resources according to an analysis of data from OFSTED reports. This evidence could then be considered against theoretical frameworks of efficiency and effectiveness to ascertain the extent to which school staffs were aware of and were implementing the processes of rational resource management.

Sample selection

At the time we began our work in 1995 there were some 300 OFSTED secondary school reports produced between April and December 1994 available for downloading. Limited time meant that we could not analyse them all. We decided to select 120 drawn from a range of school types and from diverse geographical areas of England. To speed up the time taken to develop an analytical framework it was decided to work on 70 reports initially.

Purpose of content analysis

The reports offered qualitative information on how the requirements of good practice were or were not being met in the schools. There were also straightforward quantitative elements within the report, such as examination results, absentee rates and the percentage of lessons observed that was considered to be good or very good. For our purposes we needed to gain a picture across a broad range of schools, therefore we also wanted to 'quantify the qualitative' (see Taylor Fitz-Gibbon, 2001 for other examples). To do this it was necessary to develop classificatory systems as the basis of analysis of reports and then to aggregate totals within the classification for further analysis.

To assess the extent to which governors and staff of schools were using a rational-technicist approach and to establish any linkage between rationality in resource management and educational effectiveness we needed to analyse reports for:

▶ evidence of the processes of resource management;
▶ evaluation of the effectiveness of this management by inspectors against the criteria of the rational-technicist model;
▶ statistical data of the broad socio-economic context of the school as used in the inspectors' assessment of the value for money provided by the school;
▶ statistical data of educational outcomes, including the quality of teaching and learning, and examination results.

Although we focused on only one of the four aspects of the inspection assessment – the efficiency of the school, which included the quality of the management – all other parts of the report were read to obtain contextual information and assessments of educational effectiveness.

The data from the reports were used to address the first two research questions. The third question was explored in another study by means of case studies. The reports were used to identify for consideration as case studies those schools that were deemed educationally effective by inspectors from their judgements of the quality of teaching and learning, indicators of the ethos of the school, outcomes related to socio-economic context and assessment of the value for money offered by the school. We also sought educationally effective schools that between them displayed a range of resource management practices. Although the case studies of these schools (Glover et al., 1996a, 1996b) are beyond the scope of this chapter we do refer to them in our conclusions.

Doing content analysis

Content analysis is not without its methodological problems. May (2001) suggests that the content needs to be analysed with the intentions and purposes of the author in mind. We worked on the assumption that the inspection team visiting each school was being required to report in a standardised way, with substantiating evidence and with limited opportunity for personal bias. The reports were read and analysed on the basis of the detail given, not according to any implications for the school or OFSTED secretariat. Ericson et al. (1991) detail the care needed in the reading of documents for content analysis and the establishment of patterns from the data given. Scott (1990) urges that a balance be struck between the stark measurement of the occurrence of a term and grasping the significance of the use of the term in its context – qualitative synthesis. For us this meant a line-by-line examination of each report so that terms could be analysed in context and then classified and recorded according to their significance for our research objectives.

Despite these reservations there were certain advantages in the use of the reports because of the standard framework and the evidential basis of judgements made. The fact that the data are also used by the research division of OFSTED for the development of summary reports such as that on gender-related attainment, and as the basis of annual national reports, goes some way to ensure that consistency is maintained. That said, our work was undertaken during the initial period of inspection development and we were aware of three deficiencies of detail in reports:

▶ some elements of financial and resource management outlined in the framework were not commented on, either by omission or design;
▶ some inspectors were evaluating practice as 'good' in one school but similar evidence was commented upon as 'satisfactory' in another;
▶ not all the reports contained suggestions for improved practice which were often the key to the detail of the deficiencies noted.

The task was then to use the reports in an objective way but with an awareness of the inherent problems in the interpretation and analysis of the data. The process was as follows:

▶ downloading reports from the Internet and printing them for analysis;
▶ reading each report to gain an impression of context and the major features of management and leadership;
▶ focusing on the relevant sections of the reports that gave detail of resource and financial management procedures;
▶ analysis, classification (coding) and recording of evidential data;
▶ statistical analysis of the interlinked elements in resource management and analysis against other educational outcomes;
▶ reporting findings;
▶ conceptualising our findings, comparison with other studies' findings and drawing conclusions.

In this research, the process adopted was to read the statistical background material giving student age range, some indications of socio-economic context, examination outcomes, absentee rates and a summary of parental observations, and to note these on an Excel spreadsheet. The 'flavour' of the school as an educational organisation was thus implanted in the reader's mind. The next stage was to read the general observations about all aspects of the school including those sections dealing with the resource management issues pertinent to our enquiry, but to use this to add substance to the statistical background. It was then possible to look in detail at the sections of the report concerned with aspects of resource management.

Developing an analytical framework

From the reading and analysis of the pilot group of reports it was possible to see that the inspectors had been using three main criteria for evaluation based on evidence of:

▶ the use of rational development planning and the use of plans to determine expenditure;
▶ effective employment of resources to maximise educational opportunity within the school;
▶ the way in which the staff of the school secured value for money.

These criteria provided a framework for our analysis because they identified a list of management process variables that inspectors should be looking for when assessing resource management within the schools. Our list was as given in Figure 4.1. This is a modification of the original used for the analysis of the earlier 66 secondary school reports (Levačić and Glover, 1997). Each of the elements was coded by the use of acronyms to aid both spreadsheet recording and the subsequent analysis.

Figure 4.1 *The analytical framework.*

1. *Rational planning (RP)*. This encompasses five steps which characterize rational decision-making including:
   setting strategic aims and objectives;
   budget processes for considering costed alternatives relative to benefits;
   school development planning and the involvement of staff and governors;
   monitoring budget and development plan implementation;
   evaluation of efficiency and effectiveness to feed back into planning.

2. *Departmental planning (DP)*. This refers to the same set of processes in relation to departments.

3. *Evaluation variables*. These were extracted in part from the statistical data for each school but were also the subject of comment by inspectors:
   quantitative outcomes, e.g. examination results (EO);
   securing value for money through searching, e.g. for best buys (ER);
   procedures for school based reviews of aspects of work and policies (EV);
   governor and senior management involvement in evaluation (EI).

4. *Staff deployment (SD)*. Match between staff resources and curriculum needs.

5. *Staff training (ST)*. Relationship to stated school priorities and individual need.

6. *Educational resources (RS)*. Adequacy, allocation, maintenance and effectiveness.

7. *Accommodation (AC)*. Adequacy, allocation, maintenance and effectiveness.

8. *Financial administration (F)*. Related to probity and audit requirements.

9. *Value for money (V)*. An overall judgement on effectiveness and efficiency related to the school's annual budget and cost per student.

There were three possible explanations of 'failure' to mention an element in the reports:

▶ Inspectors assume that because they speak favourably in overall terms of a major heading, such as staff development, they do not consider it necessary to provide evidence subsumed by the comment.
▶ Despite the efforts made by those responsible for inspector training and the official inspection guidance there is evidence of some inconsistency in observation by reporting teams.
▶ There is variation in the extent to which an element is seen to be important to the reporting inspector. Some reports mention the existence of a development plan, while others provide evidence of the plan in use.

The reports offered a full range of comment from the brief and often unsubstantiated, to lengthy discussion of issues to be faced in securing school improvement. Comments have therefore to be analysed within their context, underlining the importance of a preliminary reading of all general sections of the document and one or two of the departmental reports.

Quantification

If public documents are to be a worthwhile source of data for analysis it is necessary to transform the evidence into something that can be analysed. Where statistical analysis is to be used, as in our study, then the qualitative data have to be represented quantitatively. We have mentioned that OFSTED has its own seven-point grading system. This analysis is not published as part of the report but underpins the comments being made. It is confidential. Only since our research was conducted have these gradings been put in a database, access to which requires permission from OFSTED. In our research the reader of inspection reports needed to consider the implied grading and to develop a way of inferring the level of approval or disapproval implied.

In order to achieve consistency for our classification of comments it was necessary to adopt our own set of criteria for the evaluation implicit in the reports. To this end we used measures of the quality of resource management decision-making. These are ranked 1, 2 or 3, according to the evidence for the attainment of criteria outlined in the framework. Where comments are critical the ranking is at level 1. Where there are suggestions for the improvement of processes but a system of sorts is in evidence the ranking is at level 2. Where there are commendatory remarks which show that the system is understood and used, the ranking is at level 3. Examples of good practice noted for each element in the most fulsome reports were tabulated at the same time as reading progressed and from this emerged a picture of the evidential elements necessary for a school to be classified by us as achieving level 3 in the report. The advantage of this table as an aide-memoire was that as reading progressed it was possible to build some degree of certainty into the classification being undertaken. For example, reports on those schools scoring a level 3 for staff deployment all provided evidence that the curriculum was taught by appropriately qualified teachers, that there was some system of accountability in place, and that there was balance in the availability and use of non-teaching staff.

That said, the classification of comments was not always easy. For example, the existence of a development plan may be noted – level 2 on our classification – but a subsequent comment refers to the inherent weaknesses of the plan suggesting that our classification should be at level 1. Often the resolution of such dilemmas could only be achieved by going back to other parts of the report to gauge the importance attached by inspectors to the relative strength or weakness of the element under consideration.

As an example of a critical comment with powerful recommendations for consideration in subsequent action planning we cite the following:

> *There are no strategies to evaluate cost-effectiveness. None of the co-ordinators has a delegated budget and budget setting is not informed by whole school planning. There is no cohesive system to identify spending priorities or to facilitate the formulation of medium and long term planning of objectives and help to achieve better value for money. Curriculum co-ordinators need to be involved more closely in financial and curriculum developments in order to provide governors with more information to assist them in their decision-making. The school development plan is too broad in outline and does not yet effectively aid forward planning.*

Clearly, according to our criteria such comments are classified as level 1 but the statement needs 'unpicking' to ensure that an appropriate score can be entered for each element in subsequent statistical analysis.

There were problems in classifying level 2 comments where the reports were basically descriptive, noting the existence of a feature but without criticism or commendation. We decided that by implication the element under consideration was judged to be satisfactory or adequate, for example: 'Allocation of funds to subject co-ordinators is based on the school's priorities as identified in the development plan.' Schools are often praised through a commendatory explanation of processes and this offers positive evaluation of the component parts of major elements. A rare summary of effective resource allocation provided data at our highest level 3:

> *There is a developing approach to strategic planning, financial management and budgetary control that is consistent with full delegation and school priority setting through the school development plan. The governing body, for instance, has been involved with the decision to use part of the 93/4 budget surplus to increase the spending on resources for every pupil and sustain the provision of some non-contact time for co-ordinators to monitor standards in particular subjects.*

To ensure that the classification of the evidence was such that any one of the research team could use it with confidence, a set of comments judged by the analyst to be at levels 1, 2 and 3 was then 'second marked' by another member of the team. Discussion of areas of disagreement then led to a refinement of the classification process and to an enhanced mutual understanding of the meaning of comments within our research context of effectiveness and efficiency. Undertaking this exercise for the first group of 66 secondary schools (Levačić and Glover, 1997) on an earlier project led to the development of additional 'search' techniques for the second tranche of 117 schools dealt with in this study. These included:

▶ skim reading of a range of reports on different curriculum subjects within the main report to see whether they yielded substantiating evidence for vague comment in the latter;
▶ triangulation of comment from different sections of the report to see whether what was implied, for instance by the comment 'weak leadership', was sustained by comment on resource management;
▶ comparison of the classification resulting from two similar reports to check for consistency.

Presenting the findings

The findings (Levačić and Glover, 1998) can be divided into two types: descriptive and relational.

Description of practice

Research question 1 – on the extent to which schools had adopted the official rational model – can be answered descriptively. At its simplest level the reports provided a commentary on what was happening within the schools. They provided an illustration of what is required for level 3 classification in our analysis, and at the same time offered examples of the OFSTED Guidance in action. Our aim was to gather evidence from the comment in those reports that offered specific guidance on the way in which rational planning should proceed. We were enabled to develop exemplars of good practice that showed progress towards rational resource management from which generalisations could be made. This part of the commentary – the 'how to do it' – was of greatest interest to staff from other schools. The extract given in Figure 4.2 provides an illustration.

We assessed the extent to which school staff had successfully adopted the rational model by calculating the average ranking (from ranks 1 to 3) for seven resource management processes (those listed above, excluding evaluation variables and value for money), as shown in the 'all schools' column of Table 4.1. The higher the all schools' average ranking the greater the extent of adoption of the resource management process. From this we can see that the schools performed best in relation to the efficiency of financial administration, followed by accommodation. They had adapted least well to the rational model in relation to departmental planning, followed by resource deployment and then rational planning and staff training. These are not unexpected findings since finances can be administered efficiently while the quality of decision-making on how to make the best use of resources is poor. In this way we have addressed research question 1 and put forward estimates of the extent to which schools have adopted the rational model in terms of distinct processes within it.

Relational analysis

Research question 2, on whether there is an association between rational resource management and educational effectiveness, requires analysis of the relationships between the two sets of variables (quality of education as assessed from the reports) and the resource management variables. We developed a number of indicators of educational quality or effectiveness from the evidence in the reports. The quality rating, Q, was ranked as 1, 2 or 3 according to the inspectors' overall comments on educational quality.

Figure 4.2 *Example of the framework for descriptions of management practice.*

Progress to Rational Planning

a. Involvement of governors and senior staff
    Now that a decision has been taken to keep the school open the management team and the governors recognise the need to take rapid steps to secure its future by producing a realistic and forward-looking development plan.

b. Statement of aims related to the SDP
    Such decisions are made in the context of the school's vision statement but are not sufficiently based on priorities identified in the school development plan

c. Development planning through the work of working parties, task groups etc. to ensure involvement
    There are regular meetings of curriculum and tutor teams, the full staff and the management team...linked to the cycle of Governing Body meetings...this enables staff to be involved in planning and decision-making.

Implementation of Rational Planning

a. Through strategic planning as a framework with forward budget use plans
    The strategic management of the school is guided by a comprehensive three-year development plan. A set of curriculum principles gives this plan cohesion and purpose. All the targets are linked to funding from appropriate budget headings.

b. Selection from identified alternatives
    The governors' F and GP Committee receives recommendations for budget spending and makes decisions which relate to the overall plan. Good quality information is available on which the committee can make its decisions.

Table 4.1 presents an initial examination of the data by showing the cross tabulation between the three groups of schools ranked 1, 2 or 3 by quality of education and the average ranking of the resource management variables for each quality group. The average rank rises with the quality group ranking for all the resource management variables except accommodation. However, the rise in the average rank score as the quality ranking increases is quite small in the case of financial administration and staff training.

Differences between groups in the mean values of a variable may be too small to be statistically significant. In this study, as in most quantitative research, we have taken a sample of the population of schools and are attempting to draw conclusions from our sample about the population of all schools. If the difference between the mean ranking for staff training between the three quality groups of schools is too small to be statistically significant, it could have arisen in the sample by chance and so does not exist in the population of schools. The standard rule for the statistical significance of the difference between the mean values of two comparison groups is that there is a 5 per cent chance (probability) or less that the difference is zero (the difference does not exist).

Table 4.1 *School quality ranking compared with resource management rankings*

Average ranking for resource management processes:	All schools	Quality = 1: % schools	Quality = 2: % schools	Quality = 3: % schools
Financial administration	2.49	2.30	2.46	2.53
Rational planning	2.08	1.80	1.99	2.30
Departmental planning	1.80	1.30	1.84	1.85
Staff deployment	2.2	1.90	2.15	2.35
Staff training	2.08	1.90	2.06	2.15
Resource deployment	2.03	1.80	1.96	2.23
Accommodation	2.14	2.20	2.10	2.17

We cannot tell this from a simple arithmetic comparison of the means of the three quality groups. We need to conduct a statistical test of the hypothesis that the mean differences in the resource management variables are zero. The results of such a test are reported in Table 4.2. The middle column of Table 4.2 gives the value of the F statistic which is the test for the difference between the means. In this case, given the size of the groups, the value of F has to exceed 3.5 for the difference in means to be statistically significant. Column three reports the groups for which the mean difference in the value of the resource management variable ranking is statistically significant.

The schools in quality group 3 tend to have higher values for the resource management variables than the other two quality groups, while schools in quality group 1 tend to have the lowest resource management scores. This finding is also shown in the overall total for the resource management variables both as total 1 and total 2, which includes the scores for the evaluation techniques used. The conclusion is that rational planning at school and departmental level and effective resource deployment are positively associated with educational quality.

We were able to triangulate from the statistical analysis to the qualitative data from the content analysis. Comment from the reports substantiated the statistical analysis. For example, in the key findings for one school which has a resource management decision making variable mean of 2.2:

> *Some reductions have been made in capitation and further significant cuts in staffing costs are being made. In general this has been achieved without adversely affecting provision although the school will need to monitor this in the longer term.*

Furthermore, the schools which tend to score most highly on evaluation are those which have a regular and known pattern of reviews, usually undertaken by departmental heads with senior staff on a line management basis, and those where there is an established governor involvement. From this

Table 4.2 *Resource management decision-making variables and quality of education*

Resource management decision-making variable	Is there a significant difference between the means for schools differentiated by overall quality of education? This is indicated by the size of the F ratio	The quality groups with significant mean differences (Tukey-HSD test with confidence level of 0.95)
Rational planning (RP)	5.12	Group 3 mean higher than groups 1 and 2
Departmental planning (DP)	4.44	Groups 2 and 3 means higher than group 1
Staff deployment (SD)	3.25	None
Staff training (ST)	0.50	None
Resource deployment (RS)	3.90	Group 3 mean higher than group 2
Accommodation (AC)	0.25	None
Total 1 (all the above scores summed up)	6.00	Group 3 mean higher than group 1
Evaluation: quantitative outcomes (EO)	3.15	None
Evaluation: value for money processes (ER)	0.38	None
Evaluation: reviews (EV)	4.66	Means of groups 3 and 2 higher than group 1
Evaluation: involvement of governors (EI)	4.00	Group 3 mean higher than group 1
Total 2 is Total 1 plus the four evaluation indices	9.32	All group means significantly different from each other
Effectiveness of financial administration	0.58	None
Overall value for money rating (1, 2 or 3)	8.79	Group 3 mean is higher than for groups 2 and 1

data we conclude that there is a marked association between most of the resource decision-making variables and the quality of education as measured by the criteria used.

Further statistical analysis explored the relationship between input variables, such as the pupil–teacher ratio, contact ratio, unit cost, hours taught and percentage of pupils eligible for free school meals (an indicator of pupil social background). The only variable to have a significant relationship to quality ratings was the percentage entitled to free school meals, which is an indicator of family poverty and hence social disadvantage.

Additional analyses of the relationship between the resource management variables and the percentage of lessons in which teaching and learning were graded as good or satisfactory were reported in the full study. We found that rational decision-making was related to the educational outcomes of teaching and learning. Departmental planning can be identified as a factor in securing educational effectiveness. It suggests that rational planning may be the most important of the resource decision-making variables. Where rational planning was embedded in the practice of the school then all associated practices were of a higher quality, although departmental planning and staff deployment were of greatest significance in association with quality rankings.

A more disturbing finding was that poorer assessments of the quality of teaching and in particular of learning and overall educational quality were associated with a more disadvantaged socio-economic background as measured by the percentage of pupils entitled to free school meals. This is further evidence to that already accumulated from other studies that school staff in socially disadvantaged areas find it more difficult to provide good quality education. There is, however, no significant difference in the percentage of pupils entitled to free school meals between the three groups of schools ranked in terms of rational planning. The link between the resource management processes and the outcomes appears to be through the use of resources to foster learning and teaching quality but most schools with high free school meals levels have difficulties in establishing desired educational effectiveness even in terms of the quality of teaching and learning.

Conclusion to the study

At its simplest level we were able to offer a picture of the inspectors' views of rational-technicist management by the governors and senior staff in secondary schools during the first round of inspections. The extent to which weaknesses in rational resource management were a major concern was reflected in the concluding or 'key issues' section of reports. At that time over one-quarter of the schools sampled lacked any rational planning system. A further quarter showed some evidence that headteachers were aware of the need to establish the aims of the school and to link resource use to them. School development plans had frequently been developed by either the headteacher or a small group of senior colleagues, as a response to the need to prepare for an inspection rather than as an integral and collaborative part of the school organisation process. Consequently, there was limited linkage between the stated aims of the school, resource development plans, costing and evaluation. For the headteachers and governors of just over half the schools critical comment included elements of the following example:

> *The governors and headteacher should review budget management, introducing more systematic monitoring and evaluation of expenditure so that budget planning can be set in the context of whole school priorities.*

The officially desired pattern is shown in this illustrative commendatory comment applicable to slightly less than half of schools:

> *There are clear procedures for preparing the school budget to reflect and support targets in the development plan. The approach shows in departmental planning as well as in planning for the whole school and this is achieved with a high level of consistency. Through taking a fresh look at the way funding was previously allocated senior staff have been able to make money available for development work.*

In securing the transition from level 1 to level 3 in resource management practices, reports from the second round of inspections showed that headteachers have had to convince governors and staff of the need to move to a more rational-technicist system. They have also had to consider issues of efficiency and effectiveness in resource use, and to ask questions about the relationship between context, resource use and outcomes so that value for money becomes an issue in educational management. Our initial work led us to the view that the headteachers were more likely to achieve the latter for their schools if they were rational in their approach.

In undertaking this study we were attempting to test the proposition that rational resource management is related to educational effectiveness using empirical evidence derived from inspection reports. We concluded that there was evidence of an association between variables reflecting rational decision-making processes and indicators of educational effectiveness. This conclusion depends on a number of assumptions. One is that the inspection evidence has construct validity and reliability and so can provide consistent measures of rational management processes and educational effectiveness. Judgement on this issue will depend on evidence emerging from other studies evaluating OFSTED inspections. The second assumption is that inspectors' judgements of educational quality are independent of their judgements about the degree to which rational decision-making processes for resource management are present. One can argue that these two sets of judgements are likely to be independent because the evaluation of the school's management and the efficiency of the school are usually assigned to only one or two inspectors out of a team of around 15 inspectors, whereas the educational quality evaluations are undertaken by a much larger number of inspectors each separately assessing a subject area.

Despite these reservations, it is still the case that the OFSTED inspection reports provide the most accessible data in England and Wales for a large number of schools on both resource management practices and educational effectiveness. Clearly, the evidence would be stronger if the data on both sets of variables could be obtained from valid research instruments administered independently of the inspections. But this would require a generously funded research project. A further extension of the database, which would not be so expensive, would be to include pupil level datasets of pupil prior attainment and National Curriculum key stage assessment results with the OFSTED data.

Although we concluded that this evidence supports the view that the processes of rational decision-making with respect to resource usage promote school effectiveness, we did not argue that there is a straightforward causal relationship from rational resource management to educational effectiveness.

It is much more likely that those management processes enabling resources to be effectively and efficiently utilised are also those which contribute to promoting effective teaching and learning. The connection does exist between managing resources well and good practice in teaching and learning. School staff are more likely to achieve success where they subscribe to strategic aims, prioritize their objectives accordingly, and use appropriate staffing and resource allocation systems to support subject departments. Our case studies of four very effective schools, which were identified from the content analysis (Glover et al., 1996a, 1996b) found that these four schools varied in the degree to which their resource management practice accorded with the official rational model. Staff in only one practised a fully rational model, with tight linkages between educational objectives and resourcing. At the other end of the range the fourth school had a much more informal and intuitive approach, although it was still broadly rational. This finding suggests that the way resources are managed in schools is an intrinsic part of the broader management philosophy and style which pervades all areas of school life. The processes which make a school educationally effective (or not) also embrace resource management. Reflection at a later stage following further documentary analysis of primary schools, and investigation of resource management in nine primary schools as well led to the conclusion that there can be very few (if any) schools that are not rational to some extent in their organisation. The rational-technicist model has become accommodated within schools. However, practice can vary from that of embraced rationality conforming to official practice, through tempered acknowledgement of plans used as guides, to models where circumstances, capacities and personalities may subvert good intentions (Levačić et al., 1999). Our findings confirm those of other authors who have critiqued the rational-technicist model for its inapplicability to organisations responding to unfolding sequences of uncertain events. In these circumstances emergent strategy (Minzberg, 1994), flexible planning (Wallace, 1991) or retroactive planning (Scheerens, 1997) are more appropriate. In these models, clearly articulated school aims and direction provide the reference points to guide medium- and short-term decision-making.

Thinking about the research – conclusions

We have focused on a particular type of documentary evidence – OFSTED inspection reports. They offer considerable scope for those investigating policies and processes in schools. However, it is important to recognise that the format and content of documents may change over time. Since the reports we used were produced, emphasis has shifted from the preparation of an all-embracing report to one that concentrates on aspects of improvement and effectiveness. It may not refer to those elements of the school's policy and practice that are considered to be at least satisfactory. We were comparatively lucky in being able to gain access to inspection reports during the first years of publication. They were, perhaps, more honest and less mechanical, or indeed bland, than subsequent reports, and they had not been the subject of commentary from other sources that would have informed our own way of thinking about the documents (e.g. Wilcox and Gray, 1996; Cullingford, 1999). We were also fortunate in being able to secure reports before the impact of the inspecting process had resulted in a higher degree of conformity of practice between schools: the requirements of the 1988 Education Reform Act were still being translated into action in different ways in different schools.

In investigating resource management over a period of time, we have had to recognise:

▶ the subjectivity of the inspection process and report writing and that this cannot be isolated from the concurrent political and socio-economic context;
▶ the changing emphasis of leadership training and the enhanced understanding of financial management within schools;
▶ the changing role of LEAs which now have increased influence on resource allocation through bidding processes.

All these factors have prompted more positive reports in the second round of OFSTED inspections. It may be that because so much of the changed practice is an assumed feature in all schools it is only mentioned where resource management procedures cause problems. Longitudinal study of schools as reflected in reports is a possibility, but we recognise that the investigation processes initially used could not be employed without adaptation of recording and analysis. But the reports do offer a vast amount of material and a picture of educational policy and response to context.

Thoughts about the process are concerned with the need to secure a greater degree of conformity in the translation of data from the subjective to the objective. We have explained how we used some 'double marking' of reports so that critical comments, refinements and supportive comments meant the same thing to each reader. If funding and time had allowed, we would have gained from the use of two readers and subsequent resolution of differences of opinion in the classification of data. We would also have gained from a larger sample although there was some evidence after the analysis of the 85th report that percentage figures for each element were not changing markedly. Just how large a sample gives sufficient internal validity and generalisability for investigative purposes is a matter of judgement, in part using statistical evidence, and financial constraints. Above all though, we are convinced that the benefit of using the inspection reports accrued because of the attempts made by OFSTED training and monitoring to ensure standardisation and substantiated comment. There is no other way that we could have secured high-quality school-level process and context data at comparatively low cost. The collection of comparable data by structured interviews within such a relatively large number of schools would not have been possible both on cost and nuisance grounds! Since we completed our research, in which we had to do our own classification and ranking of inspection judgements, OFSTED has created a database which contains the 1–7 rankings of inspection judgements. This database is not readily accessible because of its confidential nature and permission to access it must be sought.

In this chapter we have provided an example of using content analysis of documents to yield data for use in both qualitative and quantitative analysis so as to address a set of research questions. We have shown how the existing theoretical literature and official exhortations of good practice related to that literature are used in interaction with the content of documents to create an analytical framework. It is then applied in rendering these documents usable for subsequent analysis as the basis for classification. The study also illustrates ways of combining qualitative and quantitative analysis. Often, as in this instance, the distinction is not between qualitative and quantitative data since the latter are derived from the former, but between qualitative and quantitative methods of data analysis. Too frequently a misleading distinction is drawn between quantitative and qualitative research, treating them as quite different research approaches or paradigms.

References

Audit Commission (1993) *Adding up the Sums: Schools' Management of their Finances.* London: HMSO.
Audit Commission and OFSTED (1993) *Keeping Your Balance: Standards for Financial Administration in Schools.* London: HMSO.
Blaxter, L., Hughes, C. and Tight, M. (1996) *How to Research.* Buckingham: Open University Press.
Cullingford, C. (ed.) (1999) *An Inspector Calls: OFSTED and its Effect on School Standards.* London: Kogan Page.
Department for Education (1994) *Local Management of Schools,* Circular 2/94. London: HMSO.
Department of Education and Science (1988) *Education Reform Act: Local Management of Schools,* Circular 7/88. London: HMSO.
Downes, P. (ed.) (1988) *Local Financial Management in Schools.* Oxford: Basil Blackwell.
Ericson, R., Baranek, P. and Chan, J. (1991) *Representing Order: Crime, Law and Justice in the News Media.* Buckingham: Open University Press.
Fidler, B. (1996) *School Development Planning and Strategic Planning for School Improvement.* London: Fulton.
Glover, D., Bennett, N., Crawford, M. and Levačić, R. (1997) 'Strategic and resource management in primary schools: evidence from OFSTED inspection reports', *School Leadership and Management,* 17 (3): 333–51.
Glover, D., Levačić, R., Bennett, N. and Earley, P. (1996a) 'Leadership, planning and resource management in four very effective schools', Part One, *School Organisation,* 16 (2): 135–48.
Glover, D., Levačić, R., Bennett, N. and Earley, P. (1996b) 'Leadership, planning and resource management in four very effective schools', Part Two, *School Organisation,* 16 (3): 247–61.
Hammersley, M. (ed.) (1993) *Social Research: Philosophy, Politics and Practice.* London: Sage.
Hopkins, D. (1985) *A Teachers' Guide to Classroom Research.* Buckingham: Open University Press.
Levačić, R. (1995) *Local Management of Schools.* Buckingham: Open University Press.
Levačić, R. and Glover, D. (1997) 'Value for money as a school improvement strategy: evidence from the new inspection system in England', *School Effectiveness and Improvement,* 8 (2): 231–53.
Levačić, R. and Glover, D. (1998) 'The relationship between efficient resource management and school effectiveness: evidence from OFSTED secondary school inspections', *School Effectiveness and School Improvement,* 9 (1): 95–122.
Levačić, R., Glover, D., Bennett, N. and Crawford, M. (1999) 'Modern headship for the rationally managed school: combining cerebral and insightful approaches', in T. Bush, L. Bell, R. Bolam, R. Glatter and P. Ribbins (eds), *Educational Management: Redefining Theory, Policy and Practice.* London: Paul Chapman.
May, T. (2001) *Social Research: Issues, Methods and Process.* Buckingham: Open University Press.
Mintzberg, H. (1994) *The Rise and Fall of Strategic Planning.* Englewood Cliffs, NJ: Prentice Hall.
National Audit Office (1994) *Value for Money at Grant Maintained Schools: a Review of Performance.* London: HMSO.
National Audit Office (1996) *Good Stewardship: NAO Examination of Value for Money at Grant Maintained Schools.* London: HMSO.

National Audit Office (1997) 'Linking strategic planning with the budgetary process', in M. Preedy, R. Glatter and R. Levačić (eds), *Educational Management: Strategy, Quality and Resources*. Buckingham: Open University Press.

OFSTED (1993) *Handbook for the Inspection of Schools*. London: HMSO.

OFSTED (1995a) *Guidance on the Inspection of Nursery and Primary Schools*. London: HMSO.

OFSTED (1995b) *Guidance on the Inspection of Secondary Schools*. London: HMSO.

Scheerens, J. (1997) 'Conceptual models and theory-embedded principles on effective schooling', *School Effectiveness and School Improvement*, 8 (3): 269–310.

Scott, J. (1990) *A Matter of Record: Documentary Sources in Social Research*. Cambridge: Polity.

Scott, W. R. (1987) *Organizations: Rational, Natural and Open Systems*. Englewood Cliffs, NJ: Prentice Hall.

Simon, H. (1957) *Administrative Behaviour*. New York: Macmillan.

Tarter, C. J. and Hoy, W. K. (1998) 'Toward a contingency theory of decision-making', *Journal of Educational Administration*, 36 (3): 212–28.

Taylor Fitz-Gibbon, C. (2001) *Monitoring Education: Indicators, Quality and Effectiveness*. London: Cassell.

Wallace, M. (1991) 'Flexible planning: a key to the management of multiple innovations', *Educational Management and Administration*, 19 (3): 180–92.

Wilcox, B. and Gray, J. (1996) *Inspecting Schools: Holding Schools to Account and Helping Schools to Improve*. Buckingham: Open University Press.

Chapter 5

Understanding and contributing to school improvement in Thailand: a research and development project

Philip Hallinger and Pornkasem Kantamara

Hallinger and Kantamara report part of a larger research and development project examining the process of change in successful school improvement in Thailand. They concentrate on a critical review of literature and case studies of school change in Thailand to test the validity of concepts and theories derived from the literature. Here the authors examine the potential gap between theoretical and research knowledge and its application to practice. They consider how this problem might be addressed through research and development projects such as the one presented here, arguing that this approach may provide an important means of connecting these kinds of knowledge.

The chapter addresses problems associated with importing ideas and policies from one cultural context into others with fundamentally different socio-cultural norms. In doing so, Hallinger and Kantamara explicitly address the values and assumptions that underpin much research and theory on organisational change and school improvement originating in Europe, Australia and North America. They argue that knowledge developed in one society needs to be adapted before application in another, and that the adaptation process should be the subject of empirical study. An important point made towards the end of the chapter is that graduate students can make a useful contribution to knowledge in the field through well-conducted studies that identify indigenous ways of leading in schools and working with innovation and change.

In their critical review of literature, the authors identify the conceptual framework that guided the investigation. This conceptual framework was derived from social psychology and identified dimensions on which national cultures differed. Hallinger and Kantamara offer a stipulative definition of culture. Hallinger and Kantamara then consider how these four dimensions can be applied in relation to Thailand, and highlight the potential problems associated with attempts to import western approaches to organisational change. The specific examples of successful

---

This chapter expands on material, portions of which have previously appeared in Hallinger and Kantamara (2000b, 2001a, 2001b).

school change presented in the case studies are also analysed in relation to this conceptual framework. However, Hallinger and Kantamara also point out the ways in which the case studies provided unexpected findings – especially in relation to the role of leadership and the notion of 'power distance'. They are circumspect about offering definitive conclusions, even from a rigorously conducted study, and suggest that such work generates as many questions as it answers.

Introduction

In the past two decades we have witnessed unprecedented changes in education throughout the world. Educational reform has become an industry in itself with policies racing from nation to nation across the jet stream and through the Internet. Educational policies and methods developed in specific cultural and institutional contexts are spreading rapidly during this era of globalisation. School-based management, student-centred learning, parental involvement, learning technology, and cooperative learning are but a few examples of widespread global adoption.

Yet, even while the educational reform industry churns out these global best practices, reception among teachers, principals and parents at the local level is often considerably less enthusiastic. Indeed their doubt is warranted as the process by which these reforms are adopted usually skips over a crucial step: empirical assessment of their appropriateness for the local context. Empirical research and validation has seldom been conducted in the local context, even when educational reforms are touted as research-based. This creates a major gap which is quickly filled by the scepticism of educational practitioners.

Our characterisation applies to reforms in educational leadership and administration as well. Although an abundant empirical and theoretical literature has developed in western nations, outside Europe and North America the indigenous literature on school leadership is considerably less mature. This situation has led to calls for development of an 'indigenous knowledge base' on school leadership, particularly among Asian scholars (for commentaries on the need for such studies see Bajunid, 1995, 1996; Cheng, 1995; Dimmock and Walker, 1998; Hallinger, 1995; Hallinger and Leithwood, 1996; Heck, 1996; Walker et al., 1996; Wong, 1996).

Calls for culturally grounded research set the context for our own research and development effort aimed at understanding leadership and school improvement in Thailand (see Hallinger and Kantamara, 2000a, 2000b, 2001a, 2001b). The project grew out of our experience working with educators in school improvement projects in this country. Both our own observations as well as feedback from teachers and principals highlighted a gap between the improvement models and assumptions in use and the realities of improving teaching and learning in Thai schools. Thus, we conceived a multi-stage research and development project aimed at furthering our understanding of school improvement in the Thai context and developing materials that could be used in training Thai school leaders.

In this chapter we describe the R&D (research and development) process that we employed in this project, focusing primarily on selected stages: research review and small-scale research. The project began with a thorough review of literature on change in western societies as well as in Thailand, followed by a series of case studies on successful change in schools. The results were then used to inform the revision of a North American computer simulation designed to train school leaders in the process of managing change so that it would be appropriate for the Thai context (Hallinger and Kantamara, 2001b). This simulation was then field-tested with Thai school principals. We will first highlight the process we used in the R&D project. Second, we will describe the process and results. Finally, we will offer some reflections on the use of the R&D model for researchers in educational administration as well as some thoughts on the how national culture shapes the context for school improvement.

The research and development cycle

Research and development is a strategy that incorporates extant knowledge from theory and empirical research into a product that can be used for the improvement of practice. Borg and Gall (1989: 781) state that research and development 'consists of a cycle in which a version of the product is developed, field-tested, and revised on the basis of field-test data'. R&D is an appropriate strategy for use when the knowledge base related to a problem of interest is sufficient to inform practice.

This was the case with respect to managing change in schools. We began the project with a computer simulation (Making Change Happen!™, copyrighted by The NETWORK Inc., 1988, 1999) that had been developed as a tool for training school leaders in change management. The simulation programme was based on the frameworks of Rogers' (1971) adopter types, Hall and Loucks' (1979) concerns-based adoption model and Crandall and Associates' (1982) study of dissemination efforts supporting school improvement. It had been used previously with thousands of school leaders in the United States and we believed that the simulation remained relevant for school leaders in Thailand.

However, we were sensitive to the fact that the simulation was based entirely on research conducted in western societies. Moreover, we were also aware that the knowledge base on managing change in Thailand is much less fully developed. That awareness framed both the challenge and the potential significance of this study. Our broad goal for the project was to increase our knowledge about leadership, change and school improvement in Thailand. Our more specific objective for the R&D effort was to adapt the Making Change Happen! simulation for the Thai context.

The R&D process provides a systematic process and framework for seeking valid knowledge and employing it for the purpose of school improvement. Borg and Gall (1989: 784–5) outline the major steps in the R&D cycle where the final product is a training tool:

1 *research and information collecting* includes needs assessment, review of literature, small-scale research, and preparation of a report on the state of the art;
2 *planning* encompasses defining skills to be learned, stating and sequencing the learning objectives, identifying learning activities, designing materials, and planning small-scale feasibility testing;

3 *developing a preliminary form of the product* covers preparation of the instructional materials and learning procedures, translation as appropriate, and design of the assessment and evaluation instruments;

4 *preliminary field test*, a preliminary application of the product which is usually conducted with a small number – six to 18 – subjects. A variety of data – interview, observational, and questionnaire – are collected in order to shed light on ways in which the product and learning process can be improved prior to the main field test;

5 *main product revision* entails the researcher revising the product as suggested by evaluation data collected during the preliminary field test;

6 *main field test*: the product is tested under the normal conditions in which it would be used in practice. (For this project the main field test entailed evaluation of several full-day workshops with Thai school leaders using the revised computer simulation.) Evaluation data are collected, analysed and interpreted with respect to the stated learning objectives;

7 *final product revision* where the product is then revised as suggested by results from the main field test;

8 *dissemination and implementation*, following completion of the product, when the researcher reports on the product at professional meetings and in journals and seeks to foster dissemination of the product and support its implementation.

Our project generally followed these steps in the research and development process. We turn next to how we used research and collection of information to inform our cultural adaptation and revision of the computer simulation.

Research and information collecting: literature review

As noted above, this phase of the R&D process entails assessing the knowledge that underlies the field of study, which we conducted in two stages. First, we carried out a literature review on educational change in Thailand, Asia and western societies. While this review was helpful in identifying broad principles, it also highlighted important gaps in our knowledge.

Identification of these gaps in the change literature necessitated a second stage during which we conducted a small-scale research study of change in a set of schools where change had been successfully implemented in Thailand. The purposes of this case study research were twofold. We sought to explore qualitatively the validity of propositions generated through the literature review, and we wished to fill out the broad characterisations of change in Thai schools developed through the review with concrete examples and specific strategies.

Like other areas of public administration in Thailand, the educational system is highly centralised (Ketudat, 1984; Meesing, 1979). In Thailand's educational system, participants assume that orders from above are orders for all concerned. This situation has resulted in what even senior Ministry of Education (MOE) officials have acknowledged, with mixed feelings, is a 'compliance culture' (see also Sykes et al., 1997; Wheeler et al., 1997). Over the past decade the constraints imposed by this institutional culture on educational reform have become increasingly apparent. Consequently, the MOE has recently adopted policies that seek to implant 'empowering' educational reforms into Thai schools (Ministry of Education, 1997a, 1997b; Sykes et al., 1997). These include school-based management, parental involvement, social-constructivist teaching practices, and the use of new learning technologies.

Even in their countries of origin, implementation of these 'global' school reforms has been difficult, long and uncertain (e.g. Caldwell, 1998; Evans, 1996; Hargreaves and Fullan, 1998; Murphy and Adams, 1998). Not surprisingly, these reforms have found an even more tentative welcome in the strongly hierarchical institutional culture of Thailand's schools. Indeed any local observer would confirm that, more so than in the West, the values and assumptions underlying these 'modern' educational practices run counter to traditional cultural norms of Thai society (Sykes et al., 1997; Wheeler et al., 1997).

This is not to say that Thai educators have not been asking for change. Indeed, there is widespread recognition that the current system is ill suited to meet the demands of the emerging global society. Even so, when faced with implementing these challenging new approaches to management, learning and teaching Thai educators remain subject to traditional Thai cultural values, assumption and norms. Resistance is observable throughout the educational system, whether among students and parents, teachers and principals or politicians and government bureaucrats.

We therefore assert that implementation of these 'modern' educational reforms will fail unless Thai school leaders demonstrate a deeper understanding of how traditional cultural norms influence the implementation of change in Thailand's social systems. We further contend that being Thai no more guarantees understanding how to foster real change in Thai schools than being American does in the United States or being Chinese in Hong Kong. Thus, we began this inquiry into leading change with an exploration of key facets of Thai culture and how these would affect responses to change in general (see Hallinger and Kantamara, 2001a for a more complete explication).

Geert Hofstede, an engineer and industrial psychologist, conducted a six-year social study in the late 1960s to explore cultural differences among people from 40 countries, including Thailand. Hofstede (1980, 1983, 1991) defined culture as: the collective mental programming of the people in a social environment in which one grew up and collected one's life experiences. He identified four dimensions on which national cultures differ: 'power distance', 'uncertainty avoidance', 'individualism–collectivism' and 'masculinity–femininity'. According to Hofstede's cultural map, Thailand ranks high on power distance, high as a collectivist culture, moderately high on uncertainty avoidance and high on femininity. Let us briefly explain how we interpreted this cultural profile for the purposes of understanding predominant responses to educational change in Thailand.

High power distance

Power distance refers to 'the extent to which the less powerful members of institutions and organisations within a country expect and accept that power is distributed unequally' (Hofstede, 1991: 28). Thailand is a high power distance culture as reflected in its strongly hierarchical and bureaucratic social systems. Thais learn to understand and accept their position in society from their earliest youth.

In fact, in order to function confidently Thai people must be able to identify their own particular social status in relation to others. Thais quite naturally differentiate social status and treat others as juniors, seniors or peers (Holmes and Tangtongtavy, 1995). Status differentiation is demonstrated by way of expressions in spoken and written language as well as non-verbally (e.g. gesture, expression, posture). Simple observation of virtually any interpersonal interaction among a group of Thais quickly reveals an elaborate hierarchy of status.

Based on Buddhist teachings, Thais believe that they were born into their current status based on *karma* from previous lives. As a cultural characteristic, formal status differentiation may be traced back as far as the fifteenth century when Thailand employed the *sakdina* system. This system ranked every citizen by assigning a number or 'dignity mark'. The points ranged from 100,000 to 5 based on one's social status. Originally, these numbers were based on the size of one's land holdings. *Na* means rice field, while *sakdi* means power. Thus *sakdina* refers to power stemming from landholding (Holmes and Tangtongtavy, 1995).

Although the *sakdina* system was abolished four hundred years later by King Chulalongkorn, two beliefs persist to the present. First, every Thai understands that he or she has a particular place in the cultural hierarchy. Second, Thais generally accept that they should be content with that place (Holmes and Tangtongtavy, 1995). This is the essence of what Hofstede refers to as high power distance.

Not surprisingly, seniority is an important factor in a high power distance culture. As explained by Thailand's National Identity Office (1991):

> *Respect for elders is taught very early, however, and by the time a child walks he is aware of his position in the family hierarchy, a distinction that applies not only to the relationship between siblings of different ages. This same delineation of roles also applies to the wider world outside the family and will remain deeply ingrained throughout life, thus explaining the reluctance of younger Thai to oppose or otherwise confront a senior during their subsequent careers in business or government.* (Cited in Taraseina, 1993: 66–7)

This vertically aligned cultural system exerts great influence on social relations in the workplace. Persons of lower status (in terms of age, position, seniority) naturally defer to those of higher status, accepting such differences in power as a normal feature of social relations. Thais commonly show consideration or *kwarm greng jai* towards each other. *Greng jai* means 'to be self-effacing, respectful, humble, and extremely considerate, as well as the wish to avoid embarrassing other people, intruding, or imposing upon them' (Servatamorn, 1977: 13).

Students *greng jai* their teacher by not asking questions, even when they do not understand the lesson. Teachers *greng jai* their principal when they politely accept orders – for example, to implement a new curriculum or teaching method – even if they do not understand or agree with it. A less experienced or younger member on a team may refrain from contributing new ideas at a meeting because she or he feels *greng jai* towards senior colleagues who have already spoken. Or a young supervisor may *greng jai* a veteran teacher and fail to provide corrective feedback on weaknesses in class instruction.

In western cultures, people expect greater equality in social relations regardless of formal status and act accordingly. For example, an American principal's staff would typically respond to the same announcement of a curriculum change with a simple question: 'Why?' In a western context, this does not imply disagreement. Rather it reflects the staff's (culturally) legitimated belief that they have a right to know why they are expected to do something, that they should have a voice in school decisions, and that they will be able to 'do it' better if they know 'why' they are doing it. Such is not the case in Thailand where simply asking the question 'why?' would imply disagreement and be received as an open and impolite challenge to the principal's authority.

High power distance provides both an advantage and an impediment to change leaders in Thailand. The principal is the key decision-maker for the school; even an assistant principal has little authority to make decisions without direct contact with the principal. Teachers will naturally accord their principal a high degree of respect. Thus principal support for an innovation is even more important than in the West.

Principals can proceed with confidence that staff will listen with a polite ear to new proposals and feel some obligation to comply. However, this advantageous aspect of high power distance may lead Thai principals to underemphasise the important task of explaining the rationale and building genuine support for change. Thai principals may falsely interpret polite acceptance of their pronouncement as support for the change rather than as the normative response of teachers to *greng jai* their superior.

Individualism/collectivism

Collectivism pertains to 'societies in which people from birth onwards are integrated into strong, cohesive in-groups, which throughout people's lifetime continue to protect them in exchange for unquestioning loyalty' (Hofstede, 1991: 51). In contrast, nations such as the United States, England and Australia are highly individualistic and 'the ties between individuals are loose: everyone is expected to look after himself or herself and his or her immediate family'. Thailand is a highly collectivist culture. Thai people have a long history of being members of extended families. As an agricultural culture, collective work is common and expected. Consequently, Thais work hard to build and maintain relationships among a wide and complex network of people (Holmes and Tangtongtavy, 1995). Thai culture encourages interdependence instead of independence and a 'We' consciousness prevails rather than an 'I' consciousness.

The reference group is so important that Thais try hard to avoid conflicts that might create uncomfortable and unpleasant feelings. Letting one's negative feelings out in the open is frowned upon and subject to social sanctions. Indeed it is hard for Thais to understand how Americans can feel good after venting their feelings by shouting at each other or banging on a table at a meeting (Dakin, 1988).

Another cultural norm salient to Thai collectivism is *gumlung jai*: spirit or morale. *Gumlung jai* surfaces with surprising frequency in everyday discussions of Thai organisations. For example, it is quite common for a school administrator who has come under public criticism to receive *gumlung jai* from a group of supporters. A group of parents, teachers or students will typically come en masse bearing bouquets of flowers in a public show of moral support for their leader.

Gumlung jai reflects the strongly collective nature of Thai social relations and the strong bonds that tie people together. It is a public act of reciprocal support for the leader who has taken care of the staff during their times of need. To our knowledge, this type of moral support has no direct counterpart within highly individualistic cultures.

Hampden-Turner and Trompenaars (1997) note that since Thailand is a community-based culture, change is fundamentally a group, not an individual, phenomenon. Innovators are accorded neither significant attention nor social status in Thai culture. Indeed, for reasons suggested above with respect to both power distance and collectivism, people work hard to avoid standing out. Therefore, a strategy of 'sowing seeds of innovation' or fostering diversity of practice is a truly foreign notion within Thai culture.

Several scholars have made the case that the process of change is essentially one in which people make meaning of their work and life (Evans, 1996; Fullan, 1990). Thais 'make meaning' primarily through reference to the behaviours of their predominant groups – family, peers, colleagues. Therefore, it would appear that change strategies in Thailand would need to target the group as the primary point of leverage. While the peer group is an important consideration in fostering change in western cultures, the magnitude of difference in Asian cultures is large enough to require a qualitatively different approach. Again, the strategy must start with how leaders make the case for change. In Thailand, they must create opportunities by which groups of staff can come to a common understanding of the change proposal for their own setting.

Uncertainty avoidance

Uncertainty avoidance indicates the 'extent to which a society feels threatened by uncertain and ambiguous situations and tries to avoid these situations by providing greater career stability, establishing more formal rules, not tolerating deviant ideas and behaviors, and believing in absolute truths and the attainment of expertise' (Hofstede, 1980: 45). Thailand ranks moderately high on uncertainty avoidance.

Thai people would rather maintain things the way they are than to take initiative, be different or shake the ground. For Thais, like the Japanese, 'order depends on people's knowing and accepting their proper place or rank and on not disturbing "the proper order" of things' (Hall and Hall, 1987: 45). As suggested earlier, innovation is neither encouraged nor highly valued, and may even be regarded as undesirably disruptive. Even if a new practice holds potential for the organisation or for individuals, they will feel uncomfortable departing from accepted practice.

Thais seek stability and routines and look for written rules and regulations as guidance for their actions, providing solid ground and justification for decisions. When confronted with an unfamiliar decision in the absence of an established norm, a written policy or access to a superordinate, Thais often find themselves subject to 'decision paralysis'. A traditional corollary principle for fostering change that Thais themselves recommend is to apply constant pressure. As one principal put it: 'Staff need to know that it's the supreme law of the land and then you have to apply constant pressure to them to comply.'

Although expertise is secondary to rank, Thais also give great credence to experts and expert knowledge. Ordinary citizens have traditionally been viewed – and view themselves – as incompetent compared with formal authorities (a tendency further reinforced by high power distance). This perception helps to shape the relatively low level of importance leaders place on providing information and building interest among staff as a foundation for change. It further reinforces a tendency to wait for orders and direction rather than striking out on one's own or trying a new approach.

Not surprisingly, Thais also evince a tendency to look for and follow their leaders, those who display a quality referred to as *baramee*: 'personal power and strength derived from respect and loyalty' (Holmes and Tangtongtavy, 1995). One earns *baramee* over time through experience, not from position. Such leaders have the moral authority to lead the group. The leader in Thai culture is intimately bound to the group, is modest, sincere and trustworthy. He or she reflects the essence of the group rather than a new direction in which the group wishes to go. Not surprisingly, entrepreneurial leadership is a relatively scarce commodity within the culture.

Femininity

Masculinity pertains to 'societies in which social gender roles are clearly distinct, whereas femininity pertains to societies in which social gender roles overlap' (Hofstede, 1991: 82–3). This dimension highlights the value people place on social relations versus productivity. Within a highly masculine culture, performance outcomes and productivity represent the top priorities. As members of a more feminine culture, Thais place great value on maintaining harmonious social relations, even at the expense of accountability and productivity in the workplace. As Redmond (1994, b2) has observed, in Thailand:

> *Responsibility is a proud and cold word, capable of causing abysmal rents in the social fabric and frayed edges of tender feelings. An ethic of compassion, the inculcation of deference to superiors (kreng jai) and an ingrained desire for harmony and familiarity have created a communal security blanket.*

In terms of normative practices, people belonging to Asian cultures have traditionally been willing to accept trade-offs in the attainment of cognitive and skill performance against goals of spirit and community. The result of these culturally based variations is a fundamentally different approach to human relationships in eastern societies. The quite different importance attached to reason and logic has manifest implications for how leaders relate to followers.

The emphasis on social harmony over productivity is linked to another important social norm, *sanook*: 'the feeling of enjoyment, excitement or pleasure that one has taking part in work, play or any other activities' (Dakin, 1988: 51). Swierczek (1988: 77) suggests: 'Social aspects of work are important in Thailand because of the cultural value of working together in making the work fun.' In the absence of a feeling of *sanook*, it will be difficult to engage the ongoing interest of staff. Indeed, the resultant organisational stress is likely to increase resistance. So creating opportunities for staff to have fun – *sanook* – is essential to obtaining the commitment of the group. Of course, if taken too far, a danger lies in the tendency for staff to become complacent or lose sight of the goal.

This dimension poses interesting problems and opportunities for the Thai change leader. The sacrifice of results in order to maintain a harmonious process is unacceptable in a globally competitive environment. Yet, to date, concepts such as accountability have existed primarily at the level of rhetoric. Indeed as Redmond has observed, such terms are quite incompatible with this dimension of Thai culture.

While our research review generated interesting propositions about change within Thai culture, there was a dearth of actual empirical research on school change available to us. Therefore, although our initial hope had been to proceed from the literature review phase to revision of the simulation, it was not possible. The knowledge base on change in Thai schools was simply insufficient for our R&D objectives. Therefore, a small-scale study of change in Thai schools was required to increase our level of confidence in the findings prior to adapting the simulation.

Research and information collecting: small-scale study

Several potentially conflicting characteristics complicate research into school leadership in Thailand and other rapidly developing countries in this era:

▶ Thailand's MOE is promulgating reform policies that seek to change the normative practices of Thai schools in terms of management, the role of parents and community, and teaching and learning.
▶ The social and economic context surrounding Thai schools is in a period of rapid transition. This emerging context is characterised by rising expectations and dissatisfaction with the educational system by a growing middle class and a concerned business community (*Bangkok Post*, 1998; Hallinger, 1998).
▶ To date, new reform policies have reached relatively few schools and Thailand's leaders are under pressure to consider how they will 'import' these innovative practices into more schools (MOE, 1997a, 1997b; Sykes et al., 1997).
▶ Given these trends, understanding 'what worked' in terms of leading Thai schools in 1980 or 1990 will provide an incomplete picture of what it takes to lead change in the new millennium (Drucker, 1995).

This rapidly evolving context created a problematic situation, given our goal of illuminating the process of change in Thai 'schools of the future'. We settled on a research strategy that would study schools that had demonstrated success in implementing the type of 'modern' educational reforms envisioned by Thai policy-makers for all schools.

Research design and methods

Our case study focused on a subset of 139 schools whose staffs had participated in a systemic school reform project undertaken by the MOE between 1993 and 1997: Basic and Occupational Education and Training (BOET). The BOET project's goal was: 'To expand access to and improve the quality of basic and occupational education programs so that traditionally disadvantaged groups will be better served' (MOE, 1997b). This was accomplished largely through local collaboration and technical assistance designed to help staff in these project schools with implementing the types of innovations in management, teaching and learning noted above. The BOET programme was funded by the United Nations Development Programme and implemented in 13 provincial sites in the four regions of Thailand.

We selected three schools from among the 139 schools two years after completion of the project (spring 1999). The three schools were nominated by the project director as having successfully implemented and maintained the desired reforms over a seven-year period. Moreover, the principals who led these schools during the project were still in post by the spring of 1999.

The three schools were located in different regions of Thailand (north, south, central). They were co-educational schools of moderate size (200–350 students) serving students from pre-school to ninth grade. Teaching staffs ranged from 15 to 17 teachers per school. Staff qualifications were similar across the schools with all teachers having at least a special diploma and a few teachers at each school possessing a bachelor's degree. The principals (two male and one female) each held a BA degree.

Participation in the BOET project meant that these schools received more resources than 'typical' Thai schools. Despite this difference from the challenge facing Thai schools in general, they still met our most important criteria:

▶ They had started at a typical baseline of performance compared with other schools in their regions. Initially, the schools had been selected for participation in the BOET project because their norms of practice reflected a range typical of other Thai schools.
▶ They were implementing the same educational reforms envisioned for all Thai schools by the MOE (parental involvement, school improvement planning, IT, school-based management).
▶ Over a seven-year period, the staffs had overcome a typical set of change obstacles faced in Thai schools and still managed to sustain the implementation of these complex reforms.

While our sample of three schools would not provide a definitive perspective on the salience of our conceptual analysis, it seemed well suited to the requirements of an exploratory empirical effort.

Data collection and analysis

We contacted principals from the three schools to obtain their participation in 'a study of educational reform'. Two days were spent at each of the schools. A researcher observed and conducted focus group interviews with teachers. More extensive individual interviews were held with each of the principals. The interviews were semi-structured and designed to elicit staff perceptions of the change process that the school had undertaken. Each interview typically lasted from one to two hours.

We employed thematic analysis of the data, focusing specifically on two areas: change obstacles and change strategies. Initially we looked for patterns within the three schools and compared the perceptions of the teachers with those of the principal. Then we compared data across the schools in order to generate common categories. Finally, we referred back to our conceptual framework on cultural change to generate additional perspectives on the data. We limit our report of findings here to a summary and discussion related to the change strategies employed in the schools.

Results

When comparing the findings across the three schools, several common categories emerged from the data: leadership style, group orientation and teamwork, pressure and support for change, spirit and celebration, accountability. As suggested above, the tendency of Thai school administrators is to rely heavily on position power when implementing new policies or programmes. Given our expectation, we were surprised to find that all three principals used decidedly participatory management styles. Although manifested in different ways, each of the principals took specific steps to:

- build widespread support for the vision of change;
- reduce the 'status gap' between themselves and their stakeholders;
- gather information that reflected a broad range of perspectives from stakeholders prior to and during the adoption of school changes.

Their style was demonstrated in their approaches to building visions for change in the schools. Contrary to the top-down vision approach favoured by many Thai leaders, these principals involved all stakeholders – students, teachers, parents and community members – in setting the direction for change.

The three principals worked hard to create a sense of family in their schools. One principal noted: 'I want my staff to work as brothers and sisters with a sense of mutual responsibility and a high level of trust, even in the face of the conflict that comes with change.' This statement also reflected the high value that the principals placed on teamwork as a focus for change.

When the BOET project was initiated, all three principals explicitly avoided forcing teachers to join. Instead, they sought initial participation on a voluntary basis and then expanded the programme concurrent with increased staff interest. They all used a similar strategy of encouraging the more active and knowledgeable teachers to participate in the change effort first. This approach allowed sceptical colleagues to observe their colleagues, as well as the reactions of students, reducing the stress associated with change and defusing the fear that they were 'guinea pigs for another top-down MOE project'. Over time, many of the initially sceptical teachers decided to join the project activities.

Some teachers paid little attention to the new initiatives. Moreover, while they were indifferent to the new programmes, they were not averse to criticising other staff's efforts. The principals relied on a combination of support and peer pressure to foster change with these staff members (Evans, 1996; Kotter, 1996).

We have noted how Thai culture's feminine dimension places a strong emphasis on social relationships in the workplace. A key outgrowth of this norm lies in the importance of paying attention to spirit in the workplace. To be productive Thai people must find some degree of fun in their work. Harmonious group relationships are a necessary condition for effectiveness in Thai organisations, taking forms that differ in both subtle and obvious ways from western schools. In these schools it was apparent in the degree to which group-oriented socialising occurred in the context of the school's change implementation activities.

Propositions about change in Thai schools generated during research and planning

The findings from the review and empirical study highlighted both differences and similarities in change between East and West. They led us to generate a set of assumptions about change in Thai schools, to be used later to guide our revision of the computer simulation.

1 *Target formal leaders and obtain their support early in the change process.*

If administrative support is an important condition for educational change in western countries (Evans, 1996; Fullan, 1990, 1993; Kotter, 1996), our theoretical and empirical analyses suggest that it is a sine qua non in Thailand. The high power distance that characterises Thai culture invests the principal with significantly more position power as well as culturally legitimised, informal influence.

Both carried over to the principal's role in leading change. The teachers at all three schools made it clear that their principal played a critical role by creating an initial stimulus for change and actively supporting implementation. The leader's role as a catalyst for change seems even more necessary given that staff in these schools were undertaking reforms that ran counter to deeply-rooted Thai cultural norms. Early, firm support from the principal seems necessary for catalysing and sustaining the transformation of Thai schools into 'modern organisations'.

2 *Formal leaders must use strategies that counter traditional norms of deference and bring staff concerns to the surface so they may understand and address staff resistance.*

The high power distance prevalent in Thai culture creates an intriguing problem for change leaders. It would appear that Thai leaders might need to 'disarm' themselves of the most powerful tool at their disposal – power – in order to promote lasting change. This message is consistent with a Buddhist principle familiar to Thai people: 'In order to get something that you really want, you need to want it less.'

In the face of the principal's power and status, the Thai tendency to *greng jai* or show deference forestalls the initial impulse of staff to ask important questions about the innovation. Consequently, Thai leaders often fail to surface the concerns and questions of staff at the outset. They may come to believe they have achieved consensus where none exists. These principals demonstrated an implicit understanding of this fact as they employed a variety of 'disarmament' strategies designed to reduce the power distance between themselves and their constituencies.

Significantly, as highlighted above, these principals evinced a more participatory mode of leadership than we typically see in Thai schools. It extended to personal perspectives (e.g. vision), behaviours (e.g. modelling), leadership tools (e.g. surveys, annual written evaluation-feedback forms, open meetings) and to the strategies used to foster staff interest and involvement in the change projects. While these principals emphasised the importance of breaking down cultural norms of deference, they also continued to maintain traditional values of mutual respect and sincerity. More in-depth case studies that describe the manner in which leaders walk this fine line of cultural transformation would add greatly to our broader understanding of change leadership.

3 *Obtain and cultivate the support of informal leaders and leverage the resources of the social network to create pressure and support for change.*

Since Thailand is a highly collectivist culture, Thai people learn to use their social groups as the primary sources of reference for understanding their place in society. Not surprisingly, these principals made extensive and varied use of the social networks in and around their schools to foster change. They targeted informal leaders in the initial implementation of the reform project and maintained close contact with them throughout. Their colleagues often looked to these leaders for direction and reassurance. Accessing the resources of the social network of the school, and in this case the community, created support for change. For example, staff outings gave the staff a chance to gain a group perspective on the innovations under consideration.

Parental and community pressure emerged, somewhat unexpectedly, as a factor that exerted considerable influence on teachers over time. The BOET project mandated a level of community participation hitherto unknown in Thai schools. A range of activities that increased contact among staff and community members (e.g. planning meetings, fairs, celebrations, study visits) also created pressure (e.g. higher expectations) as well as support (e.g. pride) for change. Thus, we would suggest that the informal network of the school and its community is as important – if not more important – in Thailand as it is in western schools.

4 *Use formal authority selectively to reinforce expectations and standards consistent with implementation of the innovation.*

We saw how the principals understood the need to downplay their authority if there was any hope of stimulating meaningful participation among staff, students and community members. They began by seeking the participation of volunteers and encouraging the use of 'democratic' group processes. Even so, over time they did use a variety of strategies that increased the pressure for implementation. Some were quite direct, while others were indirect. They were not afraid to use the authority of external educational constituencies (e.g. project staff, provincial administrators, experts), the expectations of the community and peer pressure to foster change.

5 *Find ways to inject fun, support mutual concern and caring, encourage team spirit and celebrate shared accomplishments while maintaining accountability.*

All three principals identified the importance of fostering a family spirit of mutual responsibility and assistance when speaking of visions for their schools. The skill of their leadership and that of their colleagues lies in finding an acceptable balance between the pressures for change (e.g. accountability) and group harmony. Organisational rituals such as study visits, fairs and celebrations became important opportunities for creating meaning and sustaining the momentum of change. The staff in all three schools would have claimed that in an effective school *sanook* (fun) and *gumlung jai* (moral support or spirit) go hand-in-hand with productivity.

Use of this knowledge to inform the development of training materials

We viewed the knowledge we had generated to inform the development of culturally relevant training materials for use with Thai school leaders as assumptions, not conclusions. Nonetheless, they represented a step forward in the process of translating broad descriptions of change into principles and practices that could guide school leaders in general ways.

The design of the Making Change Happen! computer simulation had been grounded in research on educational change in North American and European schools. While this western version of the simulation had been used successfully with Thai school leaders in training, we were concerned about the lack of any form of cultural validation. The results of this research and planning process were therefore subsequently used to inform revisions to the computer simulation. We will briefly outline a few examples to demonstrate how we used the knowledge from the literature review and case study research to revise this North American simulation for Thailand.

Revision of the computer simulation

The computer simulation asks the player to implement new learning technologies in a school system over a three-year period. The change team must interact with many staff members (24 people) during the simulation. Staff members have different personality characteristics and responses to change. The characteristics of the 24 staff members in the schools correspond roughly to Roger's (1971) theory of adopter types (innovators, leaders, early majority, late majority, resistors). In the original (North American) version, the staff ask many questions about the new learning technology at the outset of the change. There is considerable resistance to the idea of implementing the new technology and resistance is expressed overtly. Yet following satisfactory response by the change team to their queries, staff members do begin to change.

In the Thai version we used our research data to rewrite the characteristic responses of the Thai staff. We maintained the adopter types framework, but revised the responses of the people in several ways. For example, when the change is announced, teachers ask few or no questions at all. They politely respect the announcement of their superiors and express no overt resistance. However, in spite of their apparent compliance, in the simulation the Thai staff do not change! Their responses reflect the cultural tendency towards overt, polite compliance – *greng jai* – even in the absence of any change in behaviour. This type of revision reflecting the effects of high power distance on change was carried out as deemed appropriate throughout the simulation text and decision rules. As a consequence, the change team must use somewhat different strategies to interest the Thai staff members in the change.

A key stage in the change process (in any culture) involves generating interest among staff prior to training. The simulation contains several ways in which the change agents can generate staff interest, for example through a presentation to staff, by talking to people, by a demonstration of the software, by gaining support of administrators and the social leaders. However, our research had suggested that Thai teachers would be reluctant to ask questions openly. Yet without asking necessary questions, both knowledge and interest are likely to remain low.

In our research we identified an activity employed in the Thai schools during the 'interest stage' of the change process (Hall and Hord, 1987): an overnight visit by teachers to observe the use of the change in another school. It was a means of increasing staff interest in, understanding of and commitment towards the change. Typically, such visits involve staff travelling together to another school some distance away from home. Teachers observe in classrooms and talk with other teachers who are already using the innovation. In the evening members of the team will typically eat, talk and perhaps sing together.

The activity provides an opportunity for group members together to 'make sense of the change' outside the formal school setting. Consistent with the importance of sanook (fun) and collectivism in Thai culture, the trip builds a bond among the group members and sets the stage for building support back at the school. This and other activities, like the 'Demonstration of Learning Technology' at the school site, provide an important stimulus for creating interest and making the abstract notion of a specific change more real. Given the culturally passive orientation of Thai teachers, it is critical for leaders to create opportunities where teachers can ask questions and find personal meaning in the early stages of the change process.

Another adaptation involved the role of school principals. In the original version, the change team must gain support from the principals in order to conduct activities in the target schools. To reflect the even greater importance of the Thai school leader in the change process, we increased the student benefits accruing from school-level activities, such as workshops, if the team has obtained strong support from the principals.

These brief descriptions of our adaptation of the simulation provide a taste of how the R&D process was used to inform our revision of the training materials for Thailand (see Hallinger and Kantamara, 2001b). Subsequent to our revision of the simulation, several full-day workshops were conducted with Thai school principals to field-test the revised version. Evaluation of the simulation used both formative and summative measures. The results were used to further revise the simulation and the instructional process.

The result of the R&D process was a simulation that was both translated into Thai language and culturally transformed for use with Thai school leaders. We have been using the simulation with Thai school leaders for the past two years with considerable success. They find the characters and the problems encountered in the simulation realistic and high in 'face validity'. It is interesting to note that the strategies that work to create change in the simulation often appear novel at first to the principals. This finding should not be surprising since the assumptions behind successful change run counter to many institutional norms embedded in the Thai educational system. Yet these differences provoke useful discussion of whether and what kinds of shifts in managerial behaviour are needed in the present era. The school leaders often conclude that what worked yesterday may not work tomorrow.

Implications of the research and development project for studies in educational administration

Our first project goal concerned the use of the R&D process in order to revise the North American version of a change simulation for use in Thailand. Upon completion of the project, it would be comforting to feel that we had reached a conclusion. After all, we did a thorough review of literature, conducted case studies (albeit limited in scope and numbers), did substantial revision of a major instructional tool, field-tested the product several times, and evaluated both the product and instructional process. Indeed, the project produced a fully functioning simulation that has been adopted for use by Thailand's main training institute for school leaders and has been used with over 500 leaders in training. Moreover, we have reverse-translated the simulation back into English for use in other Asian countries (e.g. Malaysia, Hong Kong, Singapore). This move reflects our assumption that the Thai version of Making Change Happen! more closely reflects the process of school change in other Asian nations than does the North American version.

These are not inconsiderable accomplishments for a single project, parts of which were incorporated into Kantamara's doctoral study. Yet, at the conclusion of this project, we are aware that we have arrived back at the start of the R&D cycle. For example, our literature review and case studies only scratched the surface of understanding change in Thai schools. Moreover, we could not claim that the simulation has been truly validated. Even with our initial pre- and post-testing procedures, we have only assessed the face validity of the simulation. A more thorough assessment of implementation of the best practice strategies incorporated into the Thai version of the simulation is needed in order truly to establish the revised simulation's cultural validity.

Nonetheless, our effort has led us to believe that the R&D process holds considerable promise for scholars and students interested in bridging research, theory and practice. Those searching for research models that foster the practical application of knowledge would find this approach fruitful. Consistent with Borg and Gall, we recommend that a general approach could be to:

1 begin with a significant problem of practice;
2 reflect on how research and theory might be applied to deepen understanding of the problem;
3 assess the extant knowledge base in terms of guidance for potential solutions and best practice models for addressing the problem;
4 expand on that knowledge in a focused manner;
5 apply systematically the results of research and planning towards the development of products or tools that can be used in training and/or practice;
6 evaluate the results of using the product or tool and use those results for further improvement;
7 disseminate the results for use more broadly.

Understanding leadership across cultures

The second project goal concerned expanding our understanding of leadership and school improvement in Thailand. Our work generated interesting information concerning the enactment of school leadership across cultures. As a preliminary effort, this study confirms the complexity of cross-cultural understanding of leadership processes. Two decades ago Bridges (1977) claimed that leadership entails getting results through other people. If this is the case, then we can only understand the nature of leadership by exposing the hidden assumptions of the cultural context in which leaders operate in order to open new windows through which to view educational leadership.

The culture of Thailand creates a unique context in which to lead educational change. According to Hofstede's cultural map, however, Thai culture also shares similarities with other southeast Asian nations. In particular, other southeast Asian nations tend to rank high on both collectivism and power distance. Thus, for example, high power distance also shapes the context for leading educational change in Singapore and Hong Kong. Therefore, school principals in such nations might find a need for similar 'disarmament strategies' in efforts to foster change.

Our analysis further suggests that a culture's strengths are also its limitations. In the case of leading change, high power distance enables leaders to achieve initial attention and compliance of staff more easily. However, it can become a limitation when the goal is deeper implementation of complex innovations that require staff to learn new skills. It is an intriguing problem which only cross-cultural comparison can illuminate.

This perspective on leadership seems especially salient during an era in which global change forces are reshaping the face of education throughout the world. An ever-expanding array of western management innovations are traversing the globe and finding their way into traditional cultures. Not unlike the response of a living organism to a virus, the instinctive response of many organisations to these innovations is to attack with self-protective mechanisms. Even as policy-makers embrace foreign educational policy reforms with the infatuation of a new romance, change engenders more suspicion than enthusiasm at the point of implementation. Successful implementation will require sophisticated leadership, especially where the underlying assumptions are 'foreign' to prevailing norms of the local culture.

In conclusion, it is our hope that this project will provide a potentially useful model for other students in this field. In particular, we hope that it might inspire students studying far from their home countries to feel that they can conduct a legitimate, useful graduate-level project as part of their studies. The R&D process provides a systematic approach that can enable students to advance knowledge and make a positive contribution to schooling in their own countries. Indeed, it is those students who seek out, describe and assess indigenous ways of leading and working in schools who may make the greatest contributions to our field in the coming years. They will do so by illuminating the unquestioned assumptions of dominant (western) theories of knowing and doing, thereby expanding our conceptions of school leadership and improvement.

References

Bajunid, I. A. (1995) 'The educational administrator as a cultural leader', *Journal of the Malaysian Educational Manager*, 1 (1): 12–21.

Bajunid, I. A. (1996) 'Preliminary explorations of indigenous perspectives of educational management: the evolving Malaysian experience', *Journal of Educational Administration*, 34 (5): 50–73.

Bangkok Post (1998) 'Graft blamed for fall in world ranking: kingdom slides from 29th to 39th place', 3 November.

Borg, W. and Gall, M. (1989) *Educational Research: An Introduction*, 5th edn. White Plains, NY: Longman.

Bridges, E. (1977) 'The nature of leadership', in L. Cunningham, W. Hack and R. Nystrand (eds), *Educational Administration: The Developing Decades*. Berkeley, CA: McCutchan.

Caldwell, B. (1998) 'Strategic leadership, resource management and effective school reform', *Journal of Educational Administration*, 36 (5): 445–61.

Cheng, Kai-Ming (1995) 'The neglected dimension: cultural comparison in educational administration', in K. C. Wong and K. M. Cheng (eds), *Educational Leadership and Change: An International Perspective*. Hong Kong: Hong Kong University Press.

Crandall, D. and Associates (1982) *People, Policies and Practice: Examining the Chain of School Improvement* (Vols 1–10). Andover, MA: The NETWORK.

Dakin, S. (1988) 'Critical elements of Thai culture influencing the relations between Thais and Americans: a study of cross-cultural interaction at the Panat Nikhom Processing Center'. Unpublished Masters thesis, School for International Training, Thailand.

Dimmock, C. and Walker, A. (1998) 'Transforming Hong Kong's schools: trends and emerging issues', *Journal of Educational Administration*, 36 (5): 476–91.

Drucker, P. (1995) *Managing in a Time of Great Change*. New York: Talley House, Dutton.

Evans, R. (1996) *The Human Side of Change*. San Francisco: Jossey Bass.

Fullan, M. (1990) *The New Meaning of Educational Change*, 2nd edn. New York: Teachers College Press.

Fullan, M. (1993) *Change Forces: Probing the Depths of Educational Reform*. New York: Teachers College Press.

Hall, E. and Hall, M. (1987) *Hidden Differences*. New York: Doubleday.

Hall, G. and Hord, S. (1987). *Change in Schools: Facilitating the Process*. Albany, NY: SUNY Press.

Hall, G. and Loucks, S. (1979) *Implementing Innovations in Schools: A Concerns-Based Approach*. Austin, TX: Research and Development Center for Teacher Education, University of Texas.

Hallinger, P. (1995) 'Culture and leadership: developing an international perspective in educational administration', *UCEA Review*, 36 (1): 3–7.

Hallinger, P. (1998) 'Educational change in southeast Asia: the challenge of creating learning systems', *Journal of Educational Administration*, 36 (5): 492–509.

Hallinger, P. and Kantamara, P. (2000a) 'Leading at the confluence of tradition and globalization: the challenge of change in Thai schools', *Asia Pacific Journal of Education*, 20 (2): 46–57.

Hallinger, P. and Kantamara, P. (2000b) 'Leading educational change in Thailand: opening a window on leadership as a cultural process', *School Leadership and Management*, 20 (1): 189–206.

Hallinger, P. and Kantamara, P. (2001a) 'Exploring the cultural context of school improvement in Thailand', *School Effectiveness and School Improvement*, 12(4): pp. 385–408.

Hallinger, P. and Kantamara, P. (2001b) 'Learning to lead global changes across cultures: designing a computer-based simulation for Thai school leaders', *Journal of Educational Administration*, 39 (3): 197–220.

Hallinger, P. and Leithwood, K. (1996) 'Culture and educational administration: a case of finding out what you don't know you don't know', *Journal of Educational Administration*, 34 (5): 98–119.

Hampden-Turner, C. and Trompenaars, F. (1997) *Mastering the Infinite Game: How Asian Values are Transforming Business Practice*. Oxford: Capstone Press.

Hargreaves, A. and Fullan, M. (1998) *What's Worth Fighting for Out There*. New York: Teachers College Press.

Heck, R. (1996) 'Leadership and culture: conceptual and methodological issues in comparing models across cultural settings', *Journal of Educational Administration*, 30 (3): 35–48.

Hofstede, G. (1980) *Culture's Consequences: International Differences in Work-Related Values*. Beverly Hills, CA: Sage.

Hofstede, G. (1983) 'The cultural relativity of organizational practices and theories', *Journal of Business Studies*, 13 (3): 75–89.

Hofstede, G. (1991) *Cultures and Organizations: Software of the Mind*. London: McGraw-Hill.

Holmes, H. and Tangtongtavy, S. (1995) *Working with Thais: A Guide to Managing in Thailand*. Bangkok: White Lotus.

Ketudat, S. (1984) 'Planning and implementation of the primary education reform in Thailand', *Prospects: Quarterly Review of Education*, 14 (4): 523–30.

Kotter, J. (1996) *Leading Change*. Boston: Harvard Business School Press.

Meesing, A. (1979) 'Social studies in Thailand', in H. D. Mehlinger and J. L. Tucker (eds), *Social Studies in Other Nations*. ERIC Reproduction Document Service No. ED. 174 540.

Ministry of Education–Thailand (1997a) *Introducing the Office of the National Primary Education Commission*. Bangkok, Thailand: Ministry of Education.

Ministry of Education–Thailand (1997b) *The Experience from the Basic and Occupational Education and Training Programme.* Bangkok, Thailand: Ministry of Education.

Murphy, J. and Adams, J. (1998) 'Reforming America's schools 1980–2000', *Journal of Educational Administration*, 36 (5), 426–44.

NETWORK Inc. (1988, 1999). *Making Change Happen!*™. Rowley, MA: The Network Inc.

Redmond, M. (1994) 'The unselfishness of not being there', *The Nation*, b2, 9 January.

Rogers, E. (1971) *Diffusion of Innovations.* New York: Free Press.

Servatamorn, S. (1977). *Education in Thailand: From Old to New.* World Education Monograph Series, Number Two. ERIC Reproduction Document Service No. ED 170 878.

Swierczek, F. (1988) 'Culture and training: how do they play away from home?', *Training and Development Journal*, 42 (11): 74–80.

Sykes, G., Floden, R. and Wheeler, C. (1997) *Improving Teacher Learning in Thailand: Analysis and Options.* Report to the Office of the National Education Commission (#21/2540). Bangkok, Thailand: ONEC.

Taraseina, P. (1993) 'Assessing the instructional leadership of Thai secondary school principals', Unpublished doctoral dissertation, Nashville, TN: Vanderbilt University.

Walker, A., Bridges, E. and Chan, B. (1996). 'Wisdom gained, wisdom given: instituting PBL in a Chinese culture', *Journal of Educational Administration*, 34 (5): 98–119.

Wheeler, C., Gallagher, J., McDonough, M. and Sookpokakit-Namfa, B. (1997) 'Improving school–community relations in Thailand', in W. K. Cummings and P. G. Altbach (eds), *The Challenge of Eastern Asian Education: Implications for America.* Albany, NY: SUNY Press.

Wong, K.C. (1996) *Developing the moral dimensions of school leaders*, invited paper presented at the meeting of the APEC Educational Leadership Centers, Chiang Mai, Thailand.

Chapter 6

Heads of secondary school subject departments and the improvement of teaching and learning

Ray Bolam and Chris Turner

The role of the head of department in secondary schools is the focus of the study outlined in this chapter. The authors discuss how the head of department in British secondary schools has a key managerial role in the improvement of learning for students. The importance of the substantive topic is highlighted by reference to policy developments in Britain in the past decade and their implications for the management of schools. However, the authors point out how a review of available literature revealed a considerable amount of research on the leadership role of the headteacher or principal, but relatively little on heads of department who have an instructional leadership role in secondary schools. The study reported in this chapter also built upon earlier work by one of the authors. An important aspect of Bolam and Turner's work is that it focuses on something that has largely been taken for granted in schools in Britain. They problematise an aspect of practice that has not previously been the subject of extensive study. This approach has considerable potential for a masters or doctoral study.

In line with the model of the research process that we outlined in Chapter 2, Bolam and Turner identify a central research question and then from this identify a number of specific sub-questions. They make explicit the assumptions underpinning their approach: that it is within the positivistic tradition, largely following an input–process–outcome research design. However, the research design is based on interviews with heads of department, headteachers and some subject teachers, and the data is analysed qualitatively. Their sample was taken from ten secondary schools in Wales and the authors explain the criteria for selecting the heads of department and other informants. An interesting point to note is that in discussing what they perceive to be the limitations of their study, Bolam and Turner highlight the lack of what they refer to as 'hard evidence' about the impact of the heads of department on students' learning, as they are not able to link it with outcome measures such as examination results. The authors are duly cautious about their own study, but the issue of what counts as 'hard evidence' is a subject of debate by many researchers throughout the world.

Introduction and background

Our purposes are threefold: to report on selected preliminary findings of a study, funded by the Economic and Social Research Council (ESRC), of the work of heads of subject departments in the improvement of teaching and learning (instructional leadership) in secondary schools; to relate these findings to emerging theory on 'middle' management in schools; and to consider their implications for professional development. The ESRC is a government agency that aims to encourage and fund high-quality research in the social sciences.

First, a brief reminder of the national context is necessary. From 1988, students, teachers and headteachers in the 22,000 schools in England and Wales had to respond to powerful governmental pressures for restructuring and change. The most important of these pressures arose from the twin policy goals of raising educational standards and increasing 'customer' choice, together with the related aims of increasing the influence of the community in the management of schools and improving their accountability, efficiency and effectiveness. In summary, government strategy involved the introduction:

▶ at national level, of a quasi- or regulated market for schools via a National Curriculum and national testing for students at the end of four key stages (at age 7, 11, 14 and 16), together with published results and regular external inspections, all designed to inform parental choice;
▶ at school level, of a range of industrial management techniques and procedures designed to enhance the school's effectiveness and efficiency in the quasi- or regulated market. These included responsibility for strategic planning, the delegated budget, staff recruitment, appraisal and development, together with increased strategic powers for parents and community representatives on schools' governing bodies.

To date, the present New Labour government's policies on the National Curriculum, assessment, raising standards, inspections, league tables and approaches to school improvement have followed broadly similar lines to those of its predecessors (Welsh Office, 1997).

Although recent national policy has focused on *school* improvement and thus upon *school* leadership, it is now widely recognised that heads of department (HoDs) in secondary schools are central to the improvement of performance and results in their subject areas and thus have a crucial *departmental* (or instructional) leadership role. For example, a report by OHMCI Wales (the Welsh school inspectorate) concluded (1995: 23) that: 'Heads of department...should exercise greater influence on the quality of teaching and learning and the standards achieved by students.' Similar views also underpin recent proposals from the central government's Teacher Training Agency to introduce national training standards for continuing professional development at four key career stages, one of which is the subject leader or HoD.

The following general features of the position of HoD in English and Welsh secondary schools are noteworthy. There are HoDs for all National Curriculum subjects. National assessment and examination scores for students aged 14, 16 and 18 are directly and explicitly linked to departmental performance via the annual published results. The 'core subject' departments (English, mathematics and science) are the largest with perhaps ten or more staff. The position of HoD is a permanent one that carries a fairly substantial salary increase, linked to the size of the department, and a small, extra amount of non-teaching time. It is generally regarded as influential and prestigious, and vacant posts, which are nationally advertised, are usually well contested. It is normally an essential stepping stone for promotion to deputy headship and headship, to university lectureships in initial teacher education and to advisers' and inspectors' jobs in local education authorities and at national level.

From a research perspective, however, HoDs have been neglected figures. Earlier research largely ignored their contribution to the improvement of teaching and learning and, thus, to the processes of school improvement. Following nearly two decades of effort to identify the characteristics of effective schools and their management (Rutter et al., 1979; Mortimore et al., 1988; Bolam et al., 1993), a degree of consensus has been reached among researchers as to the general features of such schools. According to Sammons et al. (1995a), eleven key factors have been identified, including shared vision and goals, concentration on teaching and learning, high expectations and professional leadership, but the specific contribution of subject HoDs has received little attention.

Two earlier studies (Sammons et al., 1995b; Harris et al., 1995) sought to identify the characteristics of effective subject *departments* in secondary schools. The former, for example, concluded that 'for a substantial proportion of schools (e.g. approximately 32% in 1991), however, there are substantial departmental differences in terms of effectiveness...' (Sammons et al., 1995b: 17), a finding broadly consistent with professional experience. Using departments selected on the basis of significant 'value-added' scores, both studies arrived at similar conclusions about the characteristics of effective departments, notably that they displayed a central focus on teaching and learning and a student-centred approach. However, there were also differences between the two sets of findings. For example, the Sammons study emphasised the combined effects of whole-school management and departmental management processes while the Harris study includes other more departmentally-based factors such as 'an effective system for monitoring and feedback, the syllabus matching the needs and abilities of students.' Neither study dealt directly with the part played by HoDs in improving teaching and learning, yet it may reasonably be hypothesised that they do exert considerable influence on such outcomes, depending on a number of factors which prevail in the school and department at any particular time.

Torrington and Weightman's (1990) study of school management referred to the HoD as a 'taken-for granted' role. A review of the literature on the role and tasks of the HoD in Britain (Turner, 1996) concluded that it consisted mainly of prescriptive accounts by practitioners (e.g. Marland and Hill, 1981; Edwards, 1985) of the characteristics of the 'good' HoD, which lacked any theoretical basis. Earley and Fletcher-Campbell's (1989) survey remains the most substantial British study directly focused on the role of the subject HoDs in secondary schools and, although it was largely atheoretical, it certainly provided valuable insights into their management problems. One major finding highlighted the lack of time available for HoDs properly to manage their departments. Time is certainly likely to be a significant constraint on the ways in which HoDs can actually influence teaching and learning since it limits their scope for observing the work of, and team teaching with, departmental colleagues. This survey also highlighted the problems faced by all HoDs in monitoring and evaluating the work of the department effectively, not least because the observation of classroom teaching can conflict with prevailing notions of professional autonomy and accountability.

In summary, none of the earlier British research had focused directly on the ways in which HoDs try to improve teaching and learning. Moreover, an ERIC search revealed a similar situation in the USA. For instance, in a review of literature on the role of the HoD in United States high schools, Siskin (1994) pointed to a lack of in-depth research on subject departments when she described the 'invisibility of departments'. Hord and Murphy (1985) investigated the role of the HoD as a change agent but their study viewed the HoD as the key person in the implementation of policy changes taken at district or state level, rather than in the improvement of teaching and learning in classrooms. In the light of these policy developments and a continuing lack of empirical research, it is the authors' intention to outline, first, the thinking behind the research design and methods employed in this study; second, the main findings from our research, focusing on the work of a representative sample of HoDs, headteachers and departmental staff working in secondary schools in Wales; and finally, to describe what we think are the main implications arising from this study for the development of an appropriate theoretical framework and for the professional development of aspiring and existing HoDs.

Research design and methods

The research design was founded on a positivistic methodology, based on the assumption that a number of input factors, in conjunction with a set of management process factors orchestrated by the HoD, could largely determine whether successful teaching and learning outcomes could be achieved. During the course of this research, it became clear that the so-called input factors operated at two levels: the contextual factors (national and local factors, whole school factors and subject-related factors) and HoD role-related factors (determined largely by the subject being taught).

The management processes utilised by HoDs focused on the tasks to be accomplished within the department and the methods by which they might be achieved. The identification of a series of factors was recognised by the authors as being an over-simplification of what is really a very complex situation and set of processes. However, working in this way rendered the research more manageable. The adoption of this approach also allowed the HoDs and the other interviewees to articulate their perceptions of social reality in such a way as to enable a number of key themes to emerge from their diverse responses.

The research design built on an earlier study, described in detail in Turner (2002), which was based on a postal questionnaire survey completed by 204 heads of English, mathematics, science and technology departments in Welsh secondary schools. Three of these four subject areas were chosen because they are core subjects in the National Curriculum while the fourth, technology, was included because of the emphasis placed on it in recent policy documents (e.g. Welsh Office, 1995).

The fundamental objective of the present study was to answer the following two-part question:

What are the main methods reportedly used by heads of subject departments to improve teaching and learning in their departments and which of them are perceived by them, their colleagues and their headteachers to be the most successful?

In so doing, nine broad research questions were addressed:

1 Which methods and techniques do the HoDs say they use to try to improve teaching and learning in their departments? Specifically, how do they use available value-added data (e.g. results of national assessment at age 11 and 14, and of public examinations at 16 and 18)?
2 Why do the HoDs choose to use these methods and how did they acquire them and the professional knowledge which may underpin them?
3 Which major external (to the school) and internal (school-level) factors influence the methods used?
4 Which characteristics of the teachers in the department and their students influence the methods used?
5 Which characteristics of the particular subject (English, mathematics, science or technology) influence the methods used?
6 To what extent do these four sets of factors (self, external, departmental and school) cause problems for the HoDs and how do they seek to overcome them?
7 How effective are the methods used perceived to be by the HoDs, the teachers and the headteacher?
8 What are the perceived implications of the conclusions from questions 1–7 for the continuing professional development and training of HoDs?
9 How helpful are three selected theoretical perspectives (contingency theory, professional knowledge and socialisation) in explaining the role of the subject HoD in the improvement of teaching and learning, and what modifications to these perspectives, if any, are suggested by the study's conclusions?

In a sample of ten Welsh secondary schools, semi-structured interviews were carried out with the headteachers and with HoDs and two teachers in each of four subject areas: English, mathematics, science and technology, a total of 130. The criteria for selecting the sample of ten schools included:

▶ all four HoDs to have completed the questionnaire in the earlier study;
▶ the headteacher and heads of the four subject areas to be willing to take part in the research;
▶ the schools to be reasonably representative of secondary schools in Wales in terms of size and location.

The criteria for selecting the department members included:

▶ a reasonable balance of experience and a proportionate gender balance;
▶ willingness to be interviewed;
▶ availability for interview in their non-teaching periods.

The purposes of the interviews with HoDs, completed in 1997, were to clarify the nature of the methods used, how they are used, how the HoDs acquired the professional knowledge and skills to use them, and which methods they consider to be successful and why. Follow-up, triangulation interviews (to cross-check HoDs' account) were held with the headteachers and two department members in each school during the spring term of 1998. These aimed to obtain independent information about the methods used by the HoDs, their perceived success in terms of improved teaching and learning and the effectiveness of HoDs in communicating professional ideas to teacher colleagues.

The interviews were set up to allow HoDs to consider a list of possible factors and methods and comment as they wished. This list was compiled from the same factors and methods that had been used in the earlier survey (see Turner, 2002). In this present study, a number of other issues were addressed in more detail; most notably questions were posed to investigate the ways in which the nature of the subject being taught influenced the methods used by HoDs and the manner in which they were able to resolve conflict within the department.

The interviews were conducted with the full agreement of the headteacher and the other participants within the school. Letters were sent to each school explaining the purposes of the research. They also contained a guarantee of confidentiality and anonymity to allow each of the potential interviewees to speak freely without fear of any subsequent retribution or damage to existing professional relationships. The success of this approach was reflected in the fact that staff in none of the ten schools refused to take part in the study. The semi-structured interview format enabled all the research questions to be addressed and allowed time to deal with any points of clarification. Each of the interviewees was provided with a set of questions to be used before the interview.

One of two researchers carried out the interviews. On a pre-arranged day in 1997, a researcher was able to interview the four HoDs in each school for up to an hour each in a vacant room. Transcripts of the interviews were inspected very carefully and common themes or key issues arising from each of the questions were identified. This process enabled us to produce a summary of the findings that was subsequently sent to each of the ten schools. A further set of letters was sent out in early 1998 requesting permission to interview the line manager for the HoDs and two departmental staff from each of the four departments. Again, we were allowed to complete our investigations in each of the schools, spending one day interviewing these other participants.

The approach used in this study suffers from three major limitations. First, the research analyses the perceptions of the HoDs but does not include observation of them actually at work. Second, there is a lack of 'hard' evidence about the impact of their work since there was no corroborating evidence to link it to improvements in examination results or to other output measures. Third, only four curriculum subjects were selected for investigation. It may well be that if other areas of the curriculum had been chosen additional ways of improving teaching and learning might have emerged. This makes the drawing of generalisable conclusions which might apply to all subjects even more problematic. While acknowledging these limitations the approach adopted was justified because, within the project's resource constraints, it would not have been possible to observe HoDs at work over a suitably long period of time. Moreover, in the event hard output data, and especially value-added data, were not available. The under-lying rationale for the design was that it was important to analyse the perceptions of HoDs and a sample of their colleagues about HoDs' work and management methods, thus filling a knowledge gap in the field of enquiry.

Main findings

All forty HoDs were experienced teachers and all but one had been a HoD for at least five years. Hence it is reasonable to conclude that their responses are likely to be representative of experienced, but not necessarily of inexperienced, HoDs. The responses from headteachers and department members were broadly consistent with those of the HoDs. Headteachers predictably took a strategic view and saw the HoDs as critical agents in the success of their respective departments. Department members had a narrower perspective and tended to focus in their answers on their own departmental experience. In this regard, the main finding was that they tended to hold less clear and less positive views about the impact of their HoDs on the improvement of teaching and learning than did the HoDs themselves. The results are presented here in summary form in relation to the research questions although, inevitably, this is a somewhat arbitrary approach since the answers often relate to more than one question.

1 *Which methods and techniques do the HoDs use to try to improve teaching and learning in their departments? Specifically, how do they use available value-added data?*

The evidence indicated that HoDs concentrated on attempting to influence the quality of teaching, recognising that their impact on student learning was much less direct. All the HoDs regarded certain underpinning, well-tried and recognised methods as being essential to their success. They included regular, formal departmental meetings, formal and informal meetings with individual staff, the design of the syllabus, the selection of textbooks, the purchasing of equipment and representing the interests of their department in meetings with the senior management team. The importance of working together and developing team-work can be seen in the light of comments made by one Head of English when she commented that: 'Sharing good practice, encouraging individual staff to evaluate their own work and developing a house style, all help people to work together as a team sharing the same aims. It fosters an open attitude where all members of the department are free to comment, argue, differ, etc.'

Views about the monitoring of staff work were mixed. While many of the HoDs interviewed expressed their frustration at having very little time to observe members of the department teaching, a few did mention classroom observation of their colleagues as a high priority if a particular individual had identified weaknesses. They did observe and monitor the work of newly qualified teachers. Formal teacher appraisal was not perceived to be a particularly effective method by most HoDs. As one HoD explained: 'All my experience tells me that cajoling, encouraging, moving step by step, is the way that works best.' However, one relatively newly appointed HoD did comment on its usefulness in identifying training needs within the department.

Nearly all the HoDs said that monitoring of students' work was an important management method. However, the ways in which monitoring actually occurred varied quite widely. Some HoDs adopted a more formal approach, looking at samples of students' work for each member of the department on an annual basis. Heads of English said they spent a great deal of time moderating course work in discussion with their colleagues. Both the monitoring of work and the display of students' efforts were considered to be highly influential by many HoDs. For example, according to one Head of English: 'Monitoring of work makes students think their work is valued and valuable. Display praises them and emphasises the value of their work.'

HoDs valued and deliberately engineered regular informal contacts. 'Popping in and out' of classrooms, spending time with staff at break times and lunchtimes, and socialising out of school were all seen as useful mechanisms for acquiring and communicating information. A number of HoDs commented that this was much easier to achieve if the classrooms used by the departmental staff were clustered together. Informal staff contacts in Technology departments were frequently mentioned, as equipment was often shared between two classes operating in adjacent rooms. This finding is consistent with the comments made by Gold and Evans (1998: 120): 'If members of a department regularly enter each others' classrooms while teaching is going on, and regularly talk about their work together, and if they have an atmosphere of trust and expectations of the best from each other, then informal visits cannot be misinterpreted.'

In addition, most HoDs laid great emphasis on the team approach. According to one Head of Maths, he tried to:

> lead by example; to ensure that one's teaching is of a good standard; to give advice to members of the team when required; to promote the team approach by listening to their views and ideas on topics or methods to be used; to value their ideas, which are just as important as those of the HoD.

HoDs considered that significant school-based in-service training opportunities for departmental staff were provided by the compulsory five annual training days more than by departmental meetings or other forms of staff contact, particularly in relation to curriculum development and the sharing of good practice. An example of this view came from a Head of English: 'On-site INSET is the most valuable method. It forces us to prioritise; it gives ownership of new developments to all staff, which are all important team-building factors.' Off-site training was not regarded as favourably, although there was a more positive response from many of the Heads of Technology, some of whom used a local consortium for training.

None of the HoDs were using value-added data, largely because it was not yet available to most of them. For those in the one LEA that did have access to such information, its use was confined to school level.

2 *Why do the HoDs choose to use these methods and how did they acquire them and the professional knowledge which may underpin them?*

HoDs selected elements of practice that they judged to constitute good departmental management. They rejected others that they considered would damage departmental morale, including the HoD taking all the most able classes for the external GCSE (General Certificate of Education) examination, allocating a high proportion of disruptive classes to newly qualified teachers, and adopting an unsympathetic attitude towards inexperienced staff.

In answer to the question 'how did you acquire your professional knowledge?' three main categories of response emerged. First, most emphasised the influence of previous HoDs with whom they had worked. They frequently described both positive and negative role models as powerful influences. Second, they referred to experiences acquired in post, which may be viewed as important socialising influences (Turner, 2000). Third, only a minority mentioned influential management training courses.

3 *Which major external (to the school) and internal (school-level) factors influence the methods used?*

Three main external school factors were cited as being very influential on the behaviour of HoDs. First, some HoDs considered the introduction of the National Curriculum and the subsequent revisions had provided a common stimulus and challenge, encouraging more teamwork in planning the schemes of work and developing teaching materials. Similar views were expressed about external assessment and examination scores and, to a lesser degree, about published school league tables based on these scores. Second, the imminence of an external inspection motivated some HoDs to give monitoring a higher priority. According to one Head of English: 'The inspection report has identified potential weaknesses; for example, a lack of differentiation'. As monitoring can be a contentious issue, many HoDs mentioned the need to achieve internal consistency (comparability of marking standards across the department) as the main justification for using this strategy. Third, local education authorities were, in general, viewed somewhat neutrally and even as being marginal. Both positive and negative experiences were occasionally described.

A wider range of internal school factors was cited as being very influential on the behaviour of HoDs:

▶ overall school policy on teaching, learning and assessment as expressed in the school's development plan;
▶ the school's financial position and its system of allocating resources;
▶ more specifically, the occasional use of salary increments to reward good performance by individual teachers was mentioned both positively and negatively by some HoDs, depending on how it was implemented by the headteacher, how far they could influence it and whether or not teachers in their department had benefited;
▶ the extent to which HoDs felt able to influence the appointment of staff to their subject area;
▶ the characteristics of the student intake, especially in terms of their performance at key stage 2 (in the year before entering a secondary school);

▶ the ways in which the student grouping was organised in the school and, in particular, the use of streaming, banding and mixed ability teaching;
▶ class size, particularly in practical subjects such as science and technology, where overcrowding was a continuing problem;
▶ the organisation of the timetable.

4 *Which characteristics of the teachers in the department and their students influence the methods used?*

HoDs stressed that the first requirement was that they themselves had to be seen by colleagues as being a good teacher and as being well organised. The expectations of them held by their departmental colleagues were also central. Asked to what extent they perceived themselves to be a team leader, most said they had to be capable of having, and sharing with colleagues, a vision about the subject and how it should be taught. One commented that 'sharing the vision is important but having the vision in the first place is even more important'.

They also mentioned the significance of being willing to listen to the opinions of others to make individuals feel valued. One HoD commented that she felt it was part of her job to 'notice things, to notice displays that have been put up, to notice techniques that are being experimented with, to notice the work the children produce in a particular class and to praise it and reinforce it'.

Some HoDs commented favourably on the effect of having trainee teachers in the department. They indicated that trainees had a 'catalytic' effect, stimulating more experienced staff to question their own assumptions about current classroom practice and encouraging reflection on the appropriateness of various teaching strategies.

5 *Which characteristics of the particular subject (English, mathematics, science or technology) influence the methods used?*

There was little evidence that the nature of the subject itself was in itself a major factor in influencing the approaches adopted by HoDs to the improvement of teaching and learning. However, the nature of the subject did influence the scope of the role. In science, the HoD was also usually the head of one subject subsection, for example biology. In such cases, the HoDs had a strong influence within their subject area of the science curriculum. But they tended to adopt a liaison role in relation to the other two heads of subsections, for example of physics and chemistry, and they saw themselves as having a more indirect effect on physics and chemistry teaching. Similarly, heads of technology were specialists in one part of the curriculum (like resistant materials) on which they exerted considerable indirect influence on classroom practice, whereas they tended to work through the heads of textiles and food and nutrition to influence teaching in those areas. The English and mathematics departments were more homogeneous in character, although in some schools both curriculum areas used non-specialists to teach these subjects. Many of the heads of technology were enthusiastic about team teaching and also commented on the importance of display work in their curriculum area as a way of recognising achievement. Some heads of English felt that team teaching was a useful way of improving standards overall.

6 *To what extent do these four sets of factors (self, external, departmental and school) cause problems for the HoDs and how do they seek to overcome them?*
7 *How effective are the methods used perceived to be by the HoDs, the teachers and the headteacher?*

HoDs all thought that they did influence the quality of teaching and, to a lesser extent, student learning in their subject area. But it was evident that the extent of such influence was dependent on a range of contextual factors, such as experience in the post, size of the department, the nature of the subject and whether or not the physical location of the teaching rooms was conducive to regular departmental staff contact. Gender was not identified as an important factor. Lack of time was confirmed as a major problem.

Most HoDs considered that it was the combination of methods they used (a holistic approach), rather than one particular method, which was instrumental in dealing with problems and in improving teaching within the department. Most respondents found it difficult to describe their experience of unsuccessful methods for improving the quality of teaching. Some were able to describe examples of policy changes which they had tried to initiate when they first started in post and which they had subsequently failed to implement. These failures often occurred when they were inexperienced or new to the school, and not fully aware of the likely reactions of more established departmental staff to the proposals.

Conclusions

Implications for professional development

In 1996 the central government's Teacher Training Agency launched a new initiative to introduce national standards and, possibly, qualifications at four stages of continuing professional development: for newly qualified teachers, 'advanced skills' (experienced and highly skilled) teachers, subject leaders and headteachers. These national standards related to assessment and to training and development activities. The core purpose of the role of subject leaders (HoDs) is defined as being: 'to provide professional leadership and management for a subject, to secure high quality teaching, effective use of resources and improved standards of learning and achievement for all pupils'. (Teacher Training Agency, 1998). The standards entail four key areas of subject leadership:

- strategic direction and development of the subject;
- teaching and learning;
- leading and managing staff;
- development and deployment of people and resources;

They also identify the requirements for professional knowledge and understanding and the underlying skills and abilities required by HoDs.

The findings from the present study offer research-based data to inform the development and implementation of the national standards for subject leaders and could also be applied to the study of leaders' problem-solving expertise and to problem-based training. In particular, the responses to Question 2 throw up major challenges for policy-makers and providers in the field of school management training. Management training opportunities were accorded much lower priority than incidental learning through professional experience before and since becoming a HoD. How, therefore, may the provision of planned professional development opportunities be improved? These implications will be considered further in future research.

Implications for theory

The research set out to clarify the contribution of HoDs to improvement of teaching and learning by building on, and developing, three aspects of theory: the characteristics of effective departments and their contribution to effective schools; the relevance of theories of *school* leadership, especially contingency theory, to *departmental* leadership; and the importance of an individual HoD's professional knowledge as one contingent factor affecting the performance of this role.

Emerging accounts of the characteristics of effective departments and their contribution to effective schools were referred to earlier. In his extensive review, Immegart (1988) demonstrated that many different models of leadership have been proposed, all of which reflect its complex, multi-dimensional nature. These include transformational, moral, political, cultural and symbolic leadership. Immegart concluded that 'effective leaders exhibit a repertoire of styles and...style is related to situation, both context and task' (1988: 262).

The essential features of contingency theory are that effective leadership is context-based and that effective leaders must take into account four sets of factors when deciding on their courses of action: those associated with the leader, the task, the subordinates and the organisational situation (see Hanson, 1979; Hoyle, 1986). Although this approach has informed studies of school leadership (e.g. Bolam et al., 1993) it has not been applied to HoDs, yet it clearly has considerable explanatory potential.

Accordingly, the study's overarching perspective derived from contingency theory and Figure 6.1 attempts to apply it to HoDs in a provisional model based on one devised by Bolam et al. (1993) for their work on headteachers. Like all such heuristic models, it is necessarily a simplified portrayal of complex and dynamic processes and interactions. It distinguishes between eight broad sets of factors, all of which might influence how a HoD works to improve teaching and learning. The model highlights two types of contextual factor:

A. those external to the school, such as the pressures brought about by national targets and the national curriculum;
B. those internal to the school, such as student characteristics and policies on assessment and resource allocation, all of which influence teaching and learning.

Figure 6.1 *A provisional model of the work of HoDs to improve teaching and learning in their department.*

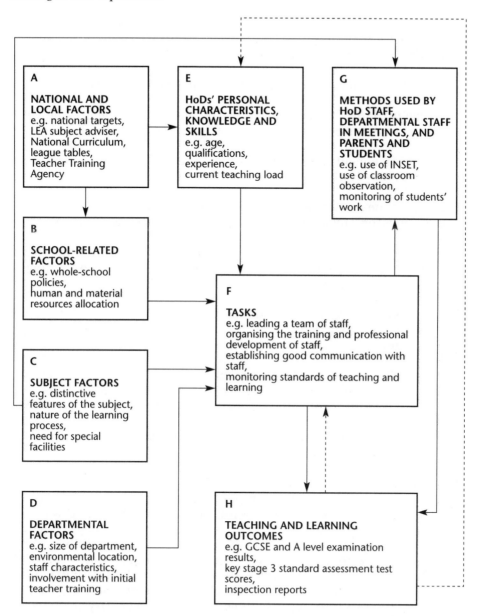

Input factors are focused around:

C. key features of the subject;
D. key features of the department and its staff;
E. the personal characteristics of the individual HoD;
F. the HoD's role and task requirements.

The model's central management process component concentrates on:

G. the methods used by HoDs to improve teaching and learning, all of which are seen as contingent on the contextual and input factors.

The final component of the model focuses on the educational impact of the methods used by HoDs to achieve their tasks:

H. the educational outcomes are, therefore, seen as necessarily influenced by a range of factors and processes which operate as independent variables.

This study's findings indicate that the model is useful in explaining the contribution of particular HoDs to the improvement of teaching and learning in terms of such contingent factors as:

▶ their professional knowledge and experience;
▶ the size of the department;
▶ the organisational implications of the particular subject;
▶ external pressures;
▶ student characteristics and school policies;
▶ the perceived utility of particular methods of working with individual teachers;
▶ the perceived utility of particular methods of working with departmental staff as a group;
▶ the perceived utility of particular methods of working with individual students and their parents.

Some of our expectations were confirmed. Successful HoDs appear to employ methods similar to those reported in the literature as being used by effective headteachers. They include formulating a clear vision for the department; ensuring that HoDs maintain their professional credibility as subject teachers; promoting teamwork; and building a distinctive departmental culture. Other expectations were not confirmed. The cognitive content of the subject appears not to be a major factor, whereas the ways in which subjects are traditionally organised and structured in British schools is important. Thus, the fact that science is taught as three separate subjects (physics, chemistry and biology) but English is not subdivided into language and literature has major consequences for the HoDs' roles.

The data are also being interpreted in the light of two additional perspectives. First is Eraut's (1994) typology of professional knowledge which embraces six categories (knowledge of people, situational knowledge, knowledge of educational practice, conceptual knowledge, process knowledge and control knowledge). Second are theories arising from professional socialisation, which occurs in preparatory training and via a range of professional networks and experiences, and organisational socialisation, which occurs once a headteacher takes up a particular job in a particular school (Hart and Weindling, 1996). Both have considerable potential for understanding HoDs' learning and, within a contingency theory framework, their behaviour. Thus, the findings indicate that HoDs' behaviour is strongly influenced by the negative and positive role models provided by HoDs with whom they had previously worked: they choose not to adopt methods they have observed or experienced as unsuccessful, but they do use adaptively those methods which they judge to have been successful.

This approach is consistent with ongoing research elsewhere. According to Hart et al. (1996: 2): 'Professionals must master the knowledge base in their chosen fields, even as that knowledge base changes. They must also learn to apply that knowledge to a unique set of individual circumstances, combining their knowledge in new ways with each case.' Further, cognitive and problem-based approaches to professional education are now the focus of both research and practice in the USA and Canada (Leithwood et al., 1993; Hart and Bredeson, 1996) and in Australia (Grady et al., 1995). The preliminary findings from the present study should ultimately provide research-based data to inform the development and implementation of the national standards for subject leaders and could also be applied to the study of leaders' problem-solving expertise and to problem-based training.

General comments

In the context of England and Wales, the study has produced:

▶ new findings about the perceived methods used by HoDs as they seek to improve teaching and learning and about their perceived effectiveness;
▶ clear evidence that HoDs carry out their departmental management role in much the same way as headteachers do in their school management role;
▶ confirmation of the usefulness of contingency theory for analysing and explaining the behaviour of HoDs;
▶ a challenge to management training policy and practice since the findings indicate that HoDs learned their knowledge and skills from earlier role models and their own experience rather than from management training.

The implications beyond England and Wales are more problematic. This is mainly because it is unclear whether middle management roles comparable to that of the head of a subject department exist in other countries. One research priority would be to answer this question in a sample of countries. Where such middle management roles do exist, a study that builds on the one reported here would be useful. Where they do not, it would be important to investigate how the tasks associated with such roles are carried out through different management structures and roles and what effect such alternative structures and roles have on the improvement of teaching and learning.

References

Bolam, R., McMahon, A., Pocklington, K. and Weindling, D. (1993) *Effective Management in Schools*. London: HMSO.

Earley, P. and Fletcher-Campbell, F. (1989) *The Time to Manage*. London: Routledge.

Edwards, R. (1985) 'Departmental organisation and management', in R. Edwards and D. Bennett (eds), *Schools in Action*. Cardiff: Welsh Office.

Eraut, M. (1994) *Developing Professional Knowledge and Competence*. London: Falmer Press.

Gold, A. and Evans, J. (1998) *Reflecting on School Management*. London: Falmer Press.

Grady, N., MacPherson, M. and Mulford, B. (1995) 'Problem-based learning in educational administration through block delivery modes', *International Studies in Educational Administration*, 23 (1): 58–64.

Hanson, E. M. (1979) 'School management and contingency theory: an emerging perspective', *Educational Administration Quarterly*, 15 (2): 98–116.

Harris, A., Jamieson, I. and Russ, J. (1995) 'A study of effective departments in secondary schools', *School Organisation*, 15 (3): 283–99.

Hart, A. W. and Bredeson, P. V. (1996) T*he Principalship: A Theory of Professional Learning and Practice*. London: McGraw–Hill.

Hart, A. W. and Weindling, D. (1996) 'Developing successful leaders', in K. Leithwood (ed.), *International Handbook of Educational Leadership and Administration*. Leuven: Kluwer Press.

Hart, A. W., Bredeson, P. V., Marsh L. S. and Scribner J. P. (1996) *Problem-solving errors of educational leaders*, paper presented at the Annual Meeting of the American Education Research Association, New York.

Hord, S. and Murphy J. (1985) 'Heads of department as change agents', in C. Dimmock (ed.), *School Improvement and Effectiveness*. London: Routledge.

Hoyle, E. (1986) *The Politics of School Management*. London: Hodder & Stoughton.

Immegart, G. L. (1988) 'Leadership and leader behaviour', in N. J. Boyan (ed.), *Handbook of Research on Educational Administration*. New York: Longman.

Leithwood, K., Hallinger, P. and Murphy, J. (eds) (1993) *Cognitive Perspectives on Educational Leadership*. New York: Teachers College Press.

Marland, M. and Hill, S. (1981) *Departmental Management*. London: Heinemann.

Mortimore, P., Sammons, P., Stoll, L., Lewis, D. and Ecob, R. (1988) School Matters: *The Junior Years*. Wells: Open Books.

OHMCI Wales (1995) *Leadership and Management in Secondary Schools*. Cardiff: OHMCI.

Rutter, M., Maugham, B., Mortimore, P., Ouston, J. and Smith, A. (1979) *Fifteen Thousand Hours*. London: Open Books.

Sammons, P., Hillman, J. and Mortimore, P. (1995a) *Key Characteristics of Effective Schools: A Review of School Effectiveness Research*. London: Office for Standards in Education.

Sammons, P., Thomas, S. and Mortimore, P. (1995b) *Accounting for variations in academic effectiveness between schools and departments*, paper presented at the European Conference on Educational Research, Bath, England.

Siskin, L. S. (1994) *Realms of Knowledge: Academic Departments in Secondary Schools*. London: Falmer Press.

Teacher Training Agency (1998) *National Standards for Subject Leaders*. London: Teacher Training Agency.

Torrington, J. and Weightman, J. (1990) *The Reality of School Management*. Oxford: Blackwell.

Turner, C. (1996) 'The roles and tasks of a subject head of department in secondary schools in England and Wales: a neglected area of research?', *School Organisation*, 16 (2): 203–17.

Turner, C. (2000) 'Learning about leading a subject department in secondary schools: some empirical evidence', *School Leadership and Management*, 20 (3): 299–313.

Turner, C. (2002) 'Heads of subject departments and their influence on teaching and learning'. Unpublished PhD thesis, University of Wales, Cardiff.

Welsh Office (1995) *A Bright Future*. Cardiff: Welsh Office.

Welsh Office (1997) *A Bright Future: Beating the Previous Best*. Cardiff: Welsh Office.

Chapter 7

Evaluating technology and instructional innovation: when clear findings are not evident

Sharon Kruse and Karen Seashore Louis

In the following chapter, Kruse and Louis examine some of the problems that can be encountered by researchers. Their report addresses issues that are rarely discussed in published accounts of research: what happens when things do not go to plan, or a study generates inconclusive results? Although the research presented was relatively large-scale and publicly funded, the issues raised by Kruse and Louis are equally applicable to small-scale researchers. Their chapter highlights challenges faced in undertaking applied research, particularly action research and studies of changes in practice. The substantive focus is an evaluation of a technology innovation in schools in one region of Ohio, USA. They outline how Sharon Kruse became involved in the project at a late stage when the research design and methodology had already been established and case study data collected. Her task was to 'rescue' a project that had run into difficulties. Kruse and Louis examine how a faulty research design was modified and amended, and how inconclusive findings were still able to yield important understandings about innovation and change.

A salutory lesson is that outcomes from a project should never be assumed. In this instance, the use of a qualitative case study methodology was originally chosen to illuminate and exemplify process aspects of change whose outcome appears to have been taken for granted. This assumption was a major flaw in the research design. Kruse and Louis reveal that even when new data cannot be collected, evidence sometimes can be found through using existing data sets. They conclude that research designs that take account of potential problems, build in flexibility and allow multiple methods of data gathering are more likely to be successful. In relation to data analysis, the authors argue that multi-method designs allow for different types of data to be used in complementary ways, providing a holistic picture of a phenomenon.

Overall, the chapter highlights the relationship between research process and outcome, and the story the researcher is able to tell. Kruse and Louis point out that, despite unpromising findings, good scholarship and an interdisciplinary approach can yield new insights into a problem. In this case, literature on

149

school improvement and organisational theory and innovation helped to develop a wider and deeper understanding of the lessons from this innovation than would have been the case had they drawn only on literature relating to instruction in schools and the use of information technologies.

Introduction

In this chapter we present the story of an evaluation that failed to produce clear findings. We choose this topic because it is every student's nightmare: 'What if I spend six months or a year on this project and don't have anything definitive to say?' A great deal of research – particularly applied and action research – does not, in fact, produce a 'yes/no' answer to a well-articulated question. Instead, it reflects the inherent messiness of 'real-world' efforts to create positive school improvement. But the lesson that we want to convey is that imperfect research designs and mixed results do not need to consign an investigative effort to the well-known *Journal of No Results*. Instead, there are design and analytic strategies that can be used to extract meaning (and a thesis or dissertation) from mixed findings.

The first author of this chapter became acquainted with the project that we describe only after it was well underway. Two previous evaluators had left – one for personal reasons, the second over concerns about the funding agency's requests for changes in the evaluation. In fact, the funding agency had radically altered its expectations in the fourth year of the project, adding a requirement for quantitative test score analysis to illuminate the prior case study work. The third (and final) evaluator's task was to 'rescue' the evaluation and to produce reasonable quantitative and qualitative findings for the funding agency to consider in light of the work completed. This chapter provides a detailed history of the project, summary of initial findings from the other evaluators, discussion of how the evaluation changed during the final phase of the evaluation, presentation of sample analytical models and brief discussion of the study findings. The chapter concludes with a discussion of reflections on developing research from a multiple methods approach and the benefits of such a methodological stance.

Project description

The Technology Innovation Challenge Grant (TICG) was a national initiative designed to increase the effective use of technology in classrooms across the United States (US) based on competitive proposals from educational authorities. In this case, the TICG grant was received by a regional service centre in the mid-western state of Ohio. While the *states* have the primary responsibility for providing public education under the US Constitution, *local* (district) *and regional* (county) *educational authorities* are the actual providers of most services. In the state of Ohio, *regional* service centres (operated at the level of county government) provide assistance to *local* education authorities (districts) in matters of curriculum and instruction. The organisation of education in the

US varies considerably between states, which are constitutionally autonomous in most matters pertaining to education. Across the US, 92 per cent of funding for education comes from state, regional and local taxes. In some states, the primary authority is delegated to counties (regions); in others it is located almost exclusively in local education authorities that usually coincide with the boundaries of towns and cities, while in some states, such as Ohio, it is shared between regional and local authorities.

Regional service centres offer access to specialised personnel, such as subject area consultants, that smaller local authorities could not afford, and avoid duplication of otherwise expensive content consultants. The service centres also organise and support large-scale regional projects such as the TICG. In other words, in Ohio the regional centres provide resources and opportunities, but local education authorities and their employees make decisions about participation.

Personnel at the regional service centre designed the TICG goals to serve several complementary purposes that were intended to promote the use of technology to create fundamental change in teachers' work. The grant assumed that it was necessary to expand access to computers, the Internet and related technologies to all students across the county. In addition, the grant proposed to use the new technology to stimulate teachers to think about the kinds of work in which students engaged. Thus, there was a major focus on professional development and in-service training for both teachers and school-based administrators (headteachers). In fact, the term 'New Work' was coined as a shorthand way of describing the purposes of the grant. Teaching with technology was not to be 'business as usual' with computers as friendly assistants. Instead educators were to learn about using technologies in the context of how children learn, not what machines do. In other words, the proposal built on theories of constructivist teaching that draw on philosophers such as Vygotsky and John Dewey, and emerging neuroscientific research. It was assumed that where computers are used to help children find and solve problems, rather than providing answers to questions framed by teachers and textbooks, learning would improve. The goals of the project were stated quite clearly in the project proposal's theme: 'Unless students do New Work as they use the New Technology to learn, little will change.' The focus of evaluation efforts was to document the impacts of implementation on changes in teaching and learning in classrooms. For a cross-case analysis of exemplary use of instructional technology in US Schools, see McGhee and Kozma (2001) and Dexter and Seashore Louis (2001).

Originally, the grant was to be evaluated solely by the use of qualitative case study methods. Research questions were designed to be open-ended and to offer the researchers an array of possible avenues to explore. The initial thinking was informed by case study research methodology such as that discussed by Yin (1994) in which case study methods allow the researcher to 'pursue explanatory purposes'. Although not quite designed as grounded research (Glaser and Strauss, 1967; Strauss and Corbin, 1998), the initial study was designed to allow for emergent and evolving findings and the development of new foci. Further, the initial researchers adopted the research stance that the project would succeed and that their role was to document those successes. Such a stance has its roots in emancipatory action research and evaluation, where the researchers' role is defined by their ability to assist participants to arrive at an understanding of the forces that shape their own world and consciousness (Kincheloe, 1991; Fetterman, 2001). The emancipatory stance allowed the research to be approached from the assumption that positive results would surface and that careful observation would provide sufficient data to support encouraging findings and results. The following three questions provided the direction for the development of research within the case study sites:

1 In what ways will the introduction of educational technology, materials, tools and professional development around instruction have an impact on classrooms and student learning?
2 In what ways do professional development opportunities made available to both administrators and teachers have the ability to change school culture around instruction?
3 Can technology be introduced as a tool, rather than an end in itself?

Design and emerging process

In keeping with the qualitative design, four case study schools were chosen from those across the county which were participating in grant activities. Two elementary schools, a middle school and a high school comprised the sample. The schools spanned four local education authorities as well as communities with a range of socio-economic circumstances. The case study schools were identified by the regional service centre leadership as having the potential to be exemplary instances of systemic change through technology integration. The principals (headteachers) and many teachers in the chosen schools had played important roles in previous efforts by the regional service centre to offer in-service training that emphasised innovative instruction. The local education authorities in which the schools were located had already made a definite commitment to greater infusion and use of, and support for, technology in the schools. And, in three of the cases, the schools had received additional supplementary funding to support instructional change through technology. Each qualified for the study because the school administrator agreed to participate. Employing an emancipatory ethnographic methodology, researchers planned intensive classroom observation, interviews with a variety of stakeholders, including administrators, teachers, parents, students and, in the case of the high school, employers of students involved in the project (Miles and Huberman, 1994; Yin, 1997).

Years one through four

In early 1996, personnel at the regional service centre began the process of infusing technology into classrooms across the county. Computers were purchased and delivered, buildings were wired for both classroom computers and computer labs and the in-service training workshops began in the spring of 1997. Eager superintendents, principals and teachers volunteered for the initial round of offerings. Each technology workshop focused on the development of 'new work' for students: participants were encouraged to develop a new personal vision of the classroom of the future. The focus was on encouraging teachers to develop lessons that engaged, motivated and challenged students to address important learning from subject area content, used technology as a tool to foster under-standing of content at deeper levels and employed problem-solving and other higher-order thinking processes as a primary focus of the work provided to stu-dents. Teachers and administrators who attended the sessions also engaged in vision-building exercises, the development of individual mission statements and activities designed to foster an increased sense of urgency around the need to change pedagogy and instruction.

While the spotlight was clearly on New Work, the in-service training ses-sions provided little actual help to teachers in designing lessons that encompassed the ideals set forth in the visioning activities. In defence of the regional service centre personnel, their assigned, but daunting, task was to pro-vide professional development about New Work to over 5,000 teachers. Thus each year of the grant simply exposed another group of school personnel to similar basic training. Further, participation in grant activities was voluntary and although district superintendents across the county supported New Work activities they also had their own in-house district and building-level profes-sional development goals and objectives. Simply put, the regional service centre lacked the needed systemic leverage radically to alter instruction in so many districts, buildings and classrooms.

As the school year of 1997–98 drew to a close, grant evaluators reported tenta-tive positive results. Indeed, access to computer technology had increased in all schools across the county and access to computer technology in low socio-eco-nomic local education agencies had risen dramatically – up 37 per cent. Participants in the New Work in-service training reported strong satisfaction with their experiences. The case study findings were not surprising: school staff experienced normal difficulties with delivery schedules of the new computers, wiring efforts did not always run smoothly, and ambitious implementation schedules were subject to frustrating delays. However, the report optimistically suggested that such problems would be resolved and New Work effects would be readily observable in classrooms across the county in later years.

At the end of year two, the original evaluator resigned from the project citing personal difficulties and was replaced by a local university-level researcher who had assisted in collecting the school-level data for several case study schools. In years three and four project coordinators did little to alter the TICG goals or the evaluation plans. Additional administrative and teacher in-service training was planned and executed, case study data were collected and initial case reports were drafted. At the end of year four, case study data reported several challenges associated with implementation of the project. These included challenges in maintaining consistent building leadership, sus-taining the vision of teaching that focused on the principles of New Work, supporting the technology within buildings and classrooms, and supporting teachers within an environment of change.

Leadership challenges

Findings from the year four report (Rasinski, 2000: 34) state:

> *The continuity of leadership that is absolutely essential for a project such as this simply did not happen. Too many key personnel left the project at critical points. And, in many cases, it appears that issues of transition and continuity were not attended to. As a result continuity and momentum were lost and the vision was disrupted. The new leaders who came in, although very competent in their own right, may not have shared the vision of their predecessors and, indeed, may not have been fully aware of the actions taken by their predecessors to move the schools closer to the systemic change that had been envisioned.*

The report suggested that unless leadership remained stable within the local education agencies and individual schools grant efforts would be less successful than originally anticipated.

Vision

Visioning was also an area of difficulty identified by the end of year four. The report (Rasinski, 2000: 41) states:

> *The New Project could best be described as a top-down vision of how schools could and should work. That is, the project was inspired and given birth and legitimacy by leaders in the various schools. For the project to work, it was absolutely incumbent on the school leaders to transmit that vision of the New Work to the teachers who were entrusted to carry out the vision...However, the communication of a vision did not happen systemically throughout all of the schools and school systems as was hoped. To some extent, the lack of communication was due to the turnover of school leaders in key schools and organizations. The new leaders simply were not imbued with the vision of New Work and could not be expected to communicate that vision to their teaching staff. More generally, however, the effort to communicate and inspire a vision of New Work among teachers was not as systemic and integrated in its implementation as was required. It was simply not enough. Only some teachers, even among the case study schools, had the opportunity to allow themselves to be convinced that New Work was worth pursuing. Some teachers resisted, others never got the message.*

In other words, implementation within schools was spotty and limited to a few enthusiasts.

Technology

Additionally, the early optimism that technological difficulties would diminish after the initial hardware installation glitches proved unfounded. Findings from the year four report (Rasinski, 2000: 47) state that:

Much of the frustration that resulted in less than full implementation of New Work in the case study schools was itself the result of the fragility of the technology. Although the technology can do wonderful things in schools, it needs to be able to work dependably for teachers and students to gain benefit from it. In reality, however, the technology did not perform reliably enough for teachers to feel comfortable enough making it an integral part of their teaching. Throughout this project, I heard complaints from teachers who reported planning wonderful lessons only to find that the machines had locked up, the printer wasn't working, mischievous students had sabotaged the computers, the server was down, the software wasn't properly loaded, the class using the computers earlier had done something to the machines to make them not work properly, the files had disappeared or been erased, or some other catastrophe that made the significant investment in instructional planning all but worthless to the teacher and students. Usually these sorts of complaints were accompanied with an acknowledgment that there was no one who could help the teachers fix the problems then and there.

The need for ongoing financial support and expertise at the building level in order for technology to be seamlessly integrated into classroom practice was, in other words, profoundly apparent.

Support for teachers

Finally, even within buildings with enthusiastic principals and teacher leadership, day-to-day expert support for changing instruction through technology was waning. Rasinski (2000: 52) states:

The final major area of concern that I believe is responsible for the lack of systemic and integrated change in teachers' teaching and students' learning through technology is the lack in the appropriate levels of support to teachers to make and sustain the kinds of changes they were asked to make in this project. Apparently, there was not enough expertise to create the critical mass of teachers within buildings to allow New Work to make a strong foothold. Moreover, it seemed that more on the spot training, training that would immediately impact teachers and students in the classroom, would have been helpful. Indeed, in some cases the lack of commitment ... to technology education by school administrators was well apparent to teachers.

Thus the data suggested that even when teachers had an idea of what New Work should look like, they didn't have the knowledge or the skills to make changes in instruction on their own.

Year four conclusions

The year four cases ended with the following pessimistic note (Rasinski, 2000: 87):

> *I was not able to find compelling evidence that school-wide, systemic, and integrated change occurred in the case study schools that were part of this evaluation. The nature of change in systems is difficult to predict and control…Nevertheless, this evaluation suggests what needs to be done in the future in order for that school- and district-wide, systemic, and integrated change to occur in future projects: there needs to be ongoing, consistent, and dynamic leadership that is present throughout the duration of the project. There needs to be ongoing attempts to convince teachers of the vision that the leaders have for the project and then to empower the teachers to make that vision a reality through their own style of teaching. There needs to be ongoing support and instruction for teachers at all levels of implementation. And of course, the technology itself not only has to move toward greater levels of innovation, it also needs to move to greater levels of reliability and dependability. When the computer works with the same reliability of a telephone, then teachers can be assured that their work will not be compromised by the vagaries of the equipment itself. However, until such problems are addressed and overcome, the ultimate vision of New Work, the combination of new technology, new curriculum, and new instruction that will fundamentally change the way that schools work will not likely become a reality.*

Year five and the research process

Following the fourth year report the evaluators and project coordinators were asked to present their findings to the funding agency. The presentation was concurrent to a change in the funding agency's priorities for the projects. Although the funders had initially agreed to the qualitative study design, in the light of the lukewarm case study results, as well as increased pressures across the nation for accountability in all educational efforts, they asked for the inclusion of quantitative findings focused on student achievement.

Further, the funding agency now asked for a design that would consider the progress of students in schools other than the case study sites, and that took into consideration whether the teacher in-service training had an impact on students. Following the request for a shift in evaluative focus the second evaluator decided to step down from the role of primary investigator and to remain as part of the project only to monitor the progress of the case study schools. It was at this time that the first author of this chapter, Sharon Kruse, was employed as the third and final evaluator. The county superintendent was blunt on the day the contract was signed: the job was to 'rescue' the project, provide reasonable findings to the funding agency and to do so within the year.

Interestingly, Sharon was not an obvious choice as a quantitative evaluator. In fact, her most recent work has been informed by a methodological focus based in narrative theory (Kruse, 2001). However, there was a match between her familiarity with the work and the context in which it was occurring that may have reinforced a sense of trust in her capacities as an ad hoc 'research rescuer'. Sharon's work (like that of the second author of this chapter) had recently focused on the study of innovation in a continuous improvement-planning project. She had worked within the same geographical area of the state and was familiar with the TICG activity. Somewhat rusty statistical skills were balanced by a willingness to work within the task at hand. Work started with the agreement that the qualitative data – stories recounted by educators involved with innovative school improvement efforts – provided an ample foundation on which to rest a quantitative analysis of test score data (Heshusius and Ballard, 1996). The opportunity to combine narrative analysis with quantitative analysis was a challenge!

Narrative theory led also to a belief that the analysis of teachers' stories about school change initiatives are revealing because of *how* the educators tell them as well as what they report. Recent work suggests that some social scientists are beginning to study the process of how interviewees construct their stories by attending to cultural, linguistic and interactional contexts and processes of storytelling (Josselson and Lieblich, 1995; Riessman, 1993; Witherell and Noddings, 1991). Kruse's (2001) work in narrative analysis had taken as its object of investigation the story/interview itself. The methodological approach examines the stories told and analyses how the stories are put together: the linguistic and cultural resources upon which the stories draw and how they persuade the listener of authenticity. In sum, analysis in narrative studies opens up the forms of telling about experience, not simply the language to which the content refers. Instead, narrative analysis attends to the way a story is told and asks why it was told in that particular form. Narrative study seeks the long answer, the life story, and then uses these to understand how an interviewee's ideas are constructed, authored, owned and interpreted by themselves (Bloom, 1998; Czarniawska, 1997, 1998; Riessman, 1993). Attention is paid to how stories are constructed and represented. Narrative analysis assumes that the language a person chooses to tell his or her story is the connection between experience and understanding.

Further, the narrative methodological lens allows qualitative interview data to inform statistical findings in important ways. Narrative theory suggests that the 'cultural texts' (Heilbrun, 1989) both shape and underscore the stories we tell about ourselves and our circumstances. In searching for the cultural texts of the educators involved with the grant activities the qualitative theory helped to inform the quantitative findings by surfacing the existing cultural norms of the school sites. Remembering that any finding, be it a statistical analysis or an interview text, is constrained by the culture in which it is embedded provides the researcher with a foundation on which inconsistent results can be examined.

By bringing this distinctively qualitative approach to the evaluation the regional service centre staff members hoped to make use of the existing data and design a final year study that would have the benefit of quantitative analysis and a focus on the experiences of the member administrators and teachers. From this methodological stance Sharon began to focus on the undeniable quantitative needs of the funding agencies while developing a broader base of interview data concerning the other schools that had participated in the project.

The addition of quantitative student achievement data was problematic. Since such data had not been collected in prior years for the case study schools, nor had systematic data collection been developed for schools outside of the case study schools, development of a comprehensive collection and analysis plan was necessary. After several brainstorming sessions, it was decided that no additional direct testing of the participants was possible or practical given the time constraints, cost and disruption to instructional time in classrooms.

In the Ohio public education system, students are periodically given proficiency tests that are used to evaluate individual progress and to assess the quality of schools. It was thus decided to obtain and use these data to examine if there was a discernable difference between the scores of students who were taught by teachers who had participated in the grant activities. Fortunately, the state had adopted in the early 1990s a state-wide testing programme that tested fourth, sixth and ninth grade students in each of five subject areas – reading, writing, mathematics, citizenship and science. Scores for these student level data were kept in a central location in the regional service centre and were easily accessed through computerised sources.

These data did not, however, fully solve the design problem. While data existed for each fourth, sixth and ninth grade student across the county and could be tracked over the period of the grant, the data set was not designed to link students to teachers. In other words, there was no way to link specific student results to teachers who participated in grant activities. It was determined that it would be necessary to access and link two separate data sets. Test score data was of primary importance but equally necessary was access to school-level data such as class records and teacher assignments.

Linking these data sets posed potential ethical problems, however. In order to carry out the merger, it was necessary to know the names of both students and teachers. In general, US federal and state data privacy law restricts public access to data such as these, and it is necessary to obtain permission using formal review processes that are designed to protect human subjects – particularly children and minors. Reviews are especially rigorous when personal data, such as the income of the child's family, attendance and disciplinary records, and other similar information, are provided to an 'outsider'. In keeping with the standards established by both the university and the state, written statements about the need for the data and protection of confidentiality were obtained from district superintendents prior to accessing the needed data sets. (In the US, students as well as faculty members are required to demonstrate that they have complied with these requirements as part of their research. If they do not, the university may choose not to accept their thesis or dissertation.) Additionally, data related to student schedules, class assignment, attendance and access to federal programmes such as title one or free and reduced lunch were obtained for analysis purposes.

The resulting data set matched teachers who had participated in the New Work in-service offerings to students in their classes. As noted above, although test score data in the aggregate is considered public record, access to individual student records is sensitive, the most obvious but important consideration being the privacy of individual student scores. Since the only way to obtain a match between teacher and student was to access student records, a simple system of coding each student was developed. Participating teachers were numbered and students were then given an additional number only accessible to the researchers. So, if a student was in the class of teacher 11 she or he might be known as student 11-23. Names or other identifying features of the student files were then erased, leaving a working file that preserved student confidentiality.

These lists were matched in a similar fashion with teachers and students from the same school who had not had New Work professional development. Participation in the grant activities by teachers was determined by attendance records from the in-service records. Extent of participation, whether the participant ever felt any inclination to use the information provided or whether the participant had the capability to use the information was accessed by the administration of a survey to participants. To guarantee a representative return for the survey a gift certificate to a local bookstore was offered. Surveys were distributed through the countywide mailing system for public schools rather than through the postal service and were sent directly to teachers. Additionally, principals were alerted that the survey was distributed and were offered an additional prize for high building-level return rates. The response rate for the survey was 77 per cent.

Uniformly, the findings supported those of the case studies. While teachers were philosophically enthusiastic about the content of the New Work offerings they reported 'little opportunity to implement the ideas, topics or concepts' in 85 per cent of the responses. Many filled the blank pages on the back of the survey with complaints similar to those of teachers in the case study schools. Additionally, local education authority schools were compared for progress toward student achievement goals to determine if any conclusions could be drawn across the large regional sample.

The findings: comparison between participating and non-participating teachers

A comparison of the five subject-area grade proficiency scores for students of teachers who participated and students whose teachers did not participate in the New Work opportunities produced consistent results across grade levels. Districts were presented with data in a format similar to that shown in Table 7.1. First are some summary descriptive statistics on the scores of the students used in the analysis. Group 0 are those students who did not have a participating teacher in any class. Group 1 are the students who did have a participating teacher. The descriptive statistics indicate that for all five areas, the scores of those having participating teachers were higher than the scores of those who did not have participating teachers.

Table 7.1 *Descriptive statistics of 9th grade student proficiency scores in five areas*

	Group	N	Mean	Std. dev.	Std. error mean
Writing	0	299	48.03	9.82	0.57
	1	217	51.75	9.84	0.67
Reading	0	287	208.04	30.54	1.80
	1	216	215.58	30.17	2.05
Math	0	471	196.88	18.64	0.86
	1	293	201.39	20.67	1.21
Citizen	0	377	203.18	21.56	1.11
	1	249	205.73	20.47	1.30
Science	0	386	200.38	19.96	1.02
	1	256	204.32	21.73	1.36

Next, a two independent sample t-test was performed to compare the scores of the groups in each of the five areas (Table 7.2). The table shows that in this case only in the area of citizenship were there no statistically significant differences found. All the other testing areas showed a statistically significant difference, meaning that those who had participating teachers did better on the proficiency tests. The findings were similar for all 18 districts. In many cases students who had had teachers who participated in the New Work professional development opportunities scored statistically significantly higher than those who did not in all subject areas. In no case did a district show no significant difference between all groups.

Table 7.2 *Two independent sample t-test for the five areas on the proficiency tests*

Area	t	df	2 tailed sig.	Mean diff.
Writing	−4.248	514	0.000	−3.72
Reading	−2.756	501	0.006	−7.54
Math	−3.047	571	0.002	−4.52
Citizen	−1.478	624	0.140	−2.55
Science	−2.363	640	0.018	−3.94

Unpacking the conundrum

The findings proved puzzling. If, as teachers reported, they had implemented only minor changes to instruction what might account for the significant differences in student achievement? A final analysis of proficiency data, coupled with qualitative interview findings, provided some answers to this question – which focus on the self-selection bias of innovations that are based on teachers' willingness to volunteer for additional training.

The student test results associated with two groups of teachers – those who had attended TICG in-service programmes, and those who did not – were analysed to look for differences prior to any involvement in TICG grant activities. This analysis resulted in similar findings across all of the districts: the students whose teachers later went on subsequently to enrol in New Work professional development scored statistically significantly higher at all three levels than those who did not go on to enrol (Figure 7.1).

Figure 7.1 *Comparisons of teachers prior to the project who attended and did not attend in-service offerings.*

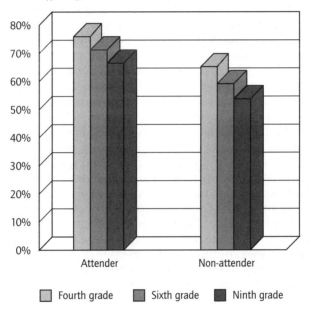

Just as striking was the finding that differences in student test scores between local education authorities were strongly associated with the socio-economic status (SES) of the families that were served. Districts with higher SES populations scored significantly better than low SES districts, districts with higher average teacher salaries scored significantly better than their lower paid neighbours, and districts with higher per pupil expenditures scored significantly better than districts with a lower investment in instruction. These differences were larger than those shown between participating and non-participating teachers.

At the outset it was not expected to find significant differences between populations of teachers who attended the in-service activities since they had reported little implementation of the ideas. Nor was it expected to find differences attributable to grant activities that had fallen prey to logistical implementation barriers that were similar to those already well documented in the school change literature. Yet the evaluation still needed to interpret the findings for the regional and local education authorities, as well as for the funding agency.

One possible conclusion is that exposure to voluntary in-service training that does not meet well-established standards for the design and delivery of professional development may not result in appreciable classroom effects. (For a review of research-based standards for professional development in education, see National Staff Development Council (undated).) But such a finding felt incomplete (and even unfair) and it was decided to interview key administrators, teachers and community leaders concerning their sense of the project. This data, supported by the case studies and the inconclusive quantitative data, enabled us to offer an interpretation related to the barriers to large-scale innovations. The final report echoed the case study findings of year four. The main focus was on the kinds of structural and human resource conditions that were lacking in the school sites but are needed to support major pedagogical changes such as those captured by the vision of New Work.

The final evaluation suggested that, while the broad goals of the grant captured what is known about how to promote change in classrooms, they were too ambiguous and imprecise to provide guidance to teachers about what needed to change. At the heart of all these efforts was the message that school cultures and practices were in need of drastic reform. But, as educators and community struggled to embrace the reforms inherent in the system standards provided by TICG activity, the actual focus of in-service work varied widely, from developing very specific technology skills – such as using PowerPoint and spreadsheets – among students, teachers and administrators, to enhancing community understanding of the ways in which knowledge has changed over the past decades and the implications of these shifts for schools. As has been evidenced by countless national polls, while educators and the general public will admit that broad school reform is necessary, they are reticent to admit that their own school is in need of fundamental change. In the end, the message that school cultures and practices must change provided too weak a link to bind the voluntary professional development activities into a coherent whole.

The coherence problem

If the major themes of the grant activity seemed somewhat confusing to the participating educators it was because they carried internal, but largely unarticulated, contradictions that became apparent in the interview and narrative data. They were partially disconnected to the wider public discourse about what defines school improvement, which in the US has recently focused on the improvement of test scores in core subject areas. In spite of the funding agency's efforts to bring the 'testable performance standards' criterion back into the programme during its final year, the New Work vision remained partially disconnected from 'raising performance standards' because there was no logical linkage at the start. The disjuncture between different strategies meant that potentially compatible reform proposals (technology and increased subject-matter competence) were not linked in ways that made their congruence visible to those participating in grant activity. The schools and teachers in those schools were caught in competing policy initiatives – those the grant proposed and those sponsored by the state and district authorities themselves.

This is, of course, hardly the first instance of competing programme and policy initiatives in education. Bryk and his colleagues, in their study of reform in Chicago, coined the phrase 'Christmas tree schools' to capture the tendency for educators to display their most recent innovations as distinct (and fragile) ornaments rather than as integral parts of the educational whole (Newmann et al., 2001). National and state educational policies also frequently embody conflicting assumptions that are largely undiscussed, but which reflect differing mental models of how schools should be organised in a democracy (Seashore Louis, 1998). Nor is the presence of multiple innovations that are not well integrated necessarily a fatal flaw in school reform, because school staffs that encourage risk-taking will naturally have a variety of new efforts being initiated at any time (Seashore Louis and Miles, 1990). The TICG initiative, however heavily funded and visible, was a marginal effort in comparison to ongoing state and district curriculum and testing initiatives, and its poor integration was therefore problematic.

The ambition problem

Further, at the start of TICG activity the intent was to provide in-service activities that utilised technology as a tool for learning and not as a machine, and were to provide teachers with a new vision of the work in which students engaged. The premise of New Work was to conceptualise the use of constructivist theory, in tandem with technology, to create classrooms in which the work tasks provided to students both challenged and motivated thinking, creativity and connectedness. In-service academies and institutes were designed to foster the development of professional communities and organisational learning among teachers, administrators and community members in the pursuit of New Work.

However, the development of such ambitious goals proved difficult. While qualitative data suggests that some may have embraced the belief structures that underscored New Work, moving beyond intellectual acceptance to implementation of congruent activity at the classroom or building level has been inconsistent. Analysis of the evaluation data suggests that the project directors lacked close ties to the school organisations they sought to affect. Without a stronger intervention or systemic leverage in the form of pressure and support from policy-makers and administrators (Huberman and Miles, 1984), the directors had few additional tools to inform classroom practice in meaningful ways. Lacking the systemic leverage necessary for deep change, directors and project staff could hope only to lay the foundation for future innovation and reform initiatives.

Conclusions

Every research effort has a story that is never part of the official published record. The bench sciences are replete with stories about serendipitously discovered substances, products and inventions. Velcro, penicillin and Post-it pads are a familiar few. Stories about the creation of these products often revolve around a similar theme – while in the pursuit of another substance, an accident occurs and the new substance is identified by chance. The accident might be glue that does not hold permanently (Post-its), a chance walk in the woods (Velcro) or a fortuitous human tear in a petri dish (penicillin). In each of these examples the common thread is that the scientist notices the usefulness of the new material and goes on to refine the early 'mistake' into something significant.

In the bench sciences persons who are graced by the windfall of serendipity are not reluctant to admit their good fortune. Rather than being defensive about the role chance played in their discoveries, they are often eager to describe it and these tales become part of the cultural mythology of invention, discovery and innovation. Serendipity does not diminish the prior efforts and knowledge that allowed them to be in the 'right place at the right time' nor does it lessen the credit due to them for making the discovery.

As encouraging as these tales of discovery and luck are, a more common story, both in the bench sciences and education, is weak or inconsistent findings concerning the central assumption of the study. Put simply, not every study leads to unambiguous or even lucid conclusions. Often a researcher starts out with a perfectly good proposition – for example, the addition of technology-rich classroom environments paired with a message focused on the urgency for change in schools ought to lead to measurably increased student achievement – yet the assumption is not borne out in the results. Without further explanation, teachers may be blamed because they are 'resistant to change' or incompetent.

In considering our example in this chapter, one might argue that the measurement tool was too imprecise accurately to capture resultant student achievement gains (perhaps true), or that the retrospective nature of the measures did not allow for the collection of longitudinal data that would have more precisely catalogued achievement gains (also perhaps true), or that had the research been designed differently from the beginning such difficulties could have been avoided (again, perhaps true). However, it is important to acknowledge the frequency with which good scholars end up in the same embarrassing reality. Often researchers who study schools are confronted with situations very much like the one described in this evaluation. Innovation efforts are begun months before the researchers arrive, efforts are clouded with multiple and related variables, and causality is all but impossible to determine. In the end, the data fail to tell a story.

At this juncture the researchers have several choices. They can bury the evaluation or put the study in the drawer and hope that the next effort bears fruit. Or they can develop a design framework in such a way that if no findings emerge there is still a story to tell. In short, a good researcher creates his or her own opportunities for serendipity. It can be done through careful planning, attention to a design plan that allows for mixed methodologies, awareness of literatures beyond those on which the study initially rests, and deliberately revisiting and elaborating on 'practical theory'.

Careful planning

At the start of the project described in this chapter, the evaluators chose only to consider qualitative data from a limited number of case sites. This decision rested on a series of choices that every researcher is forced to make. These include the consideration of linked factors: access to data with the potential to tell a story, necessary resources to obtain the data including both time and funding, and the researcher's analytic skills. In the case of the grant project, the initial research team believed that they could collect typical stories of technology implementation from carefully chosen case sites. This determination was not without precedent in the literature. Qualitative studies of classroom innovation have been a cornerstone of much of the restructuring research. Both the researchers and the programme designers believed that accountability through test score analysis was premature and significant gains in student achievement would not be observable for years to come. With limited evaluation resources – a reality for every researcher – it was decided that focused intensive qualitative data collection would provide for a story rich in detail and explanatory power that focused on implementation rather than impacts. Finally, by focusing efforts solely toward qualitative data collection, a strong research team could be easily assembled. Researchers with the analytic skills necessary to manage large, messy quantitative databases were less readily available.

The initial researchers for the grant project began their work from the vantage point that held certain reasonable assumptions as unassailable truths. Among them were that test score analysis would not provide them with the sorts of detail about student work that the study sought to tease out, and that case study data could document the expected changes in classroom instruction. By believing that the in-service work would, in fact, result in changed classroom practice and ignoring early on the possibility that other organisational forces would intervene, the researchers unnecessarily truncated their data collection and analysis plan.

In hindsight, overlooking even the most basic of quantitative data sources early on in the project created difficulties for the researchers in later years. By beginning any project with a careful eye to the types of questions one might want to explore (or a funding agency or advisor might pose) down the road, a researcher creates an insurance policy of sorts. That is, the development of a careful research plan inclusive of multiple sources of data collected over time can provide longitudinal data elements that will be useful to round out findings.

Mixed methodologies

The inclusion of mixed methodologies at the beginning of a research project can often assure the researcher access to a rich story. If quantitative data do not prove significant, or the findings are inconclusive, a strong qualitative component can often provide the foundation for either explanation of weak findings or an alternative findings section entirely. In the case of the example study offered in this chapter, the funding agency requested the inclusion of quantitative results. Yet, posing questions of the impact on student experiences, achievement and skill attainment of grant activities were reasonable foci for the evaluator's attentions. Had the initial research effort considered a mixed methods approach much additional data might have been collected throughout the project.

A mixed methods approach suggests that in addition to interview and observation data, additional qualitative data might have been collected. Reasonable to include would have been teachers' lesson plans and work products from just prior to attending in-service activities. A second collection might have been attempted just following attendance as well as at regular intervals following the conclusion of the professional development work. Student work samples might also have provided a unique lens into the impacts of grant activities. A question related to the changes in student work tasks as well as the execution of those tasks had the potential to inform researchers of project effectiveness. Quantitative data might have been collected earlier and included more than state-level testing data. Student grades, unit and semester testing on class objectives, attendance and discipline records all had the potential to provide added insight into the impacts an innovation has on a school organisation.

The rationale for a mixed methods approach rests not only on the researcher's ability more richly to explain subsequent findings and conclusions but also on the researcher's ability to have faith in the findings and conclusions presented. Qualitative methodology has long held the tradition of triangulation as a form of increasing the validity of findings and conclusions. Three interview sources that tell the same story, report the same challenge or provide similar testimony to the veracity of a new classroom approach would qualify as triangulation. But the strength of a finding supported by interview data from multiple sources and analysis of student work that illustrates in practice the instructional points offered at interview provides evidence for a much stronger conclusion.

Simply put, the inclusion of multiple methods when planning a research study offers the researcher two important tools. The first provides for the potential that one data source may not provide the evidence one expects and still allows the researcher the potential for telling a story. The second provides for depth and richness within the story once it is presented. In either case, a study based on multiple methods of data collection and analysis has the potential to bear more analytical fruit than one that is limited in approach.

Alternative bodies of literature

The project described in this chapter was based on the current literature related to student learning and technology implementation. Indeed, the original authors of the grant had completed a careful literature review concerning the state of instruction in schools and the need for new technologies in them. However when challenges arose, the initial theory proved inadequate to explain the phenomena observed across the case study sites. As researchers sought to explain the findings that the case and test score data presented it became necessary to seek literatures other than those initially explored. In this case, organisational theory, innovation studies and leadership paradigms needed to be explored before the challenges that the case data presented could be fully explained. Often the initial literature on which a study rests cannot provide deep enough theoretical roots to explain findings unique to a research effort. In these cases, a return to the library can yield new theory with the potential to offer richer understandings of phenomena observed in schools.

At the root of most study of organisational behaviour within schools are actions common to other complex organisations. A careful read of the business, hospital or government literatures can often provide an introduction to ideas new to the field of education that have great potential to explain curious findings. The introduction of new literatures in the analysis phase of research can have the result of providing multiple lenses with which to view data. Presentation of complex understandings can often be made clear only by several theoretical cuts or views of the data.

In the circumstance of the case studies presented within this study it became necessary to analyse the issues that arose with the computer technology through the lens of other technology implementation work as well as through the lens of innovation implementation in general. Some challenges that were observed – late arrival of equipment, malfunctioning printers and incompatible software purchases – were documented in other studies of technology innovation. Annoying as these small problems were, they were common to other studies and existing theory could offer enough explanatory power to suggest conclusions. However, in the case of other challenges – turnover in supportive administrative and classroom leadership, inadequate time to meet and plan new learning experiences for students, lack of access to expertise in lesson planning and technology use – other literatures were needed to help researchers make sense of the data presented. As the final evaluation was written it was the alternative literature on school improvement that helped to provide the clearest picture of what had occurred across the county during the project. Without consideration of studies other than those concerned with technology in classrooms, data could have been presented but conclusions could not have been drawn.

Iterating between theory and practice

The common saying, 'there is nothing as practical as a good theory' is widely viewed as ludicrous by practitioners. Educational researchers become obsessed with their findings and forget that they need to understand what the 'real story' is – at least if their work is to have any meaning beyond a small circle of colleagues. In our view, the 'real story' is not just an answer to the initial research question, but an explanation of the results that leads to a new, more complete and more grounded theory. Often as we participate in directing student research, we discover similar patterns. Students have data and often skill at presenting carefully constructed cases, data charts, displays and statistical tables, but they lack the ability to offer new insights into what the data mean. Our first question in an oral examination is often 'How would you present your findings to practitioners in 15 minutes or less, emphasising only those points that are significant to improving schools or making them more effective?' Without both returning to the theory on which the study rests as well as introducing new theory with greater explanatory power, the research is incomplete. Attention to alternative literatures has the potential to complete the picture and round out findings otherwise unexplained or inadequately presented.

Endnote

This chapter has described the evolution of a research project that did not produce the expected results. In light of initial methodologies that were insufficient for researchers to answer the research questions, a methodological shift was employed to provide for the opportunity to explain seemingly uninterpretable findings. The use of multiple methodologies as a safeguard against such occurrences is explored, as is the use of alternative literatures in explaining findings that seem to be without precedence. Finally, we would like to end on this hopeful note for future evaluators and researchers – should you choose to engage in any form of research, enter it with the notion that smooth sailing is a result of careful planning rather than luck – one can create one's own serendipity.

References

Bloom, L. R. (1998) *Under the Sign of Hope: Feminist Methodology and Narrative Interpretation.* New York: SUNY.
Czarniawska, B. (1997) *Narrating the Organization: Dramas of Institutional Identity.* Chicago: University of Chicago Press.
Czarniawska, B. (1998) *A Narrative Approach to Organization Studies.* Newbury Park, CA: Sage.
Dexter, S. and Seashore Louis, K. (2001) *It's OK to be stupid,* paper presented at the annual meeting of the American Educational Research Association, Seattle, WA (see http://www.coled.umn.edu/CAREI/sdexter/boundaries.html).
Fetterman, D. (2001) *Foundations of Empowerment Evaluation.* Thousand Oaks, CA: Sage.
Glaser, B. and Strauss, A. (1967) *The Discovery of Grounded Theory.* Chicago: Aldine.
Heilbrun, C. (1989) *Writing a Woman's Life.* New York: Ballantine.
Heshusius, L. and Ballard, K. (1996) *From Positivism to Interpretivism and Beyond.* New York: Teachers College Press.
Huberman, M. and Miles, M. (1984) *Innovation up Close.* New York: Plenum.
Josselson, R. and Lieblich, A. (1995) *Interpreting Experience: The Narrative Study of Lives.* Newbury Park, CA: Sage.
Kincheloe, J. L. (1991) *Teachers as Researchers: Qualitative Inquiry as a Path to Empowerment.* London: Falmer.
Kruse, S. (2001) 'Creating communities of reform: images of continuous improvement planning teams', *Journal of Educational Administration,* 39 (4): 359–83.

McGhee, R. and Kozma, R. (2001) '*New teacher and student roles in the technology supported classroom*', paper presented at the annual meeting of the American Educational Research Association, Seattle, WA (see http://www.coled.umn.edu/CAREI/sdexter/boundaries.html).

Miles, M. and Huberman, M. (1994) *Qualitative Data Analysis: A Sourcebook of New Methods*, 2nd edn. London: Sage.

National Staff Development Council (undated) *NSCD standards for staff development*. See *http://www.nsdc.org/list.htm*.

Newmann, F., Smith, B., Allensworth E. and Bryk, S. (2001) *School Instructional Program Coherence: Benefits and Challenges*, Chicago, IL: Consortium for School Improvement (ERIC ED451305).

Rasinski, T. (2000) 'The evaluation of the technology innovation challenge grant – year four', unpublished internal report. Summit County Educational Service Centre, Cuyahoga Falls, Ohio, USA.

Riessman, C. K. (1993). *Narrative Analysis*. Newbury Park, CA: Sage.

Seashore Louis, K. (1998) 'A light feeling of chaos: school reform and public policy in the U.S.', *Daedalus*, 127 (4): 13–40.

Seashore Louis, K. and Miles, M. (1990) *Improving the Urban High School: What Works and Why*. New York: Teachers College Press.

Strauss, A. and Corbin, J. (1998) Basics of *Qualitative Research: Techniques and Procedures for Developing Grounded Theory*, 2nd edn. Thousand Oaks, CA: Sage.

Witherell, C. and Noddings, N. (1991) *Stories Lives Tell: Narrative and Dialogue in Education*. New York: Teachers College Press.

Yin, R. (1994) *Case Study Research: Design and Methods*, 2nd edn. Thousand Oaks, CA: Sage.

Chapter 8

International development education: managing change in Caribbean countries

Stephen Gough

Gough discusses many of the challenges faced by the researcher in putting a project into operation. Some relate closely to the themes discussed in Chapters 1 and 2. The substantive topic is the management of change in relation to environmental education in Caribbean countries. In contrast to the focus of other chapters on leadership and management within individual schools – educational organisations at the peripheral level of an education system – Gough explores the management of an externally (in this case cross-nationally) initiated intervention within and between educational organisations at different system levels and in different national systems. The project on which this report was based was sponsored by a national government department. Gough examines the challenges posed by commissioned research, in which stakeholders may require different things of the study, and have different definitions of relevance. The author uses a typology of four intellectual projects to discuss the focusing of his investigation. (The categories he uses are identical to four of those in the typology of five outlined in Chapter 1, the additional one distinguished there being 'knowledge-for-critical evaluation'.) He considers the importance of clarifying the kind of knowledge that a study is aiming to generate.

A particularly important dimension of the chapter is its examination of the compromises that often have to be made in empirical research, particularly when fieldwork is involved. Gough outlines how real-life projects, and the decisions faced by a researcher, may seem a long way from the ideal-type of the research process presented in the methodology textbooks. He addresses the challenge of retaining rigour in a study when some decisions may have to be based on pragmatism. This is of considerable significance for masters and doctoral students, many of whom will face similar decisions in conducting their research, and yet will find little to guide them in the research literature. One reason for the lack of acknowledgement lies in the difference between the process of conducting research and the reporting of research, which we discussed in Chapter 2. Often, published accounts of studies, especially in peer-reviewed journals, give little indication of the practical problems and dilemmas faced by the researchers. However, that is not to say that they do not happen, simply that the conventions of reporting research allow little space for discussing such matters. Thus Gough's chapter, which highlights how the author addressed a number of dilemmas and problems and reached compromises in relation to design, methodology and concepualisation, offers a helpful insight into the 'unseen' aspects of research. However well they are planned and executed, field studies frequently present the researcher with unexpected situations. This chapter offers useful insights into conducting fieldwork in a setting distant from the researcher's normal base, and in which he or she may need to be both flexible and resourceful.

Introduction and rationale

Organisations of many different kinds are concerned with education because their members regard it as a means to advance their institutional or policy goals. Political parties do so, of course, and some of them duly acquire the power to put their plans into effect. Members of non-governmental organisations (NGOs) encompassing charities, private companies and a range of agencies at international, national and local levels also seek to influence the ways in which educational resources are deployed, and acquire and manage educational resources of their own.

This chapter considers part of a large research project funded by the UK government's Department for International Development (DFID) and carried out by a consortium consisting of the University of Bath, King's College London and the Field Studies Council (an environmental NGO). (The members of the research team were Justin Dillon and Kelly Teamey from King's College London, James Hindson from the Field Studies Council and William Scott and the author from the University of Bath.) The purpose of the wider research project was to make recommendations to the DFID on managing a process of 'mainstreaming' environmental education into its global development programmes. (Mainstreaming implies a commitment to making environmental education a core component of all such programmes.) The focus of the chapter is, therefore, on managing change at the level of international policy formation and implementation, rather than at the level of particular educational institutions.

It had been previously determined within the DFID that mainstreaming environmental education would be a means of improving the overall quality of development programmes, and in particular the quality of their educational content. To succeed, the project required the support and participation of a wide range of stakeholders at the international, regional and local levels, including DFID regional officers around the world (who enjoy substantial autonomy), ministries of education in different countries, other ministries, NGOs, schools, teachers and so on. One aspect of the research required by the DFID was a field study in the Caribbean region, carried out by the author in February 2001.

The Caribbean research had a number of characteristics resulting from its focus on the achievement of pre-designated institutional goals, which are outlined here and developed in the rest of the chapter. First, the research was focused on the management of educational resources in order to achieve a goal that was not itself inherently educational. This goal was the achievement of economic and social development in less developed countries.

Second, many critical questions which might have suggested themselves to the researcher were ruled out of consideration by the sponsor. The overall research context was defined by the existence of a number of International Development Targets (IDTs) to which both the DFID, and the governments of the countries involved, had committed themselves. Figure 8.1 shows the central management role of the DFID in linking selected curriculum aspects to desired international policy outcomes, which was negotiated and renegotiated between senior central DFID staff and the research team from an early stage. The educational appropriateness of these outcomes was not open to question by the researcher.

Third, and partly in consequence of the foregoing, any notion of the researcher as a detached, positivistic observer of social reality could not be sustained (whether it ever can in educational research is another matter). The researcher could not avoid being implicated in the research setting, because the research was itself *part of* the DFID's education management process. DFID concerns, preconceptions and micropolitical arrangements necessarily influenced the way the research subject was conceptualised and explored, raising a question of what it might mean to be scientifically rigorous in such research.

Fourth, questions of the generalisability and scalability of the research were particularly significant. It was necessary to ask how far findings from some parts of the Caribbean could be generalised to other parts, or to regions outside the Caribbean.

Fifth, costs in terms of finance, time, physical resources and the patience of those being researched were an issue. The overall research contract had been won through a competitive tendering process, and the budget was constrained. What is more, it was to be expected that the research would not necessarily be welcome among some of those individuals and groups being researched. No researcher could be entirely happy about this state of affairs, since it suggests that what the researcher actually did was at least as much a product of institutional pragmatism as of a detached, critical scoping process. Equally, however, no researcher who wants to do applied educational management research can possibly ignore practical constraints, and they always exist.

Taken as a whole, this Caribbean field study was at a significantly larger scale than would realistically be attempted by a masters student since it involved primary data collection in five countries. On the other hand a doctoral student, given funding and access, might have been able to spend longer over it than the author. Each of the country-based elements of the research, and the five of these taken together, illustrate significant issues for the student who wishes to research the management of educational change in line with, or in the context of, exogenously determined policy, and in the presence of multiple stakeholders.

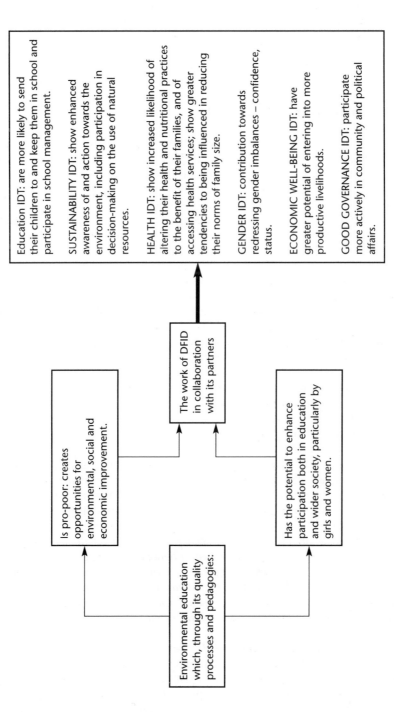

ENVIRONMENTAL EDUCATION'S POTENTIAL
CONTRIBUTION TO THE ACHIEVEMENT OF THE IDTs

Education IDT: are more likely to send their children to and keep them in school and participate in school management.

SUSTAINABILITY IDT: show enhanced awareness of and action towards the environment, including participation in decision-making on the use of natural resources.

HEALTH IDT: show increased likelihood of altering their health and nutritional practices to the benefit of their families, and of accessing health services; show greater tendencies to being influenced in reducing their norms of family size.

GENDER IDT: contribution towards redressing gender imbalances – confidence, status.

ECONOMIC WELL-BEING IDT: have greater potential of entering into more productive livelihoods.

GOOD GOVERNANCE IDT: participate more actively in community and political affairs.

The work of DFID in collaboration with its partners

Is pro-poor: creates opportunities for environmental, social and economic improvement.

Has the potential to enhance participation both in education and wider society, particularly by girls and women.

Environmental education which, through its quality processes and pedagogies:

Figure 8.1 *The place of the research in the achievement of International Development Targets.*

In the remainder of this chapter the following sequence is followed. First, the issue of focusing the Caribbean research within its external context is addressed. Then the approach taken to the task of literature review, the conceptual framing of the research, the design of the empirical enquiry and the method of data analysis and display are each described in turn. Finally, the development of conclusions and recommendations from the research is discussed.

Focusing the research

As might be inferred from Figure 8.1, the management of the introduction of environmental education across the DFID's Caribbean programme was likely to impact upon the work of both environmental specialists of various kinds (for whom it was possible that neither development nor management was of much concern) and a range of policy or development specialists (for whom it seemed possible that the environment and education would be marginal issues). This inference reinforces the point made above that the overall goal of the research was not inherently educational. It needed to be explored through the research. Additionally, a range of factors which potentially linked education, environment, policy-making and development was identified from an initial literature review (conducted jointly by the project team as a whole) and a small number of pilot interviews. These were organised into a structured list to be used to guide the interview process in the field. This list is shown as Figure 8.2.

Bolam (1999) has outlined a typology of four ideal-types of 'intellectual project' in educational management. These are:

▶ the 'knowledge-for-understanding' project;
▶ the 'knowledge-for-action' project;
▶ the 'instrumentalist' project;
▶ the 'reflexive action' project.

Bolam notes the arbitrary nature of this classification, and emphasises that it should be seen as a heuristic. In this spirit, we might note here that the Caribbean research sub-project belongs, in the main, squarely within the 'knowledge-for-action' classification. Of that intellectual project, Bolam writes (1999: 195):

> The immediate aim here is to inform policy-makers and practitioners about the nature, processes and effectiveness of educational administration in order to promote its improvement. Researchers in this tradition are often funded by a government agency, may be based in a university and pursue various forms of applied research...They, too, describe, analyse and explain for understanding but, in addition, make evaluative judgements and recommendations for action.

The list of concerns shown in Figure 8.2 was developed specifically for the purpose of enabling 'evaluative judgements and recommendations' to be made. It rests on a hypothesis that potential synergies exist between the managed introduction of environmental education into DFID programmes and development in the other areas of concern identified in the figure. This hypothesis arose from the review of

Figure 8.2 *Core themes in relation to the mainstreaming of environmental education into DFID programmes.*

Poverty reduction:
▶ Resource management skills
▶ Support for infrastructure projects
▶ Marketable skills or skills which enable market-provided skills to be substituted
▶ Local economic opportunities and threats

Good governance:
▶ Empowerment of communities and individuals
▶ Stakeholder involvement
▶ Respect for traditional (or minority) skills/values
▶ Local institutional/political context (including existing national strategy for sustainable development commitments, if any)

Gender issues:
▶ Economic and resource management within households
▶ Female role models
▶ Female participation
▶ Female empowerment

Health:
▶ Health international development targets
▶ Poverty-related disease and illness

Possible improvements in local educational and training structures and practices:
▶ The demand for education
▶ Sectoral planning
▶ Resource availability and provision
▶ Quality assurance
▶ Focus on transferable lifeskills
▶ Formal/non-formal/informal
▶ Primary/secondary/tertiary
▶ Theories-in-use of local practitioners and administrators
▶ Availability of educational resources
▶ Local teacher training provision regime
▶ Local curriculum resources design arrangements
▶ Monitoring and evaluation practice/culture
▶ Participation rates
▶ Degree of potential acceptance of curriculum based on local problem-solving (including participatory action research approaches)
▶ Involvement of parents/communities in educational planning and processes
▶ Links/potential for integration between formal sector and other sectors

The work of other donor agencies:
▶ USAID
▶ World Bank
▶ WHO
▶ UNICEF
▶ Others

literature and the pilot interviews and, as we shall see, it was substantially confirmed through the research, resulting in a number of recommendations.

However, none of the other 'intellectual projects' was excluded (in keeping with Bolam's remarks). Knowledge-for-understanding was addressed through the team's exploration of issues in contract research, which sought to build on the critically evaluative strand of knowledge-for-understanding-focused work of, for example, Grace (1998), Whitty et al. (1998), Ball (1994) and Codd (1988). On the other hand, when the research respondents were shown the research report a number of them commented on how helpful they found it in developing their own work, which suggests that Bolam's instrumentalist project was in some sense furthered. This is true notwithstanding the fact that the researcher's main reasons for distributing the report in that way were, in fact, to check validity and comply with good ethical practice. Finally, the reflexive action project was advanced at least to the extent that the researcher's reflection upon his experience led (one would hope) to improvements in his own future work.

Another way of focusing the research was to identify criteria by which its quality might be judged. According to Meulenberg-Buskens (1997: 111):

> *Quality in social science research is not a straightforward issue. Quality could refer to the relevance of a study, to the degree in which it yields useful and applicable information, to the degree it enhances values such as democracy and social justice, to the degree it empowers powerless people. Finally, it could also refer to the technical quality of a piece of work, that is, to the degree in which it conforms to the methodological expectations of a community of scientists.*

Criteria used to judge relevance, usefulness and applicability can be expected to vary between, and quite possibly be actively contested by, different groups of stakeholders to research. In this case, for example, interviews conducted by the author with officers of the St Lucia Ministry of Agriculture, Forestry and Fisheries on 23 February 2001 revealed a very different view of 'usefulness' from that encountered two days earlier at the Ministry of Education. For the Forestry and Fisheries group, the usefulness of the deployment of educational resources was to be assessed against practical development targets such as reduced incidence of reef fishing (which was believed to damage prospects for tourism development) and the enhancement within the community of alternatives to it. For the Ministry of Education respondent, the criteria for usefulness were expressed mainly in terms of progress towards literacy and numeracy targets. DFID officials wanted to know whether and how education could be made to serve both these sets of purposes and, if at all possible, advance the wider causes of social justice and democracy. In relation to the 'community of scientists' mentioned by Meulenberg-Buskens, the research (Hindson et al., 2001) has been praised by some academic colleagues, but has also failed to satisfy the 'methodological expectations' of others, who have argued that among other things the author and his colleagues allowed the sponsor too much influence over the research design. In so far as they are assuming a predominantly 'knowledge-for-understanding' perspective, or are judging quality in terms of the promotion of a particular view of justice, democracy or social empowerment which differs from that of the DFID, their position is essentially irrefutable. Further, there is no doubt that other colleagues from a predominantly quantitative paradigm would offer a quite different set of objections to the work we did (Reid and Gough, 2000; Gough and Reid, 2000). This discussion, of course, is strongly linked to the issue of scientific rigour raised earlier.

A pragmatic conclusion in relation to research quality was that it was unrealistic to expect to please everybody. As already noted, however, pragmatism cannot be its own justification. A minimum obligation to the objectively-minded reader of the research product must be to set out clearly what the research *was* and what it *was not*. One way might be to position the work in terms of Bolam's typology and offer an answer to the question: 'How would an observer determine whether this research is of high quality?' The answer to these questions provides an indication of the methodology of the study, where the term 'methodology' is used to delineate:

> *Distinct genres of educational research – genres whose distinctiveness lies not in their main forms of data collection (i.e. different tools in the researcher's toolbox) but in the* assumptions *which prefigure what is to count as appropriate research topics, appropriate research questions, and even appropriate research outcomes, in addition to appropriate research methods. (Robottom and Hart, 1993: 12)*

As we have seen, the research was centrally concerned with the intellectual project of 'knowledge-for-action'. Taking a focus on a particular region, it aimed to produce relevant, useful and applicable results which might enable the successful management of a particular educational initiative by a particular organisation at a particular time (though this does not, as we shall see, entirely rule out some subsequent generalisation to other contexts). It was expected that, if successful, the research would contribute to social goals judged desirable, but selecting, defining and prioritising these goals was considered to be the prerogative of the sponsor, the DFID.

This being so, the research questions were framed in the light of the Terms of Reference laid down by the DFID, the preliminary review of literature, and a process of discussion within the team and with the DFID. The questions were:

▶ What are the nature and significance of linkages between environmental education and poverty eradication in developing countries and countries in transition?
▶ How has environmental education achieved wider impacts and benefits upon curriculum development and implementation?
▶ What are the key institutional, legislative, policy and economic factors which are critical to the sustainability of environmental education initiatives?
▶ What lessons have been learned that are of relevance to mainstreaming environmental education in developing countries and countries in transition?
▶ What are the most appropriate ways by which the DFID could mainstream environmental education?

In one important respect a decision was taken *not* to focus the research too narrowly. This was in relation to the question of *defining* environmental education. This term not only has a number of competing definitions in the literature (e.g. Lucas, 1979; Robottom, 1987; Gough, 2002), but has spawned a number of offspring such as 'education for sustainable development' (Fien, 1993; Hopkins et al.,

1996) and 'environmental education for sustainability' (Tilbury, 1995). A somewhat separate strand relates to the 'ecologisation' of schools (Rauch, 2000), which has quite specific implications for school management. Finally, there are certainly many working teachers and trainers who, without being aware of any significant body of academic literature, consider themselves to be delivering environmental education. It was felt that the Caribbean research should encompass any and all of these, implying that 'environment' in this context is to be understood in the broad sense of 'the surroundings in which people live', rather than in terms of a reified conception of 'nature'.

Reviewing the literature

The literature review required by the research was extensive and complex, though it should be stressed that a substantial part of the task was in common with the wider research project. The degree of complexity involved may be judged from Figure 8.3, in which keywords have been extracted from the research questions and set against three general categories of literature which were included in the review.

Figure 8.3 *Organisation of the literature review.*

	Linkages	Impacts	Contextual factors	Lessons learned	Ways to mainstream
Educational management literature					
Environmental education literature					
Documents					

It should be stated at the outset that this apparently tidy conceptualisation does not withstand searching scrutiny. For example, linkages between environmental education and poverty eradication may be located within contextual factors, lessons learned may be about ways to mainstream, and the distinction between 'literature' and 'documents' may, at the margin, be a matter of whim. However, the purpose of this exercise was not to establish a watertight method of classification, but to create a practicable tool that would help ensure the review stayed focused on the matter in hand and that nothing was overlooked. As with any research there was also a literature of research methodology which is pertinent to the study. This is treated here as an aspect of arriving at an appropriate methodology rather than as part of the literature review.

A merit of the approach illustrated by Figure 8.3 was that it directed attention to niche areas of the literature that might otherwise have been passed over, and enabled them to be linked. The following outline analysis gives a flavour of the literature reviewed, and of how it was subsequently incorporated into the research process. It is focused by looking along each row in turn. For the top row a small number of examples of relevant literature are cited for each cell, along with examples of the issues they informed. The remaining two rows are dealt with in more summary fashion, as the purpose is to illustrate the method rather than summarise the review.

The literature of educational management (the top row in Figure 8.3) was particularly informative in relation to the following:

▶ *organisational learning; and professional staff development [...lessons learned...].* Issues included the potential for collaborative learning between (a) different disciplinary specialists; (b) different elements of an organisation, such as administrative sub-groups within the DFID, or ministries within a government; (c) attempts to promote a 'learning society'; (d) requisite professional development for teachers, aid workers, non-formal educators and others (e.g. Senge, 1990; Argyris and Schön, 1996; Quicke, 2000; Strain, 2000; Elliott, 1998).

▶ *the management of change; and the micropolitics of organisations [...ways to mainstream...].* Issues included the existence of competing goals within and between institutions, the difficulty of precisely or universally defining either a 'present state' or a desired 'final state' within which change could be framed, and the management of transitional processes, quality and evaluation (e.g. Fullan, 2001; Hoyle, 1982; Taylor and Hill, 1993).

▶ *the significance of context; and of culture [...contextual factors...].* The cultural contrasts and similarities across a range of organisational scales in the five countries were an important aspect of the study. The literature is very extensive. Meyerson and Martin (1987) and Hanna (1997) provide useful overviews of many of the main issues.

▶ *[...wider impacts...] of environmental education.* There is a specialist literature relating to the management of education in the context of development which was significant because of the particular emphases typical of environmental education programmes. For example there is usually an emphasis on participatory pedagogies, and so issues relating to the decentralisation of educational decision-making, which environmental education programmes tend to require in varying degrees, were significant (e.g. Fiske, 1996).

▶ *[...linkages...between environmental education and poverty eradication].* Hallinger (2001), writing about east Asian countries, has noted that western theories of educational change management cannot be expected to transfer without amendment to developing country contexts, even though the driving force behind such change may be a globally-shared process of economic integration. Identifying the local environment as a key parameter of educational change may be a step to developing nationally appropriate strategies for change management within an internationally coherent framework. In this way some of the difficulties with national and international monitoring of education systems (Greaney and Kellaghan, 1996) may also be addressed.

One notable aspect of the literature of environmental education (Figure 8.3, Row 2) in this context is that there is no consensus on whether development, even 'sustainable development', is a valid educational goal (e.g. Jickling, 1992; Hopkins et al., 1996). Another is that the issue of *management* as it bears on educational change has received relatively little attention, and there is often considerable suspicion of anything that might be called managerialism (Huckle and Sterling (1996) provide insights into many aspects of these issues). A result is that the environmental education literature maps only with difficulty onto the pursuit of specific organisational goals of the type identified in this case by the DFID. In complete contrast, many of the documents reviewed, including many produced within the DFID itself, by NGOs, government ministries, UN Agencies and others, take great pains to demonstrate to the reader that they are consistent with such goals. The overall lesson for any critical reviewer is that the content and structure of educational literature cannot be assumed to be solely a function of the subject matter it addresses. It is equally a product of the author's purposes and relationship with the intended audience. Returning once more to the question of social scientific rigour, we might conclude that this is best served by researchers making themselves and their interests explicit as a matter of course.

Conceptually framing the research

It has already been noted that a set of 'core themes' relating to the research (Figure 8.2) were identified through the literature review and pilot interviews. As with the approach to the literature review, the schedule for the pilot interviews was derived from the Terms of Reference for the research, discussions about these with DFID staff in London and further discussions within the research team as a whole. The team was also provided with an opportunity to give a short presentation to an international gathering of DFID staff, to answer their questions about the research and to ask questions of them.

We have seen that the research focused on 'knowledge-for-action'. In particular, it was hoped to provide qualitative data which, used with appropriate skill and sensitivity to context, might subsequently facilitate purposive actions by educational managers to achieve specified improvements in a variety of real educational settings. This wording is suggestive of two approaches to educational research: 'problem-based methodology' or PBM (Robinson, 1993), and case-study.

The central tenets of PBM are that the purpose of educational research is to solve educational problems and that research methodology, therefore, needs to be matched to research subjects. Whether PBM is, as Robinson herself claims, truly a distinct research methodology or rather a method within the class of naturalistic research approaches is open to question (Smith, 1995). We may say, however, that it has the following characteristics:

▶ It is interpretive and naturalistic. It works from the theories of practitioners themselves, in their specific contexts.
▶ It is collaborative, in that the researcher and the researched work together to solve problems, but it is also expert led in the sense that the researcher aims to produce 'an outsider critique which eventually becomes part of the individual's understanding' (Robinson, 1993: 119).
▶ It takes a functional view of research but a structural view of the constraints on practitioners (Walker, 1997: 160–1).

For the purposes of the Caribbean study these characteristics are helpful. The many different organisations to which respondents were affiliated are listed in Table 8.1. The great variety present might be expected (and were, in fact, found) to be associated with a wide range of views on education, environment and development. PBM allows the researcher to work with this multiplicity of perspectives in the context of a given educational problem, sharing a purpose while accommodating diversity. It also makes it possible for the researcher to collaborate with respondents while reserving a private view at a more abstract level of theory. Finally, it enables the researcher to take account of structural constraints on respondents while maintaining a sense of agency, that is to accept that there are limits and obstacles to action while at the same time seeking to promote it.

Table 8.1 *Organisational affiliations of individuals interviewed*

Caribbean Country	Organisational affiliation of interviewees
Antigua	US Peace Corps
	Environmental Awareness Group
	Ministry of Education
	Ministry of Tourism and Environment
	Ministry of Agriculture, Lands and Fisheries
	Prime Minister's Office
Barbados	Caribbean Conservation Organisation
	Social and Environmental Management Services Inc.
	Darwin Initiative
	Caribbean Regional Environmental Programme
	Global Environment Facility Small Grants Programme/UNDP
	UNDP
	DFID
	UNICEF
Guyana	Ministry of Education
	University of Guyana
	Conservation International
	Iwokrama Rainforest Programme
St Lucia	St Lucia National Trust
	National Conservation Authority
	Ministry of Education
	Primary Teacher
	Ministry of Agriculture, Forestry and Fisheries
	Organisation of East Caribbean States/Natural Resources Management Unit
	Solid Waste Management Authority
	Ministry of Planning, Development, Environment
Trinidad	Point-a-Pierre Wildfowl Trust
	Environmental Management Authority
	Ministry of Education

PBM research focuses on a particular problem, while case study research focuses on a particular instance (Adelman et al., 1980). However, in practice the distinction might not be so clear-cut. To say that the Caribbean research was concerned with mainstreaming environmental education in the Caribbean region counts as both forms of research. Also, in both, generalisation beyond the immediate instance (or problem) is possible only to a level of *theory* (Robinson, 1993; Yin, 1994). This is to say that one cannot generalise from the findings of this study directly to any sixth Caribbean country, but one might usefully set those findings alongside other literature in informing one's thinking about what it might be interesting to look for in that country. Perhaps the key distinction between PBM and case study is that the former is much more explicitly purposive. But, even though this research clearly *was* purposive in relation to a particular problem, it is still instructive to consider it from the case study perspective.

Some characteristics typically associated with case study research were present. In particular, it was possible flexibly to adopt positions along a continuum (Cantrell, 1993) ranging from 'pure observer' (for example, sitting in the offices of the St Lucia National Trust quietly watching work in progress), through to 'participant-as-observer' (visiting sites of mangrove loss, hurricane damage and proposed tourism development with members of the Antiguan Environmental Awareness Group). It was also possible to adopt a variety of roles, including those of interviewer, outside expert, participant observer and evaluator, as seemed most appropriate. Finally, it was possible to accommodate multiple audiences and alternative explanations and priorities without compromising the internal logic of the study.

A possible serious objection to this account so far is that it does not, in fact, address the major methodological issues in terms of which a piece of educational research should be conceptualised. The choice between a positivist view of objectivity as both possible and necessary and a post-positivist perspective in which it is merely a 'regulatory ideal' (Connell, 1997) has not been discussed. Nor has anything being said about the deep-seated methodological issues that divide advocates of, for example, grounded theory, constructivism, transformative approaches, postmodernism and poststructuralism.

By omitting these matters at this stage it is not intended to deny their importance, but to suggest that they are not necessarily prior questions which must be resolved before any research can take place. Seale (1999) makes the case that there are many skills in qualitative research that do not have to be linked to any particular paradigmatic or methodological position. The craft (Gough and Reid, 2000) of qualitative research can be practised while ultimate questions of ontology, epistemology and process remain productively open.

A final issue in conceptualising the research concerned its ethical status. Much has been written on research ethics, and a useful summary appears in Miles and Huberman (1994). Issues bearing particularly on the Caribbean research were as follows:

▶ *Informed consent.* Interviews were taped with permission, and notes taken on the understanding that these would be checked back with respondents. An interesting and probably useful consequence was that in a small number of cases respondents actually changed their minds when they subsequently read what had been transcribed! It was made clear that a report would be produced specifically on the Caribbean research which respondents would be able to read and comment upon before it went to the DFID, or anyone else.

▶ *Confidentiality and anonymity.* They were not normally offered, but in some cases respondents offered information on condition that it remained confidential, and this request was then observed.

▶ *Ownership of data and conclusions.* It was made clear that the final report for the larger research project would be the property of the DFID.

The most severe ethical dilemmas which researchers may face were absent here, since all respondents took part voluntarily and had an interest (though not an identical interest) in the success of the work.

Designing the empirical investigation

A key practical constraint was the amount of time that it would be possible to spend in the field. Any attempt at representative sampling would clearly be out of the question. Equally, given the variety of respondents to be questioned and the complex detail of responses sought from them, the use of any kind of remotely administered survey instrument seemed not to be an option. The author's itinerary in the Caribbean is summarised in Table 8.2.

Table 8.2 *Researcher itinerary*

Caribbean country	Arrival		Departure	
Barbados	13/02/01	1530	15/02/01	0820
Antigua	15/02/01	0920	18/02/01	1635
Guyana	18/02/01	2000	20/02/01	0545
Trinidad	20/02/01	0650	21/02/01	0530
St. Lucia	21/02/01	0635	23/02/01	1615
Barbados	23/02/01	1655	25/02/01	1535

Given this kind of hectic schedule the most appropriate approach appeared to be by means of a purposive sample from which data could be collected in depth. Therefore, an organisation was identified (by the Field Studies Council, one of the partners in the research as a whole) that would not only be a source of primary data itself, but could also provide advice about the selection of individuals to be interviewed. This organisation, the Caribbean Conservation Association (CCA), was also engaged to manage the visit. During the period indicated in Table 8.2, 35 respondents were contacted and a field trip (in Antigua) conducted. (The organisational affiliations of these respondents is indicated in Table 8.1.)

In particular, a respondent was identified in each country who could not only provide information relevant to the research questions, but could also provide an overview of contextual factors specific to the particular country and its institutions. This respondent was typically the in-country representative of the CCA.

Given the brevity and intensity of the field research period, it could be assumed that events of significance to the study could happen at almost any time during the visit. Further, the availability of technological support could not always be taken for granted, and so the primary technology of the study consisted of notebook, pencil and a battery-powered tape-recorder. (Secondary technology included a small travel iron, as one got through a lot of shirts conducting several interviews in a day in different locations in a hot country, and there was rarely time to use hotel laundry facilities!)

An interview schedule had been designed for initial 'pilot' interviews in England, based on the literature and the project Terms of Reference. This instrument had also been sent to the CCA as a means of illustrating what the detailed focus of the study was, and a copy was on hand at every interview conducted in the field. The structure of this document was as follows. It began with a short section of text which described the research and its purposes. In the pilot interviews this was read out to the respondents. There followed seven detailed questions relating to key issues for the research. Although this sequence was followed, considerable variation was possible within it depending on the responses received. For this reason the next page of the interview schedule contained a total of 38 possible prompt questions that might be used to draw out details of particular points of interest from respondents. Next came a further short section of explanatory text which was read to respondents and followed by two further detailed questions. Respondents were then shown a diagram. This was an early version of Figure 8.1 above. Finally, two further questions, relating to the diagram, were asked.

The procedure worked well on one occasion, in England, at least. Even in that case, however, the resulting interview was longer (105 minutes) than seemed likely to be typically practicable in the field study. Further, it was not sufficiently flexible to accommodate the wide variety of respondents in the Caribbean. As a result, interviews in the field were conducted with both this interview schedule and the list of 'core themes' (Figure 8.2) on hand as prompts to the researcher. The questions actually asked depended on my judgement of what was likely to be worth asking and following up. Further, the course of later interviews was modified in the light of the experience of earlier ones.

There are clearly problems with such an approach if one considers that a research study should be replicable. Not only were the interviews impossible to replicate in practice (because of the impossibility of assembling the same individuals in the same places more than once), they were impossible to replicate *in principle*, since it would not have been possible to brief another researcher to conduct the same interview in exactly the same way.

Earlier I argued that fundamental methodological questions about ontology, epistemology and process were not necessarily prior to the design and conduct of research. As the above illustrates, however, they cannot ultimately be avoided. The interviews I conducted in the field can only be considered as legitimate research from the perspective of an interpretive methodology for which objectivity is at best an unattainable ideal, and which accepts the existence of multiple realities, truths and perceptions.

> *Naturalistic inquiry presupposes that communities, schools and social settings of any variety have pluralistic sets of values…In order to understand what those sets of values are and to understand at which points they are in conflict, it is necessary to ground inquiry and evaluation activities in the multiple perspectives that are held…The standardized or survey interview assumes value consensus (and handles variations in expected 'norms' statistically) and therefore does not take account of multiple world views. But to get at manifold value systems the evaluator must let them arise from the context in whatever way the respondents express them.*
> *(Guba and Lincoln, 1981: 156)*

Within the fieldwork some interviews took place with a group of respondents. This was simply unavoidable either because it was an unrepeatable opportunity (for example the chance arose to conduct a follow-up interview with two respondents in Antigua); because of pressure of time; or because it was the preference of the respondents themselves.

Problems can arise with group interviews. It may not be possible to explore fully the position of all those present; some respondents may tend to dominate proceedings while others remain silent; individuals' responses may be influenced by perceived social pressures; and personal information is unlikely to be truthfully revealed (Hedges, 1985). On the other hand, group discussions can sometimes be particularly revealing as respondents prompt each other to think through their views. An example of a specific potential problem in this research arose when the group included a senior official and her subordinate. It must be assumed that the dynamics of this relationship had some bearing upon what both chose to say.

Finally, many documents (and two videos) were collected during the course of the field visit. The documents included official publications, policy documents, publicity materials and items of interest from local newspapers. They were analysed using the same categories as the transcribed data.

Summarising, displaying and analysing data

There is surprisingly little clarity about the proper sequence of activities in qualitative research (Gough and Scott, 2000). For example, it is often the case that categories for analysis are prefigured in the research design, though in most narrative accounts 'design' comes long before 'analysis'. It may be inferred from the prior existence of a list of 'core themes' and a carefully-worded interview schedule that this was so to a significant degree in the Caribbean research. The question 'how does an idea, a phrase, a group of words come to be designated as *interesting* from the point of view of data analysis?' is one all researchers should ask of themselves. The existence of computer software for qualitative data analysis in no way weakens this imperative (Richards and Richards, 1994).

In the Caribbean research one might suppose that the answer to this question was clear. Certain aspects of the data were interesting because they had a bearing on the issues identified by the DFID in the research Terms of Reference: but we can still ask how we come to think that one datum is significant in this way while another is not. It is precisely the meaning of 'significance' that is illusive.

The approach taken in the Caribbean research was to analyse and subsequently present data using two sets of criteria for significance which suggested themselves from careful reading and re-reading of fieldnotes, interview transcripts and documents. The criteria were (for mainstreaming): strength, weakness, opportunity and threat; and (for education), outcomes, processes and context. Combining these two sets of categories produced an analytical grid with twelve categories (Figure 8.4).

Examples from the report of each of the categories are as follows.

- *Mainstreaming:* **outcomes** *of environmental education which are a* **strength**. Any environmental education intervention should have an *evaluation* as a key output. This should be part of planning from the outset. Such evaluations help embed work within systems and practices where they might otherwise be forgotten, so building capacity. The Darwin Initiative 'Coral Reef Biodiversity in the Caribbean' programme is notable for providing training in evaluation for the development team. Note that evaluation skills are transferable to other educational work.
- *Mainstreaming:* **outcomes** *of environmental education which may be a* **weakness**. Environmental science education may often be the easiest kind of environmental education to justify and evaluate within a particular institutional context. Of course, there is nothing wrong with environmental science in itself, but it may not be the best focus in the context of development. For example, the Ministry of Education of Antigua has a focus on environmental science education, and also on supporting the tourism industry. Given the economic, management, cultural and social aspects of tourism (as well as the environmental science aspect) a careful re-focusing

Figure 8.4 *Grid for analysis and presentation of data.*

	Environmental education *outcomes*	*Processes* of environmental education	*Context* of environmental education
Strengths for mainstreaming			
Weaknesses for mainstreaming			
Opportunities for mainstreaming			
Threats to mainstreaming			

would seem likely to be helpful. This is to say that educational outcomes stated in terms of learners being able, say, to describe biological processes are admirable in themselves but not clearly capable of linkage to either resource conservation or income generation.

▶ *Mainstreaming: **outcomes** of environmental education which present **opportunities***. Where environmental education promotes skills of resource management and utilisation which have commercial value it may be appropriate to post-11+ students who might otherwise drop out of the system. (There is a parallel danger that such education will be seen as 'non-academic'.) These opportunities might focus on, for example, environmental monitoring skills, and might improve learners' capabilities to participate in both civil society and the labour market. The National Conservation Authority of St Lucia suggests that using environmental education to 'remove the stigma of failure' might be a good way to think about this.

▶ *Mainstreaming: **outcomes** of environmental education which may be a **threat***. There is a difficulty that environmental education outcomes are difficult to measure or quantify, particularly in the non-formal sector. This difficulty is classified here as a 'threat' rather than a 'weakness', because of its great significance for the inclusion of environmental education in target-focused programmes.

▶ *Mainstreaming: **processes** of environmental education which are a **strength***. Collaborative work between agencies on particular programmes may help build capacity which impacts beyond those programmes. An example is the Darwin Initiative 'Coral Reef Biodiversity in the Caribbean: a schools education project', which has involved NGOs in six Caribbean countries, the Ministries of Education in those countries and external participants.

▶ *Mainstreaming: **processes** of environmental education which may be a **weakness***. Because of the segmentation of responsibility for environment between different public bodies in many countries, it is often difficult to be clear to whom environmental educators should report.

▶ *Mainstreaming: **processes** of environmental education which present **opportunities***. A focus on girls and women is consistent with wider educational targets. The opportunity for this focus in the Caribbean lies in the fact that women form a large part of the informal selling sector, typically take responsibility for environmental health issues around the home, and may be involved in support jobs in mainstream production, for example of bananas or in fishing. Women may be seen as an educational resource at least as much as a target group. They should be involved through any community-planning approach.

▶ *Mainstreaming: **processes** of environmental education which may be a **threat***. In-post teachers tend to have a traditional view of pedagogy. Field trips and the like may well be regarded as a 'day off' rather than an opportunity for learning. This view was not shared by the only serving teacher interviewed.

▶ *Mainstreaming: **contexts** of environmental education which are a **strength*** – where environmental concerns are specifically represented throughout the formal curriculum. The Ministry of Education of Guyana has sought to do this. For example, the Secondary Schools Entrance Examination has an environmental component. In June 2001 a pilot project (under the joint auspices of the Ministry of Education and the Guyana Environmental Protection Agency) will get under way to develop supplementary environmental materials for mathematics, languages, science and social studies.

▶ *Mainstreaming:* **contexts** *of environmental education which may be a* **weakness** – parental attitudes. It was reported in Antigua that where innovative pedagogies were used students typically had a smaller volume of notes in their workbooks. Parents then expressed concern. Human resource shortages are a problem for teacher training, particularly so in countries such as Guyana and Antigua, where there is a tendency for graduates to leave the country. Lack of teacher educators was also identified as a problem in Trinidad and Tobago. In the case of Guyana, the context of education, and therefore of mainstreaming, is quite different in the coastal area from in the 'hinterland'. 'One size' seems very unlikely to 'fit all'.

▶ *Mainstreaming:* **contexts** *of environmental education which present* **opportunities**. The Organisation of East Caribbean States (OECS) Ministers' Environmental Policy Committee has commissioned a study on participation in civil society with regard to environmental management. Lack of such capacity for participation has been noted as a problem by, for example, the Global Environment Facility (GEF) small grants programme. Education appears to have a key role in creating such capacity.

▶ *Mainstreaming:* **contexts** *of environmental education which may be a* **threat**. The content of examinations is a threat to mainstreaming. The St. Lucia Ministry of Education recognises that non-examined skills of social participation are increasingly required by employers, but they are not examined, partly because of the human-resource difficulties of effecting change. Training, for example for fisherfolk in St. Lucia, may need to take account of the fact that the recipients may be illiterate. In this case training is in Creole, and the Fisheries Ministry has contributed to adult literacy programmes for those involved.

As already noted, the draft analysis was returned to respondents for comment and correction, both an ethical obligation and a check on the validity of the report. The analysis was also subsequently subjected to extensive discussion as part of the deliberations of the wider research team.

It is notable that qualitative data analysis in research of this sort depends centrally on the intuition of the researcher (Firestone and Dawson, 1988). It is a strength of the approach, in that the researcher's tacit knowledge and engagement with the research subject can be a source of insights (Okely, 1994), but also a weakness because analysis is to some extent a private process and subject to bias. In the present research, much depended on my tacit knowledge, as the only individual who could combine an overview of the data I had collected, the research terms of reference and the deliberations of the wider research team. Also of note is the usefulness of display techniques in the research. They may have the effect of surfacing data and showing an order to it that may be counter-intuitive. Inter-subjective techniques, involving other researchers, are valuable checks on intuition and allow meaning to be 'negotiated'. This process, however, does carry with it a danger of consensual error. Here, a simple display technique was used to organise data, and to prompt responses from others in a format which was amenable to the making of comparisons. My initial analysis was offered to respondents, members of the wider research team and staff at DFID headquarters for comment and critique.

Drawing and verifying conclusions

It was made clear from the outset that the research should be seen as an integral part of DFID's change management processes. Attention was drawn to the need to derive 'evaluative judgements and recommendations' from the research. At the level of the wider research project, a full report was produced (Hindson et al., 2001) consisting of an Executive Summary and Recommendations, supported by a digest of pertinent evidence organised around DFID's original Terms of Reference. This document was the product of intensive discussions over a period of several weeks among the research team as a whole, and between the team and senior staff from the DFID headquarters in London, in which the Caribbean report, the parallel field research report (by the King's College London team, from Pakistan), and all the other data collected were sifted and analysed. In its final form, the report has been incorporated into internal planning processes at the DFID.

However, the reporting focus for the Caribbean work was different. No Caribbean-based organisation had, as such, commissioned the research. It seemed most appropriate to treat the final report as an opportunity to share with contributing individuals and organisations the particular insights which it had afforded, not in the form of firm recommendations to be applied uniformly across contexts, but as a basis for further discussion, research and collective, context-specific sense-making. One might say that, with the future in view, it seemed appropriate to relax the original emphasis on 'knowledge-for-action' a little, and to invite participants to take what the study had to offer as a basis for their own thinking and planning about 'knowledge-for-understanding' and 'reflexive action' (Bolam, 1999). In this way, the research could be seen as a step towards fostering appropriate management of the development and implementation of policy at the Caribbean regional level. Impact on management practice would occur through the adaptive use of its findings in:

▶ country-based organisations, including government ministries, NGOs and the offices of international agencies;
▶ regional organisations, particularly the CCA and, through it, the OECS;
▶ interactions between the above.

To facilitate good management practice, the report concluded with sections entitled, 'Instances of Good Practice' and 'Observations'. The following examples drawn from the report illustrate the content of these sections, and are themselves a step towards theory generation from specific cases in the manner discussed earlier. They do not provide a blueprint for what to do elsewhere. But they may provide a useful basis for *thinking about* what to do, and can be further developed in the light of the outcomes of other cases.

Instances of good practice

▶ The Darwin Initiative 'Coral Reef Biodiversity' project is an excellent example of capacity building through international collaboration.
▶ Environmental education and participation in civil society: in St. Lucia the government wanted communities to become co-managers of protected areas. GEF gave a 'small grant' to the St. Lucia National Trust to work with two communities to build their capacity to do this. Through participatory committees and environmental education and training these communities were able to have an influence nationally.
▶ In Antigua, the Environmental Awareness Group have built excellent links with Ministries, teachers and the public to promote conservation through education.
▶ The St. Lucia Solid Waste Management Authority has linked environmental education innovatively to reform of provision. Solid waste collection has been privatised creating local jobs, and this effort has been supported by education at a range of levels. There has been a DFID consultant to this work. All educational work has been done in-house and on the island.

Observations

▶ Environmental education works best when teachers and learners are able to participate freely in civil society. Environmental education also promotes skills of participation in civil society. The importance of this quite complex interrelationship was the single most uniformly identified issue through this research exercise.
▶ There is a need further to develop sophisticated instruments for evaluating outcomes and impacts of environmental learning, providing donors and policy-makers with 'hard-qualitative' data.
▶ There is virtually no support for the idea of environmental education as a separate subject in schools. It should, rather, be integrated across the curriculum. This is, of course, easier said than done.
▶ It seems likely to be effective in small countries to work through NGOs which can carry messages about the interrelationship of environment, economy and society into the structures of government, rather than directly with the (often highly segmented, sometimes competing) public authorities.
▶ The potential of radio as a medium for environmental learning in these countries seems significant.
▶ It is often not the Ministry of Education that is most open to and enthusiastic about environmental education, but other public authorities with environmental responsibilities. These may also be the bodies that teachers prefer to ask for support. For example, the St. Lucia Ministry of Planning, Development, Environment and Housing has been proactive in working with teachers and pupils on climate change issues.

Bolam (1999: 202) offers four main points as an 'underlying rationale for the research agenda and priorities' in educational management research. In summary these are that research should:

▶ be responsive to funding opportunities while at the same time pursuing carefully argued priorities of its own;

▶ achieve quality and relevance by building on earlier work in the field of educational management and in wider educational research;

▶ inform policy and practice through evidence-based critique and theory formation;

▶ follow a strategy of collaboration and consultation with stakeholders during the planning and conduct of research, and disseminate work to stakeholders in a targeted fashion.

To evaluate the Caribbean research against this benchmark was, for myself as researcher, a first step on entering negotiations about further research with groups in that region. The feeling among the research team as a whole (including myself) was that it had performed its task quite successfully. Clearly our shared perception deserved to be treated as grounds for scepticism and self-critique! Accordingly, a paper reporting the research (Dillon et al., 2002) was presented at an international research conference which laid open our work to critique by others, using Bolam's 'rationale' as a means of focusing critical commentary. In the light of that experience the following claims seem supportable:

1 The extent of stakeholder involvement at all stages of the research, and of reference to relevant existing work, was exemplary.

2 Evidence-based critique and theory-formation did take place, but within a broad framework dictated by the DFID's policy commitments.

3 The process of self-critique which led up to the conference presentation was a useful step towards testing the value of the work against wider research priorities. This process drew on a literature quite separate from that reviewed through the research itself.

References

Adelman, C., Jenkins, D. and Kemmis, S. (1980) 'Rethinking case study: notes from the second Cambridge conference', in H. Simons (ed.), *Towards a Science of the Singular*. Norwich: Centre for Applied Research in Education, University of East Anglia.

Argyris, C. and Schön, D. A. (1996) *Organizational Learning II: Theory, Method, Practice*. Reading, MA: Addison-Wesley.

Ball, S. J. (1994) *Education Reform: A Critical and Post-Structural Approach*. Buckingham: Open University Press.

Bolam, R. (1999) 'Educational administration, leadership and management: towards a research agenda', in T. Bush, L. Bell, R. Bolam, R. Glatter and P. Ribbins (eds), *Educational Management: Redefining Theory, Policy and Practice*. London: Paul Chapman.

Cantrell, D. C. (1993) 'Alternative paradigms in environmental education research: the interpretive perspective', in R. Mrazek (ed.), *Alternative Paradigms in Environmental Education*. Troy, OH: North American Association for Environmental Education.

Codd, J. A. (1988) 'The construction and deconstruction of educational policy documents', *Journal of Education Policy*, 3 (3): 235–47.

Connell, S. (1997) 'Empirical-analytical methodological research in environmental education: response to a negative trend in methodological and ideological discussions', *Environmental Education Research*, 3 (2): 117–32.

Dillon, J., Teamey, K., Gough, S. and Scott, W. (2002) *Mainstreaming environmental education: reflections on contract research*, paper presented at the annual meeting of the American Educational Research Association, New Orleans.

Elliott, J. (1998) *The Curriculum Experiment: Meeting the Challenge of Social Change*. Buckingham: Open University Press.

Fien, J. (ed.) (1993) *Environmental Education: A Pathway to Sustainability*. Geelong: Deakin University Press.

Firestone, W. A. and Dawson, J. A. (1988), 'Data analysis: intuitive, procedural and intersubjective', in D. M. Fetterman (ed.), *Qualitative Approaches to Evaluation in Education: The Silent Scientific Revolution*. New York: Praeger.

Fiske, E. (1996) *Decentralization of Education: Politics and Consensus*. Washington, DC: World Bank.

Fullan, M. (2001), *The New Meaning of Educational Change*, 3rd edn. London: RoutledgeFalmer.

Gough, S. (2002) 'Right answers or wrong problems? Towards a theory of change for environmental learning', *The Trumpeter*, 18(1) 'in press'.

Gough, S. and Reid, A. (2000) 'Environmental education research as profession, as science, as art and as craft: implications for guidelines in qualitative research', *Environmental Education Research*, 6 (1): 47–57.

Gough, S. and Scott, W. (2000) 'Exploring the purposes of qualitative data coding in educational enquiry: insights from recent research', *Educational Studies*, 26 (3): 339–54.

Grace, G. (1998) 'Extended review: scholarship and ideology in education policy studies', *International Studies in Sociology of Education*, 8 (1): 135–40.

Greaney, V. and Kellaghan, T. (1996) *Monitoring the Learning Outcomes of Education Systems*. Washington, DC: World Bank.

Guba, E. G. and Lincoln, Y. S. (1981) *Effective Evaluation*. San Francisco: Jossey-Bass.

Hallinger, P. (2001), 'Leading educational change in east Asian Schools', *International Studies in Educational Administration*, 29 (2): 61–72.

Hanna, D. (1997) 'The organization as an open system', in A. Harris, N. Bennett and M. Preedy (eds), *Organizational Effectiveness and Improvement in Education*. Buckingham: Open University Press.

Hedges, A. (1985) 'Group interviewing', in R. Walker (ed.), *Applied Qualitative Research*. Aldershot: Gower.

Hindson, J., Dillon, J., Teamey, K., Gough, S. and Scott, W. (2001) *Mainstreaming Environmental Education in DFID Programmes*. London: Field Studies Council and DFID.

Hopkins, C., Damlamian, J. and López Ospina (1996) 'Evolving towards education for sustainable development: an international perspective', *Nature and Resources*, 32: 3.

Hoyle, E. (1982) 'Micropolitics of educational organizations', *Educational Management and Administration*, 10: 87–98.

Huckle, J. and Sterling, S. (eds) (1996) *Education for Sustainability*. London: Earthscan.

Jickling, B. (1992) 'Why I don't want my children to be educated for sustainable development', *Journal of Environmental Education*, 23 (4): 5–8.

Lucas, A. M. (1979) *Environment and Environmental Education: Conceptual Issues and Curriculum Implications*. Melbourne: Australian International Press and Publications.

Meulenberg-Buskens, I. (1997) 'Turtles all the way down? On a quest for quality in qualitative research', *South African Journal of Psychology*, 27 (2): 111–15.

Meyerson, D. and Martin, J. (1987) 'Cultural change: an integration of three different views', *Journal of Management Studies*, 24: 623–47.

Miles, M. and Huberman, M. (1994) *Qualitative Data Analysis: An Expanded Sourcebook*, 2nd edn. Thousand Oaks, CA: Sage.

Okely, J. (1994) 'Thinking through fieldwork', in A. Bryman and R. Burgess (eds), *Analyzing Qualitative Data*. London: Routledge.

Quicke, J. (2000) 'A new professionalism for a collaborative culture of organizational learning in contemporary society', *Educational Management and Administration*, 28 (3): 299–316.

Rauch, F. (2000), 'Schools: a place of ecological learning', *Environmental Education Research*, 6 (3): 245–58.

Reid, A. and Gough, S. (2000) 'Guidelines for reporting and evaluating qualitative research: what are the alternatives?', *Environmental Education Research*, 6 (1): 59–91.

Richards, L. and Richards, T. (1994) 'From filing cabinet to computer', in A. Bryman and R. Burgess (eds), *Analyzing Qualitative Data*. London: Routledge.

Robinson, V. M. J. (1993) *Problem Based Methodology: Research for the Improvement of Practice*. Oxford: Pergamon Press.

Robottom, I. (1987) 'Contestation and consensus in environmental education', *Curriculum Perspectives*, 7 (1): 23–6.

Robottom, I. and Hart, P. (1993) *Research in Environmental Education: Engaging the Debate*. Geelong: Deakin University Press.

Seale, C. (1999) *The Quality of Qualitative Research*. London: Sage.

Senge, P. (1990), *The Fifth Discipline: The Art and Practice of the Learning Organization*. New York: Doubleday.

Smith, R. (1995) 'Review', *Australian Educational Researcher*, 22 (2): 131–3.

Strain, M. (2000) 'Schools in a learning society: new purposes and modalities of learning in late modern society', *Educational Management and Administration*, 28 (3): 281–98.

Taylor, A. and Hill, F. (1993) 'Quality management in education', *Quality Assurance in Education*, 1 (1): 21–8.

Tilbury, D. (1995) 'Environmental education for sustainability: defining the new focus of environmental education in the 1990s', *Environmental Education Research* 1 (2): 195–212.

Walker, K. E. (1997) 'Challenging critical theory in environmental education', *Environmental Education Research*, 3 (2): 155–62.

Whitty, G., Power, S. and Halpin, D. (1998) *Devolution and Choice in Education: The School, the State and the Market*. Buckingham: Open University Press.

Yin, R. K. (1994) *Case Study Research: Design and Methods*, 2nd edn. Thousand Oaks, CA: Sage.

Chapter 9

Transformational leadership effects on student engagement with school

Kenneth Leithwood and Doris Jantzi

Leithwood and Jantzi examine the concept of transformational leadership, including the different ways in which this notion has been defined and models for representing it. They outline how they developed a model of transformational leadership, based on empirical research, that addressed the limitations of existing models. Leithwood and Jantzi point out that while there was considerable evidence that transformational leadership practices contributed to some aspects of school improvement, there was much less evidence in relation to other areas. Thus the central research question posed by Leithwood and Jantzi focused on an area where there was an absence of evidence: the extent to which transformational leadership influenced school conditions and student engagement with school.

There are many interesting dimensions to this study that relate to the issues discussed in Part 1. An important point is that the researchers questioned assumptions, approaches and models adopted in many existing studies of school leadership. For example, most previous studies of school leadership had used measures of achievement in mathematics and language as dependent variables – primarily because these data were most easily available. However, Leithwood and Jantzi investigated the relationship between student engagement and school leadership. They explain that this was an important variable because reversing student disengagement is a necessary requirement for the educational improvement sought by most school reform initiatives. The authors identify how they set about conceptualising student engagement and designing instruments to measure it.

Another example is that rather than using socio-economic status as a moderating variable, they drew on an extensive review of research literature to develop a more sophisticated and sensitive measure – that of family educational culture. This variable aimed to address the complexity of assumptions, norms and values within families that might affect students' educational engagement and achievement.

While the research reported in this chapter was obviously more complex and extensive than that done for most master's or doctoral studies, there are many useful lessons that could be applied in such work. One is the use of a critical literature review to examine and question the assumptions and conventions underpinning work within a field, and to develop conceptual frameworks. Another is the exemplary clarity with which the authors explain and justify how the study was conceptualised and designed; the analytic methods used (even though these were complex); how findings were interpreted; and the basis for reaching conclusions about the relationship between transformational leadership practices, school conditions and student engagement.

Introduction

Most school reform initiatives assume significant capacity development on the part of individuals, as well as whole organisations. Efforts to reform instruction encompassed in the 'teaching for understanding' movement (e.g. Ball and Rundquist, 1993) often require teachers to 'think of subject-matter content in new ways, [be] much more attentive and responsive to the thinking of students and [become] more adventurous in their thinking' (Putnam and Borko, 1997: 1229).

Initiatives such as this one also depend on high levels of motivation and commitment on the part of a school staff to solving the often complex problems associated with their implementation. 'Reform documents', Putnam and Borko point out, 'stop short of offering concrete images and prescriptions for what this new reformed teaching should be like' (1997: 1224). This assertion could be made for most reform initiatives. As a consequence, whether a reform initiative actually improves the quality of education or simply becomes another 'fatal remedy' (Sieber, 1981) hinges on the work of implementers. And the extent to which they do this work depends a great deal on their commitments and capacities.

Transformational approaches to leadership have long been advocated as productive under conditions fundamentally the same as those faced in schools targeted for reform (Yukl, 1994; Leithwood, 1994). Considerable evidence suggests that transformational practices do contribute to the development of capacity and commitment (e.g. Yammarino et al., 1998). Much less evidence is available about whether these socio-psychological effects actually result in organisational change and enhanced organisational outcomes, however, especially in school contexts (for a recent review of this evidence, see Leithwood et al., 1996). Our question for this study was: 'To what extent does transformational school leadership influence, directly or indirectly, key school conditions and student engagement in school?'

Theoretical framework

This is the third in a series of studies concerned with the effects of different forms and sources of leadership using two comparable, relatively large databases (Leithwood and Jantzi, 1998, 2000). Each study in the series has been guided by a framework consisting of the same mediating and dependent or outcome variables but focused on a different independent or causal (leadership) variable. According to this framework, the influence of leadership on student engagement with school is mediated by both school and classroom level conditions. School conditions influence student engagement directly, as well as indirectly, through their influence on classroom conditions. Family educational culture is a variable which directly influences not only student engagement, but school conditions as well.

Transformational leadership

Part of a cluster of related approaches termed 'new leadership' by Bryman (1992), transformational leadership has become only recently the subject of systematic empirical inquiry in school contexts. As has been pointed out, this approach to leadership fundamentally aims to foster capacity development and higher levels of personal commitment to organisational goals on the part of leaders' colleagues. Increased capacities and commitment are assumed to result in extra effort and greater productivity (Burns, 1978; Bass, 1985). Authority and influence associated with this form of leadership are not necessarily allocated to those occupying formal administrative positions, although much of the literature adopts their perspectives. Rather, power is attributed by organisation members to whoever is able to inspire their commitment to collective aspirations, and the desire for personal and collective mastery over the capacities needed to accomplish such aspirations.

Current educational leadership literature offers no unitary concept of transformational leadership. Kowalski and Oates (1993), for instance, accept Burns' (1978) original claim that transformational leadership represents the transcendence of self-interest by both leader and led. Dillard (1995: 560) prefers Bennis's (1959) modified notion of 'transformative leadership – the ability of a person to reach the souls of others in a fashion which raises human consciousness, builds meanings and inspires human intent that is the source of power'. Leithwood (1994) used another modification of Burns, this one based on Bass's (1985) two-factor theory in which transactional and transformational leadership represent opposite ends of the leadership continuum. Bass maintained that the two actually can be complementary. Leithwood identified six factors that make up transformational leadership. Hipp and Bredeson (1995), however, reduced the factors to five in their analysis of the relationship between leadership behaviours and teacher efficacy. Gronn (1996) notes the close relationship, in much current writing, between views of transformational and charismatic leadership, as well as the explicit omission of charisma from some current conceptions of transformational leadership.

The model of transformational leadership developed from our own research in schools, including factor analytic studies, describes transformational leadership along six dimensions: building school vision and goals; providing intellectual stimulation; offering individualised support; symbolising professional practices and values; demonstrating high performance expectations; and developing structures to foster participation in school decisions (Leithwood, 1994; Leithwood et al., 1999). (Factor analysis is a quantitative technique for assessing the extent to which items used to measure a 'variable' are responded to in more or less the same way.) Each dimension is associated with more specific leadership practices and the problem-solving processes used by transformational leaders have also been described (Leithwood and Steinbach, 1995).

Most models of transformational leadership are flawed by their under-representation of transactional practices (which we interpret to be 'managerial' in nature). Such practices are fundamental to organisational stability. For this reason, we have recently added four management dimensions to our own model based on a review of relevant literature (Duke and Leithwood, 1994). These dimensions, also measured in this study, include staffing, instructional support, monitoring school activities and community focus.

There is a small but compelling body of empirical evidence concerning the effects of this form of leadership on a wide array of organisational and student outcomes when exercised by principals (Leithwood et al., 1996). Our study contributes to this literature in two ways. First, the study examined the effects of transformational practices exercised by those not only in administrative roles, potentially a distributed form of transformational leadership. Second, the study focused on an especially important student outcome, student engagement, for which there is no prior evidence of leadership effects.

School conditions

Studies that inquire only about the direct effects of school leadership on student outcomes tend to report weak or inconclusive outcomes, whereas studies that include mediating and/or moderating variables in their designs tend to report significant effects (Hallinger and Heck, 1996a). Because the largest proportion of school leadership effects on students are mediated by, or influenced through, school conditions, a significant challenge for leadership research is to identify those alterable conditions likely to have direct effects on students, and to inquire about the nature and strength of the relationship between them and leadership. In their 1996 review, Hallinger and Heck reported evidence of only one mediating variable, school goals, consistently interacting with principal leadership. One reason for such limited results may be insufficient importance attributed by researchers to their choices of mediating variables (Hosking and Morley, 1988).

Building directly on prior work by Leithwood (1994) and Ogawa and Bossert (1995), and using evidence from their two 1996 reviews, Hallinger and Heck (1998) have proposed four school conditions through which leadership may exercise its influence. These conditions include purposes and goals, school structure and social networks, people and organisational culture. Our choice of school conditions for this study included three of these four variables along with several others not identified by Hallinger and Heck. In a factor analysis carried out as part of our previous study (Leithwood and Jantzi, 1998), all of these conditions loaded on the same factor.

'Purposes and goals', one of the school conditions included in our framework, includes what members of the school understand to be both the explicit and implicit purposes and directions for the school. It also encompasses the extent to which such purposes and directions are believed to be a compelling and challenging target for one's personal practices as well the collective school improvement efforts of staff. Evidence from our reviews suggested that such purposes contribute to school effectiveness, for example to the extent that members are aware of them, and to the extent they are perceived to be clear, meaningful, useful, current, congruent with district directions and to reflect important educational values. This variable bears close similarity to what Stringfield and Slavin (1992) refer to as 'meaningful goals' and what Reynolds et al. (1996) label 'shared vision and goals'. It is the only mediating variable that Hallinger and Heck (1996a) found consistently interacting with principal leadership across the 40 empirical studies included in their review.

Although conceptually part of Hallinger and Heck's (1998) purposes and goals variable, we treated 'school planning' as a separate school condition in our study. It includes the explicit means used for deciding on mission and goals, and on the actions to be taken for their accomplishment. Planning processes contribute to school effectiveness to the extent that they bring together local needs and district goals into a shared school vision (Mortimore, 1993; Hargreaves and Hopkins, 1991).

'Organisational culture' is a third school-level mediating variable included in our study. Hallinger and Heck (1998) suggest that this variable focuses on the importance of developing shared meanings and values. For purposes of our study, organisational culture was defined as the norms, values, beliefs and assumptions that shape members' decisions and practices. The contribution of culture to school effectiveness depends on the content of these norms, values, beliefs and assumptions (e.g. student-centred). It also depends on the extent to which they are shared, and whether they foster collaborative work. This variable shares elements of Reynolds et al.'s (1996) 'learning environment' and the 'consensus and cooperative planning' to which Scheerens (1997) and Creemers and Reetzig (1996) refer.

'Structure and organisation', the fourth school condition included in this study, was defined as the nature of the relationships established among people and groups in the school and between the school and its external constituents. As Hallinger and Heck (1998: 173) argue, 'leadership is linked to organisational roles and the networks of relations among roles because it is this network that comprises the organisational system'.

Such relationships contribute to school effectiveness when they support the purposes of the curriculum and the requirements for instruction. Structure and organisation also contribute to school effectiveness when they facilitate the work of staff, their professional learning and opportunities for collaboration. This variable includes elements of what Reynolds et al. (1996) include in 'shared vision and goals', as well as in school ethos or 'learning environment'.

Information collection and decision-making was the final variable included among the school conditions in the framework guiding our study. This variable includes the nature and quality of information collected for decision-making in the school, the ways in which members of the school use that information and how they are involved in decisions. Schools benefit, for example, when information for decision-making is systematically collected and widely available to most school members for decisions. This variable is reflected in the importance attached to 'monitoring student progress' (Reynolds et al., 1996; Mortimore, 1993) as well as the extensive support now available for the contribution to organisational effectiveness of employee participation in decision-making (Lawler, 1986; Conley, 1993).

Classroom conditions

The inclusion of classroom conditions in this study goes beyond the set of mediating variables suggested as important in principal leadership studies by Hallinger and Heck (1998). While there is considerable evidence that classroom conditions make a substantially greater contribution to student achievement than do school conditions (Bosker et al., 1990), the strength of the relationship between such conditions and student engagement is unknown. If student engagement is as important a variable as we argue it is below, a comprehensive understanding of the avenues through which leadership influences it is called for.

Two classroom conditions were included in this study, 'instructional services' and 'policies and procedures'. These conditions loaded on the same factor in our previous study (Leithwood and Jantzi, 1998). Instructional services were defined as interventions by teachers with students aimed at stimulating their educational growth. Practices associated with this variable included instructional planning, the consideration of learning principles, clarification of appropriate instructional goals, decisions about curricular content, selection of instructional strategies, and the uses of instructional time. A large literature supports the important contribution to student achievement of these and closely related variables (Reynolds et al., 1996; Creemers and Reetzig, 1996).

Policies and procedures we defined as guidelines for decision-making and action in the school. Although not referring directly to practices in the classroom, when policies in the school are student oriented, encourage continuous professional growth among staff and encourage the allocation of resources to school priorities without stifling individual initiative, their contribution to classroom practice is expected to be significant. At least indirect support for this variable can be found in evidence concerning the influence on school effects of 'high expectations', 'consistency' and 'control' (Mortimore, 1993; Creemers, 1994).

Student engagement with school

Student engagement with school has both behavioural and affective components. Extent of students' participation in school activities, both inside and outside the classroom, is the behavioural component. The affective component is the extent to which students identify with school and feel they belong. As it was defined and measured in this study, student engagement is quite similar to the 'social cohesion' variable used by Oxley (1997) as a dependent measure for her test of the effects of community-like school qualities on students.

Student engagement was chosen as the dependent measure in this study for several reasons. Expanding our understanding of leadership effects beyond basic mathematics and language achievement was one of the reasons. Such achievement measures have served as dependent variables in the vast majority of school leadership studies to date, not because they are the only, or always the most suitable, measures but because they are available for research at little or no cost to the researcher. Since the research team had to collect any outcome measures to be used in this study themselves, a measure was chosen which would extend the knowledge base concerning the scope of leadership effects.

The choice of student engagement is warranted on four additional grounds. First, for many students, dropping out of school is the final step in a long process of gradual disengagement and reduced participation in the formal curriculum of the school, as well as in the school's co-curriculum (hidden curriculum) and more informal social life. Reversing such disengagement is a necessary requirement for achieving the ambitious outcomes advocated in most current school reform initiatives. Variation in schools' retention rates is likely to be predicted well from estimates of student participation and identification (Finn, 1989). Second, some factors giving rise to students becoming at risk are to be found very early in the child's pre-school and school experiences. Patterns of student participation and identification are sensitive to the consequences of these factors as early as the primary grades. Change in a student's participation and identification is a reliable symptom of problems that should be redressed as early as possible (Lloyd, 1978). Finally, at least a modest amount of evidence suggests that student engagement is a reliable predictor of variation in such typical student outcomes as social studies, mathematics and language achievement (Finn and Cox, 1992; Bredschneider, 1993; Dukelow, 1993).

Our orientation to understanding and measuring student participation and identification began with the work of Jeremy Finn. In his paper 'Withdrawing from School' (1989), Finn offers a model explaining continuing engagement in school as a function of participation in school activities which, along with other influences, results in successful performance. Such performance is esteem building and fosters bonding or identification with the school. One central construct in the Finn model is identification with school. The terms 'affiliation', 'involvement', 'attachment', 'commitment' and 'bonding' encompass the two ideas which, Finn suggests (1989: 123), constitute a good working definition of identification:

> *First, students who identify with school have an internalized conception of belongingness – that they are discernibly part of the school environment and that school constitutes an important part of their own experience. And, second, these individuals value success in school-relevant goals.*

Such identification and engagement with school, an internal state, has been found to mediate a wide range of achievement and behavioural outcomes among students, as mentioned above.

The second construct central in the model is overt behaviour – students' actual participation in school activities. Finn identifies four levels of such participation and suggests a strong positive relationship between these levels of participation and the extent of students' identification with school. Level One participation involves acquiescence to the need to attend school, to be prepared for school tasks, and to respond to teachers' instructions. At Level Two, students take initiative in the classroom, are enthusiastic and may spend extra time on school work. Level Three involves participation in school activities outside the formal curriculum – the social and co-curricular activities of the school, in addition to extensive participation in academic work. Participation in school governance is the fourth level of participation in Finn's model. In the present study, the mean of these four levels was used as the measure of participation.

Finn conceptualised the participation-identification model in the form of a developmental cycle that included other variables. Participation in school is essential to successful school performance, although such performance is also influenced by students' perceptions of the quality of their instruction and their own ability (perhaps better understood as academic self-efficacy). Quality of instruction is also an influence on participation. Successful performance influences the students' sense of belonging and valuing of school-related goals. Such identification, in turn, has a positive effect on participation. While evidence was collected about those variables in the model in addition to participation and identification, that evidence was not used in this study.

Family educational culture

Here 'family educational culture', a moderator variable, was used in place of more commonly used socio-economic status (SES) measures to represent contributions to student outcomes from home and family sources. Historically, SES has been the most powerful predictor of student success at school (e.g. Coleman et al., 1966; Bridge et al., 1979). It also has been shown to influence the form of leadership exercised by principals (Hallinger et al., 1996) – hence the arrow in Figure 9.1 (see the results section of this chapter) signifying influence flowing from family educational culture to school leadership. But SES is a crude proxy, masking a host of family interactions which have powerful educational consequences. These interactions vary widely across families, often without much relation to family income, and this is why we prefer family educational culture over SES as a moderator variable in the present study.

The content of family educational culture includes the assumptions, norms, values and beliefs held by the family about intellectual work in general, school work in particular, and the conditions which foster both. Six literature reviews were used as the sources of eight dimensions of either the family's educational culture or resulting behaviours and conditions demonstrably related to school success (Bloom, 1984; Walberg, 1984; Scott-Jones, 1984; Finn, 1989; Rumberger, 1983, 1987). Taken as a whole, these dimensions represent what Walberg (1984) referred to as the 'alterable curriculum of the home'. This curriculum, twice as predictive of academic learning as SES according to Walberg's analysis, includes family work habits, academic guidance and support, and stimulation to think about issues in the larger environment. Family culture also includes the academic and occupational aspirations and expectations of parents or guardians, the provision of adequate health and nutritional conditions, and a physical setting conducive to academic work in the home (see Leithwood and Jantzi, 1998, for a more detailed description of these variables).

Based on this framework, our intention in carrying out the study was to identify:

▶ the proportion of variation in school and classroom conditions explained by teachers' perceptions of the extent of transformational leadership practices exercised in their schools;
▶ the total direct and indirect effects (explained variation) of transformational leadership on student engagement;

▶ the amount of variation in student engagement explained by school and classroom variables;
▶ whether transformational leadership explains comparable amounts of variation in each of the two dimensions of student engagement (participation, identification);
▶ the proportion of variation in both transformational leadership and student engagement explained by family educational culture.

Research design and methods

Our approach to research design is not based on epistemology. Rather, we chose methods we consider well suited to answering our questions. Nevertheless, we would not object to being accused, as Miles and Huberman (1984) have phrased it, of being 'soft-nosed positivists'. While we have relied exclusively on the collection of survey data in this study, it is one in a series of more than a dozen inquiring about facets of transformational leadership using a mixture of quantitative and qualitative techniques (see Leithwood et al., 1999).

Context

Data about leadership, school and classroom conditions, student engagement and family educational culture were collected through two surveys in one large school district in a province in eastern Canada. The district served a population of approximately 58,000 urban, suburban and rural elementary and secondary students. Data for this study focused on the 2,465 teachers and 44,920 students in the district's 123 elementary and junior high schools.

At the time of data collection, all schools in this district were confronted with expectations for change from both the district and the provincial government, which clearly called out for the exercise of school-level leadership. For example, just two years prior to the study, the district had been newly formed through the amalgamation of three much smaller administrative jurisdictions. This gave rise to the need for considerable district-wide culture building, policy realignment and structural reconfiguration. During this period as well, the provincial government was proceeding with a host of other changes affecting schools including changes in curriculum, student assessment and funding formulae. Comparable changes were being made in many educational jurisdictions across Canada at the time of the study.

Instruments

Two survey instruments were developed, one to collect data from teachers on school and classroom (organisational) conditions and transformational leadership, the other to collect evidence from students on their engagement with school and their families' educational cultures. The 'Organisational Conditions and School Leadership Survey' contained 214 items measuring five sets of school conditions, two sets of classroom conditions, and the perceived influence of teacher and principal leadership in the school. Items measuring school and classroom conditions were stated in the form suggested by the research literature to be most desirable, and were rated on a five-point Likert scale ('strongly disagree' to 'strongly agree' that the statement was true for their school, with a 'not applicable' response option also available). Likert and Likert-like scales are the mostly widely used attitude scale type in the social sciences. They are relatively easy to construct, can deal with attitudes of more than one dimension and tend to be highly reliable. These scales are not without their limits. For example, although this is an ordinal scale (points on the scale have an inherent order or sequence), one cannot assume that the differences between points are identical. Is the difference between agreeing and strongly agreeing the same as between agreeing and being undecided? Nonetheless, the consistency with which respondents use the scale (its reliability) make it a useful measurement tool.

Examples of items related to organisational conditions include the following:

- Our school's mission statement is compatible with the mission statement for the board (local education authority/district).
- Our school emphasises creating a positive atmosphere for our students.
- School improvement planning is based on cooperative decision-making.
- Our school day is structured to maximise student learning.
- In our school, a variety of student data (e.g. marks, attendance, work habits) about individual student progress is collected regularly.
- I am expected to assess student homework.
- I help my students develop a clear understanding of the purposes of instruction.

The following examples were among the items asking teachers to what extent the person(s) providing leadership in their school:

- shows respect for staff by treating us as professionals;
- delegates leadership activities critical for achieving school objectives;
- takes my opinion into account when initiating actions that affect my work;
- encourages me to pursue my own goals for professional learning;
- holds high expectations for us as professionals;
- works toward whole-staff consensus in establishing priorities for school goals.

The 'Student Engagement and Family Culture Survey' contained 61 items measuring student participation in school activities (34), student identification with school (17) and students' perceptions of their family educational culture (10). Students responded to each item on the same five-point scale used by teachers ('strongly disagree' to 'strongly agree') that the statement was true for them, with a 'not applicable' response option also available. The following items are two examples from each of the three student variables:

- I put a lot of energy into my schoolwork.
- Participating in school events (e.g. plays, athletics, musicals) is a very important part of my life at school.

▶ I feel that I 'belong' at this school.
▶ I think schoolwork is really important.
▶ My parents or guardians make sure that I do my homework before having free time.
▶ I often discuss my schoolwork with my parents or guardians.

Sample

While this was a large-scale survey, the rules governing sample selection are essentially the same in less ambitious circumstances. All elementary and junior high school teachers in the school district (n = 2,465) were asked to respond to the 'Organisational Conditions and School Leadership Survey'. Because of the extensive number of items, however, two forms of the survey were developed. Each form collected data about at least three sets of organisational conditions and all leadership items. Our decision to divide the items into two shorter instruments rather than administering one long instrument to all staff was based on an assumption that this procedure reduced the risk of respondent fatigue and, consequently, would result in more thoughtful responses and fewer incomplete surveys. All schools with fewer than ten teachers were asked to complete both forms of the survey, preferably at two different times to prevent fatigue. Each form required an average of 20 minutes to complete. In all other schools, each teacher was randomly assigned either Form A or Form B. A total of 888 teachers completed Form A of the survey and 874 teachers completed Form B for an overall response rate of 71per cent.

The 'Student Engagement and Family Educational Culture Survey' was administered to all students in one class in each of the three highest grades. In order to protect student anonymity, principals rather than teachers supervised the administration and subsequent collection of these surveys. A total of 8,805 students responded in the 110 schools in the sample. Data for all variables in this study were complete for 110 of the 123 elementary and junior high schools in the district.

Data analysis

Responses of individual teachers and students to the surveys were aggregated to the school level. The statistical analysis programme SPSS was used to aggregate individual responses by school and then to calculate means, standard deviations and reliability coefficients (Cronbach's alpha) for all the scales measuring the variables. As in our previous study (Leithwood and Jantzi, 1998), principal components extraction with varimax rotation was used to analyse the seven school and classroom conditions. This technique enabled us to estimate the number of factors measured by the specific conditions and assess the extent to which our conceptual distinctions among the seven organisational conditions could be verified empirically. Principal components analysis is a procedure for transforming a large set of correlated variables into a smaller group of uncorrelated variables. This makes analysis easier by grouping data into more manageable units and clarifying relationships among these variables.

LISREL was used to assess the direct and indirect effects of leadership on student engagement. This path analytic technique allows for testing the validity of causal inferences for pairs of variables while controlling for the effects of other variables. The technique enabled us to control for the effects of organisational conditions and family culture while assessing the effects of leadership on student engagement. Data were analysed using the LISREL 8 analysis of covariance structure approach to path analysis and maximum likelihood estimates (Joreskog and Sorbom, 1993). Hierarchical linear modelling is the analytic technique of choice for some researchers exploring databases such as this one. For a variety of practical reasons, however, we were unable to collect our data in a way that allowed us to link the responses of individual students with their teachers, a prerequisite for hierarchical linear modelling.

Results

Table 9.1 reports means and standard deviations (SD), aggregated to the school level, of teachers' ratings of transformational leadership and all school and classroom conditions. Comparable information about student responses to items included in the three scales of the Student Engagement and Family Culture Survey appear in the last three rows of this table. The far right column indicates that the internal reliabilities of all scales were acceptable, ranging from 0.74 to 0.95.

Table 9.1 *Teacher ratings of organisational conditions and student ratings of family educational culture and engagement (N = 110 schools)*

	Mean[1]	SD	Reliability[2]
Teacher ratings of school conditions:			
Conditions (aggregate)	3.83	0.25	0.93
Purposes and goals	4.07	0.37	0.95
Instructional services	4.03	0.26	0.88
Culture	3.92	0.33	0.94
Information collection and decision-making	3.85	0.26	0.92
Policy and procedures	3.72	0.27	0.93
Planning	3.63	0.32	0.94
Structure and organisation	3.57	0.36	0.93
Teacher ratings of transformational leadership:			
Transformational leadership	3.76	0.48	0.90
Student ratings of family educational culture:			
Family educational culture	4.10	0.24	0.79
Student ratings of engagement with school:			
Identification	3.93	0.30	0.90
Participation	3.62	0.25	0.74

[1] Rating scale: 1 = disagree strongly; 5 = agree strongly.
[2] Cronbach's alpha.

Results of the factor analysis, reported in Table 9.2, indicate that only one factor was extracted from the seven organisational conditions, rather than two factors (a school factor and a classroom factor) as in one of our previous studies using comparable data (Leithwood and Jantzi, 1998). Five of the conditions loaded at 0.83 or higher, whereas the relationship of structure and organisation to the factor was somewhat weaker at 0.72. Instructional services had the weakest relationship at 0.70. Table 9.3 demonstrates a similar, single-factor outcome of the factor analysis of the ten leadership and management dimensions of our model of transformational leadership. Results of both these factor analyses are reflected in the path model tested below.

Table 9.4 reports correlation coefficients (a measure of the strength of relationships) among all variables included in the path model. Correlation coefficients, which range from –1 to +1, show the degree to which two vari-

Table 9.2 *Factor matrix resulting from teacher ratings of conditions within their schools (N = 110 schools)*

	Factor loadings
Purposes and goals	0.85
Culture	0.90
Planning	0.83
Structure and organisation	0.72
Information collection	0.88
Policy and procedures	0.89
Instructional services	0.70
Eigenvalue	4.77
Percent of explained variance	68.21

Table 9.3 *Factor matrix resulting from teacher ratings of leadership within their schools (N = 110 schools)*

	Factor loadings
Staffing	0.67
Instructional support	0.89
Monitoring school activities	0.86
Community focus	0.71
Building school vision and goals	0.92
Providing intellectual stimulation	0.93
Providing individualized support	0.90
Symbolising professional practices and values	0.92
Demonstrating high performance expectations	0.84
Developing collaborative structures	0.91
Eigenvalue	7.38
Percent of explained variance	73.81

Table 9.4 *Relationships among leadership, organisational conditions, family educational culture, and student outcomes (N = 110 schools)*

	Leadership	Conditions	Family	Participation	Identification
Transformational leadership	1.00	0.68**	0.11	0.19*	0.23*
Organisational conditions	0.68**	1.00	0.34**	0.40**	0.43**
Family educational culture	0.11	0.34**	1.00	0.88**	0.87**
Participation	0.19*	0.40**	0.88**	1.00	0.90**
Identification	0.23*	0.43**	0.87**	0.90**	1.00

*p <0.05; **p <0.01

ables are related to each other, but do not determine whether one causes the other. If one variable has a high value and the other low, their coefficient would be negative with –1 indicating a perfect relationship in which the value of one variable always increases as the other decreases, or vice versa. A positive correlation indicates that when the value of one variable is high or low so is the other. If there is no relationship between the two variables, the coefficient is 0. All relationships reported in Table 9.4 are statistically significant except the relationship between transformational leadership and family educational culture.

Figure 9.1 reports the results of testing (using LISREL) a version of the initial framework for the study adapted in response to the factor analyses, reported in Tables 9.2 and 9.3, in which all items measuring school and classroom conditions loaded on the same factor and all items measuring leadership and management loaded on the same factor. Although the model also tested relationships between family educational culture and leadership as well as between conditions and participation, to facilitate interpretation only the significant paths are shown in Figure 9.1. The model is an acceptable fit with the data (X^2 (2, N = 110) = 1.91, p = 0.38; AGFI = 0.95, RMR = 0.01; NFI = 1.00, PGFI = 0.13) and, as a whole, explains 84 per cent of the variation in student participation and 78 per cent of the variation in student identification. Family educational culture has the strongest relationship with student engagement as reflected in its significant total effects on participation (0.88) and identification (0.87). Family educational culture has significant effects on organisational conditions, and these conditions have significant, although modest, total effects on both student participation (0.11) and identification (0.15).

Transformational leadership has strong, significant direct effects on organisational conditions and weak but significant indirect effects on student participation (0.07) and identification (0.10).

Figure 9.1 *Effects of transformational leadership on student engagement.*

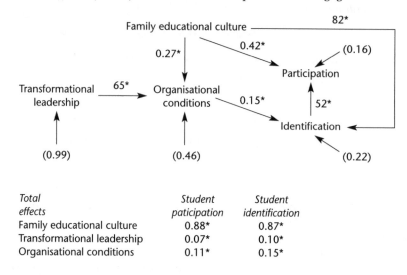

Total effects	Student paticipation	Student identification
Family educational culture	0.88*	0.87*
Transformational leadership	0.07*	0.10*
Organisational conditions	0.11*	0.15*

Discussion and conclusion

The purpose of this study was to inquire about the effects of transformational leadership practices on organisational conditions and student engagement with school, taking into account the potentially large effects of family educational culture. Results of this study are consistent, in many respects, with evidence provided by other large-scale, quantitative studies of principal leadership effects, as well as several of our own earlier studies of transformational leadership (Leithwood, 1994). With student engagement in school as the dependent variable, results of the study indicate that transformational leadership effects are significant although weak on the affective or psychological dimension (identification) and the behavioural dimension (participation) of student engagement. The sizes of these transformational leadership effects are approximately the same as those found for the effects of leadership provided specifically by principals in two of our previous studies (Leithwood and Jantzi, 1998, 2000) which also used student engagement as the dependent variable. It is possible, of course, that respondents in the present study primarily had principals in mind as they responded to questions about the extent to which they experienced transformational leadership in their schools.

Whether the focus is on leadership from principals in particular, or on transformational leadership practices whatever their source, two quite different interpretations of these results are possible. The most obvious interpretation is that principals in the case of our earlier study, and transformational leadership practices in the present study, make a disappointing contribution to student engagement. Had the dependent variable in the study been basic mathematics or language skills, this interpretation would be seen as fundamentally in contradiction with the assumptions of most school professionals, normative assertions about the role of leadership in schools (e.g. Hudson, 1997; Foster, 1989) and the results of many school effectiveness studies (e.g. Mortimore, 1993). In fact, student engagement is an outcome not nearly so obviously tied to teachers' classroom practices as are more conventional outcome measures, and so potentially more susceptible to influence by those outside the classroom. Our results, for this reason, might be considered doubly disappointing. This might be termed the 'romance of leadership' interpretation, after Meindl's (1995) argument that leadership is a convenient, phenomenologically legitimate, social construction which, nonetheless, masks a complex, multi-sourced bundle of influences on organisational outcomes.

A second interpretation of these results, after Hallinger and Heck's (1996b) analysis of principal leadership effects, cautions against dismissing as not meaningful the admittedly small effects of leadership on, in this case, student engagement. Transformational school leadership practices, after all, do explain a large proportion of the variation in organisational conditions, those features of the school to which leaders have direct access and which are, conceptually, the means through which school effects are exercised.

To put this interpretation in a broader context, recent reviews of empirical research on school effectiveness suggest that educational factors for which data are available explain, in total, something less than 20 per cent of the variation in student cognitive outcomes; very little evidence is available concerning such non-cognitive outcomes as the one used in this study. Reynolds et al. (1996) suggest 8–12 per cent for research carried out in the United Kingdom, while Creemers and Reetzig suggest 10–20 per cent for studies carried out 'in the Western Hemisphere...after correction for student intake measures such as aptitude or social class...' (1996: 203). Variation within this range across studies may be explained by such variables as school size, type of student outcome serving as the dependent measure, nature of students, and department and subject matter differences.

While these relatively small amounts of explained variation are now considered to be both meaningful and practically significant, a school is not a single variable. It is an aggregate of variables, the 'correlates' of effective schools, or the organisational conditions used as mediating variables in this study. Some of these variables most likely contribute more strongly than others to school effects, although they have yet to be unpacked empirically, except for distinguishing between classroom and school-level factors (Creemers and Reetzig, 1996; Scheerens, 1997). Efforts to do the unpacking, however, realistically begin with very modest amounts of variation to be explained, especially if it is assumed, as seems reasonable, that at least a handful of factors contribute to explained variation. This was Ogawa and Hart's (1985) argument in claiming importance for their finding that principal leadership explained 2–8 per cent of the variation in student performance, similar to the results of this study. Under such circumstances, knowing the relative explanatory power of a variable will be at least as interesting as knowing the total amount of variation it explains.

Results of the study involving family educational culture are significant for three reasons. First, most school effects studies acknowledge a central role for SES in accounting for variation in student achievement. In this study, family educational culture replaced SES on the grounds that it more precisely targeted those elements subsumed by, typically, very global SES measures (e.g. percentage of students in school eligible for free lunches) contributing to student success at school. Our results support the validity of this concept and its meas-urement in future school and leadership effects studies. Family educational culture behaved statistically in a manner comparable to the behaviour of SES in most previous school effects studies.

Second, the exceptionally large proportion of variation in student engagement explained by family educational culture raises the possibility that different student outcomes may range considerably in their sensitivity to family, as compared with school, variables. This is apparent already in studies attempting to explain varia-tion in mathematics as compared with language achievement, for example (Thomas et al., 1997). It seems likely to become much more apparent as evidence from school and leadership effects studies accumulates across a wider array of stu-dent outcomes, especially across important but 'non-standard' outcomes such as student engagement. These outcomes, while reflected almost not at all in current school effects research, are an important feature of most curriculum policy, and are central to many parents' assessments of their local schools (Townsend, 1994). Their significance suggests that future school and leadership effects studies ought to conceptualise family variables more centrally in their designs. They also might do well to reconceive themselves as 'school and family effects' or 'leadership and family effects' studies. Our understanding of school effects in general, and leader-ship effects in particular, is unlikely to progress much further without systematic inquiry about how schools and families co-produce the full array of outcomes for which schools are responsible.

Finally, effects on student engagement of transformational leadership practices were substantially weaker than those of family educational culture. This pattern of effects was especially strong for teacher leadership in one of our previous studies (Leithwood and Jantzi, 1998). A plausible implication of these findings is that high levels of student engagement reduce teachers' perceived needs for either teacher or principal leadership. Student engagement could be conceived of as a substitute for leadership (Howell, 1997), as well as a student outcome.

The design of this study did not allow for distinctions to be made between school and classroom 'levels'. For example, we could not estimate the separate effects of leadership on school conditions and classroom conditions. Similarly, the effects of these two sets of conditions on student engagement are not clear. In future studies of leadership effects, designs that permit such discriminations would be useful.

References

Ball, D. L., and Rundquist, S. S. (1993) 'Collaboration as a context for joining teacher learning with learning about teaching', in D. Cohen et al. (eds), *Teaching for Understanding: Challenges for Policy and Practice.* San Francisco: Jossey-Bass.
Bass, B. M. (1985) *Leadership and Performance Beyond Expectations.* New York: Free Press.
Bennis, W. G. (1959) 'Leadership theory and administrative behaviour: the problem of authority', *Administrative Science Quarterly,* 4: 259–60.
Bloom, B. S. (1984) 'The search for methods of group instruction as effective as one-to-one tutoring', *Educational Leadership,* May: 4–17.
Bosker, R. J., Kremers, E. J. and Lugthart, E. (1990) 'School and instruction effects on mathematics achievement', *School Effectiveness and School Improvement,* 1 (4): 233–48.

Bredschneider, C. (1993) 'A study of student participation in and identification with one Ontario secondary school'. Unpublished master's paper, University of Toronto, OISE.

Bridge, R., Judd, C. and Moock, P. (1979) *The Determinants of Educational Outcomes*. Cambridge: Ballinger.

Bryman, A. (1992) *Charisma and Leadership in Organizations*. Newbury Park, CA: Sage.

Burns, J. (1978) *Leadership*. New York: Harper & Row.

Coleman, J. S. et al. (1966) *Equality of Educational Opportunity*. Washington: US Government Printing Office.

Conley, D .T. (1993) *Roadmap to Restructuring: Policies, Practices, and the Emerging Visions of Schooling*. Oregon: ERIC Clearinghouse on Educational Management.

Creemers, B. (1994) *The Effective Classroom*. London: Cassell.

Creemers, B. and Reetzig, G. J. (1996) 'School level conditions affecting the effectiveness of instruction', *School Effectiveness and School Improvement*, 7 (3): 197–228.

Dillard, C. B. (1995) 'Leading with her life: an African-American feminist (re)interpretation of leadership for an urban high school principal', *Educational Administration Quarterly*, 31 (4): 539–63.

Duke, D. and Leithwood, K. (1994) 'Management and leadership: a comprehensive view of principals' functions'. Mimeo, University of Toronto, OISE.

Dukelow, G. A. (1993) 'A statistical analysis of educational variables that influence high school students' grades and participation'. Unpublished master's thesis, University of Victoria.

Finn, J. D. (1989) 'Withdrawing from school', *Review of Educational Research*, 59 (2): 117–43.

Finn, J. D. and Cox, D. (1992) 'Participation and withdrawal among fourth-grade pupils', *American Educational Research Journal*, 29 (1): 141–62.

Foster, W. (1989) 'Toward a critical practice of leadership', in J. Smyth (ed.), *Critical Perspectives on Educational Leadership*. London: Falmer Press.

Gronn, P. (1996) 'From transactions to transformations: a new world order in the study of leadership', *Educational Management and Administration*, 24 (1): 7–30.

Hallinger, P. and Heck, R. (1996a) 'Reassessing the principal's role in school effectiveness: a review of empirical research, 1980–1995', *Educational Administration Quarterly*, 32 (1): 5–44.

Hallinger, P. and Heck, R. (1996b) 'The principal's role in school effectiveness: an assessment of methodological progress, 1980–1995', in K. Leithwood, J. Chapman, D. Corson, P. Hallinger and A. Hart (eds), *International Handbook of Educational Leadership and Administration*. Dordrecht: Kluwer.

Hallinger, P. and Heck, R. (1998) 'Exploring the principal's contribution to school effectiveness: 1980–1995', *School Effectiveness and School Improvement*, 9 (2): 157–91.

Hallinger, P., Bickman, L. and Davis, K. (1996) 'School context, principal leadership and student achievement', *Elementary School Journal*, 96 (5): 527–49.

Hargreaves, D. and Hopkins, D. (1991) *The Empowered School*. London: Cassell.

Hipp, K. A. and Bredeson, P. V. (1995) 'Exploring connections between teacher efficacy and principals' leadership behaviours', *Journal of School Leadership*, 5 (2): 136–50.

Hosking, D. and Morley, I. E. (1988) 'The skills of leadership', in J. G. Hunt, B. R. Baliga, H. P. Dachler and C. A. Schriesheim (eds), *Emerging Leadership Vistas*. Lexington: Lexington Books.

Howell, J. (1997) 'Substitutes for leadership: their meaning and measurement – a historical assessment', *Leadership Quarterly*, 8 (2) 113–16.

Hudson, J. (1997) '*Ethical leadership: the soul of policy making*', Journal of School Leadership, 7 (5): 506–20.

Joreskog, K. G. and Sorbom, D. (1993) LISREL: *Structural Equation Modelling with SIMPLIS Command Language*. Chicago: Scientific Software, Inc.

Kowalski, J. and Oates, A. (1993) 'The evolving role of superintendents in school-based management', *Journal of School Leadership*, 3 (4): 380–90.

Lawler III, E. E. (1986) *High-Involvement Management*. San Francisco: Jossey-Bass.

Leithwood, K. (1994) 'Leadership for school restructuring', *Educational Administration Quarterly*, 30 (4): 498–518.

Leithwood, K. and Jantzi, D. (1998) *Distributed leadership and student engagement in school*, paper presented at the annual meeting of the American Educational Research Association, San Diego.

Leithwood, K. and Jantzi, D. (2000) 'Principal and teacher leadership effects: a replication', *School Leadership and Management*, 20 (4): 415–34.

Leithwood, K. and Steinbach, R. (1995) *Expert Problem Solving*. Albany, NY: SUNY Press.

Leithwood, K., Jantzi, D. and Steinbach, R. (1999) *Changing Leadership for Changing Times*. London: Open University Press.

Leithwood, K., Tomlinson, D. and Genge, M. (1996) 'Transformational school leadership', in K. Leithwood, J. Chapman, D. Corson, P. Hallinger and A. Hart (eds), *International Handbook of Educational Leadership and Administration*. Dordrecht: Kluwer.

Lloyd, D. (1978) 'Prediction of school failure from third-grade data', *Educational and Psychological Measurements*, 38: 1193–200.

Meindl, J. R. (1995) 'The romance of leadership as a follower-centric theory: a social constructionist approach', *Leadership Quarterly*, 6 (3): 329–41.

Miles, M. and Huberman, M. (1984) *Qualitative Data Analysis: A Sourcebook of New Methods*, Beverly Hills, CA: Sage.

Mortimore, P. (1993) 'School effectiveness and the management of effective learning and teaching', *School Effectiveness and School Improvement*, 4 (4): 290–310.

Ogawa, R. and Bossert, S. (1995) 'Leadership as an organizational quality', *Educational Administration Quarterly*, 31 (2): 224–43.

Ogawa, R. and Hart, A. (1985) 'The effects of principals on the instructional performance of schools', *Journal of Educational Administration*, 23 (1): 59–72.

Oxley, D. (1997) 'Theory and practice of school communities', *Educational Administration Quarterly*, 33 (supplement): 624–43.

Putnam, R. T. and Borko, H. (1997) 'Teacher learning: implications of new views of cognition', in B. J. Biddle et al. (eds), *International Handbook of Teachers and Teaching*. Dordrecht: Kluwer.

Reynolds, D., Sammons, P., Stoll, L., Barber, M. and Hillman, J. (1996) 'School effectiveness and school improvement in the United Kingdom', *School Effectiveness and School Improvement*, 7 (2): 133–158.

Rumberger, R. W. (1983) 'Dropping out of high school: the influence of race, sex, and family background', *American Educational Research Journal*, 20: 199–220.

Rumberger, R. W. (1987) 'High school dropouts: a review of issues and evidence', *Review of Educational Research*, 57 (2): 101–21.

Scheerens, J. (1997) 'Conceptual models and theory-embedded principles on effective schooling', *School Effectiveness and School Improvement*, 8 (3): 269–310.

Scott-Jones, D. (1984) 'Family influences on cognitive development and school achievement', in E. Gordon (ed.), *Review of Research in Education, III*. Washington: American Educational Research Association.

Sieber, S. (1981) *Fatal Remedies*. New York: Plenum.

Stringfield, S. C. and Slavin, R. E. (1992) 'A hierarchical longitudinal model for elementary school effects', in B.. Creemers and G. J. Reetzig (eds), *Evaluation of Effectiveness*, Publication 2: The Netherlands: ICO.

Thomas, S., Sammons, P., Mortimore, P. and Smees, R. (1997) 'Stability and consistency in secondary school effects on students' GCSE outcomes over three years', *School Effectiveness and School Improvement*, 8 (2): 169–97.

Townsend, T. (1994) 'Goals for effective schools: the view from the field', *School Effectiveness and School Improvement*, 5 (2): 127–48.

Walberg, H. J. (1984) 'Improving the productivity of America's schools', *Educational Leadership*, 41 (8): 19-27.

Yammarino, F. J., Dubinsky, A. J. and Spangler, W. D. (1998) 'Transformational and contingent reward leadership: individual, dyad, and group level of analysis', *Leadership Quarterly*, 9 (1): 27–54.

Yukl, G. (1994) *Leadership in Organizations*, 3rd edn. Atlantic Highlands, NJ: Prentice-Hall.

Part 3

Meeting the challenge of reporting a review of the literature

Chapter 10

Understanding the contribution of leadership to school improvement

Philip Hallinger and Ronald Heck

This is an exemplary account of reviewing empirical literature in the field of school leadership. The chapter illuminates, in practice, many of the points that were made in the first two chapters of this book and it offers an excellent insight into the process of systematic review. In this chapter, Hallinger and Heck pay particular attention to the methodology of literature reviews and their role in building a knowledge base within a field of enquiry. They highlight the principles and procedures that informed the review and assess strengths and limitations of research and knowledge in that field.

At the outset, Hallinger and Heck stipulate the definition of leadership used within the review, and establish its primary aim: to understand what scholars have learned about the substance of claims that the leadership exercised by principals (or headteachers) makes a difference to the effectiveness of a school. The authors establish the parameters of their search of literature, clearly indicating the time frame within which they looked for relevant studies, and why they chose work within this period. They also indicate the sources that were used to locate literature, the criteria used for selection, and the number and types of studies that were found. An important point made by the authors is that in the field of school leadership, as in many other domains of knowledge, theories and concepts are constantly evolving: there is no universal paradigm or theory for examining organisational behaviour that can be assumed to be valid in all contexts. One of the tasks of any reviewer of literature is to identify the key theories, methodologies, concepts and models within a field of study, and their interrelationships. A reviewer may also have to deal with what appear to be contradictory or conflicting findings and tendencies in individual studies and in reviews of a field. However, as Hallinger and Heck point out, apparent contradictions often can be explained by differences in the theoretical and methodological assumptions of studies or criteria for selection in reviews.

This chapter expands on material, portions of which have previously appeared in Hallinger and Heck (1996a, 1996b, 1997, 1999) and in Heck and Hallinger (1999).

An important issue highlighted by the authors is the use of terminology within a field. In relation to school leadership, they identify how widely used conceptual terms such as vision, mission and goals may be used to mean different things, and how some terms used synonymously in discussing leadership may be operationalised in different ways in empirical studies. The terms may have different theoretical foundations and may derive from alternative conceptualisations – in this case of leadership.

Introduction

Since the emergence of research focusing on school effectiveness in the late 1970s, educators internationally have joined the leadership bandwagon. Despite the admonition of respected scholars (e.g. Bossert et al., 1982; Bridges, 1982; Cuban, 1988; Miskel, 1982; Rowan et al., 1982; van de Grift, 1989, 1990) the assumption of positive leadership effects in schooling has generally prevailed in research and practice. In fact, in the years since 1980 leadership has become a newly influential domain of educational management. This is the case despite the fact that there are more questions than answers with respect to the nature and role of school leadership in school improvement and school effectiveness.

In this chapter, we discuss findings drawn from a review of empirical literature on principal leadership effects disseminated internationally between 1980 and 2000. We seek to understand what scholars have learned about the substance of claims that leadership makes a difference in school effectiveness and improvement. For the purposes of this chapter, we refer to leadership as an influence process by which school administrators, focusing especially on principals, seek to work with and through people towards the identification and achievement of organisational goals.

The body of the chapter is devoted to a discussion of findings drawn from a series of related papers that have investigated state-of-the-art perspectives on school leadership and its effects (Hallinger and Heck, 1996a, 1996b, 1997, 1999; Hallinger and Leithwood, 1994; Heck and Hallinger, 1999). This chapter builds on the earlier efforts by synthesising and extending our findings on school leadership as it operates in an international context (see also Hallinger, 1995; Hallinger and Kantamara, 2001; Hallinger and Leithwood, 1998; Heck, 1996). In this chapter we pay particular attention to the methodology of literature reviews and their role in the process of building the knowledge base in our field.

The perspective for this review

Any attempt to integrate a body of research into a coherent conceptual framework that analyses conceptual, substantive and methodological issues must acknowledge its limitations at the outset. The field's conceptualisation of organisational processes, including leadership constructs, is constantly evolving. Hence we assert that no universal paradigm or theory exists for examining organisational behaviour that is valid in all contexts (Hallinger, 1995; Heck, 1996; Leithwood and Hallinger, 1993). Moreover, the complexity of extra- and intra-organisational processes represents a particular challenge for researchers who study *causal* relationships involving leadership and school effectiveness (Bossert et al., 1982; Hallinger and Heck, 1996a, 1996b; Heck and Hallinger, 1999; Heck and Marcoulides, 1996a, 1996b). While a perusal of the professional literature of the 1980s and 1990s would suggest that we have learned much about the principal's role in school effectiveness, this review started with a cautious view towards such claims.

We chose to demarcate our review with the year 1980 in recognition of landmark efforts that reviewed research in that period. In our view, the summer 1982 issue of the *Educational Administration Quarterly* marked a turning point in the recent study of educational administrators, especially with respect to their effects on schooling. Contained in this journal issue were two articles, 'Research on the school administrator: the state-of-the-art, 1967–1980' (Bridges, 1982), and 'The instructional management role of the principal: a review and preliminary conceptualisation' (Bossert et al., 1982). These reviews examined research on principal leadership conducted over the previous decade and more.

Interestingly, however, the reviews drew quite different conclusions. Based upon his assessment of the literature, Bridges (1982: 24–5) concluded:

> *Research on school administrators for the period 1967–80 reminds one of the dictum: 'The more things change, the more they remain the same.' The state-of-the-art is scarcely different from what seemed to be in place 15 years ago. Although researchers apparently show a greater interest in outcomes than was the case in the earlier period, they continue their excessive reliance on survey designs, questionnaires of dubious reliability and validity, and relatively simplistic types of statistical analysis. Moreover, these researchers persist in treating research problems in an ad hoc rather than a programmatic fashion. Equally disturbing is the nature of the knowledge base accumulated during this period. Despite the rather loose definition of theory that was used in classifying the sample of research...most of it proved to be atheoretical. Likewise the research seemed to have little or no practical utility.*

This conclusion was sobering for those who had hoped that research might assist in solving problems of educational policy and practice in educational administration. In contrast, however, Bossert and his colleagues (1982) at the Far West Laboratory for Research and Development drew quite different conclusions from their own literature review. They suggested that principals could have a positive impact on a variety of in-school factors and, at least indirectly, affect the achievement of students. The Far West Lab group's assessment received support from independent reviews conducted by scholars at the Ontario Institute for Studies in Education (Leithwood and Montgomery, 1982), the Santa Clara (CA) County Office of Education (Murphy et al., 1983), the Northwest Laboratory for Educational Research and Development (Purkey and Smith, 1983), and the Connecticut State Department of Education (Sirois and Villanova, 1982). While not blind to methodological problems of the literature, their conclusions were distinctly more optimistic than those of Bridges' review.

The divergence of these conclusions was both startling and difficult to reconcile at the time. If the methodological and conceptual state of the art was as Bridges suggested, how could other respected scholars draw such dissimilar conclusions? In retrospect, it may be explained by several factors. First, Bridges' review did not include publications featuring the early effective schools research. Yet these studies formed an important body of evidence for the other reviews. Second, the school effects research was comprised of general investigations into the effectiveness of *schools*. The research questions and designs, therefore, were not intended to test the effects of principals on school outcomes. This feature was noted by Miskel (1982) as well as by Bossert and colleagues in a second review (Rowan et al., 1982). Thus, studies included in these other reviews may not have met Bridges' selection criteria, even if they had appeared in the journals included in his review.

Third, it would be fair to say that the foci of the reviews also differed. Bridges was primarily concerned with methodological issues, while the other reviewers evinced greater interest in conceptual linkages within the literature and on patterns of the substantive results. They also were more eclectic and drew upon studies from a variety of *sister* domains (for example school improvement, general management). Finally, it is also true that if the early effective schools studies had been included in Bridges' 1982 review, they would have been aptly described by several characteristics noted in his methodological critique. For example, the effective schools research relied heavily on cross-sectional survey research and tended to be atheoretical in the selection and modelling of variables. Moreover, the research designs and statistical methods were not always up to the task of determining causal relationships.

Together, these factors explain the divergence in conclusions drawn from reviews conducted at the same point in time. In a sense, however, these reviews all pre-dated a new generation of research on principal effectiveness. During the 1980s, stimulated by findings from the school effectiveness and improvement literatures, researchers began to reconceptualise the principal's leadership role and lay the groundwork for more systematic empirical investigation. In particular this led to the emergence of conceptual frameworks focusing on instructional leadership, a hitherto much discussed but lightly studied role of the principal (Andrews and Soder, 1987; Bossert et al., 1982; Hallinger, 2001; Hallinger and Murphy, 1986; Leithwood and Montgomery, 1982; Sirois and Villanova, 1982). With the advent of the 1990s, an international group of scholars continued to push this literature forward with a programme of research focusing on transformational school leadership and its effects (Cheng, 1994; Leithwood, 1994; Leithwood and Jantzi, 1990; Leithwood et al., 1998; Marks et al., 2000; Sheppard and Brown, 2000; Silins, 1994; Silins et al., 2000; Wiley, 1998).

Instrumentation evolving from this conceptual work has made it possible to design studies that would more reliably determine the nature and effects of the principal's leadership behaviour (e.g. Andrews and Soder, 1987; Hallinger and Murphy, 1986; Leithwood, 1994; van de Grift, 1990). Increased attention to emerging analytical techniques such as structural equation modelling and hierarchical linear modelling further allowed researchers to explore more complex theoretical models of leadership effects (e.g. Hallinger et al., 1996; Heck and Marcoulides, 1996a, 1996b; Marks et al., 2000; Rowan et al., 1991; Silins, 1994; Wiley, 1998). The two decades following publication of these reviews in 1982 was fruitful, at least if measured by the number of studies (Hallinger and Heck, 1996a, 1996b), and set the stage for this review.

Identification and selection of studies for review

We began the review of literature on principal leadership and its effects with a search of the ERIC (Resources in Education) and CJIE (Current Journals in Education) databases. We used our personal knowledge of published and presented research to identify additional studies as well. Consequently, the review includes journal articles, dissertation studies and papers presented at peer-reviewed conferences. We are reasonably confident that our reviews captured most of the empirical studies of principal effects disseminated internationally between 1980 and 2000.

Three criteria guided selection of studies for our review. First, we sought studies that had been designed explicitly to examine the effects of the principal's leadership beliefs and behaviour. The research must have conceptualised and measured principal leadership as one of the independent variables. The nature of the conceptualisation of leadership was not considered at the point of selection. That is, we did not limit the review to studies of instructional leadership, transformational leadership or any specific model. Indeed, one of the goals of the review was to identify the predominant models being used by scholars in empirical studies of principal effects.

Second, the studies also had to include an explicit measure of school performance as a dependent variable. Most often performance was measured in terms of student achievement, but occasionally other measures of performance were also used. It was our desire, though not a necessary condition for inclusion, also to identify studies that examined the principal's impact on teacher and school-level variables as mediating variables. The dual focus on outcomes and intermediate variables reflects the priority that we gave to student outcomes as an important goal for school improvement and to classroom and school-level variables as avenues through which principals reach this goal.

We acknowledge that concerns can be raised about the validity and reliability of student achievement measures. We felt, however, that the policy implications of such outcomes (for example, student achievement or school effectiveness) outweighed the potential concerns within this domain of study. Notably, however, we did *not* include studies that examined principal effects on intervening variables (for example, school mission or student time-on-task) if they did not also incorporate some measure of school outcomes. This criterion especially shifted the focus towards studies of leader effects, as opposed to the principal's work.

Third, given the growing interest in international perspectives on school improvement, we made an effort to seek out studies that examined the effects of principals conducted outside the USA. Although we do not undertake comparative analysis in this chapter, the review included over a dozen studies conducted in countries outside of the United States including Canada, Australia, Singapore, the United Kingdom, the Netherlands, the Marshall Islands, Israel and Hong Kong (Hallinger and Heck, 1996a, 1996b).

Using these criteria, we identified 50 studies that explored the relationship between principal leadership behaviour and school performance. Twenty-eight of the studies were published in blind-refereed journals. Eight were presented as papers at peer-reviewed conferences. Eleven were dissertations. Two were book chapters and one was a synthesis of studies conducted by the author.

Avenues of leader influence

Our reviews of this literature generated a range of findings. One review focused on the methodological characteristics of this literature (Hallinger and Heck, 1996b; Heck and Hallinger, 1999). Another examined the conceptual and substantive findings (Hallinger and Heck, 1996a, 1997). Here we focus only on the substantive conclusions and refer the reader elsewhere for in-depth assessments of the methodology and conceptual features of this literature.

We constructed our findings from the review around a framework that proposes leadership as a construct that influences the attitudes and behaviour of individuals and also the organisational system in which people work (see also Leithwood, 1994; Ogawa and Bossert, 1995). We found evidence for the proposition that leadership influences the organisational system through three avenues: (1) purposes, (2) structure and social networks, (3) people.

Purposes

The leadership literature generated during this era exhorts managers in all sectors to articulate their vision, create a sense of shared mission and set clear goals for their organisations. Our review supports the belief that formulating the school's purposes represents an important leadership function. In fact, our review of the literature suggested that mission building is the strongest and most consistent avenue of influence school leaders use to influence student achievement (Hallinger and Heck, 1996a, 1997, 2002).

Despite this conclusion, lack of theoretical clarity has hindered our understanding of how school leaders shape organisational purposes to influence school effectiveness. Researchers have included a wide variety of operational measures under the heading of *goal-setting*: teachers' educational expectations, the framing of educational purposes, the principal's clarity in articulating a vision, the substance of the school's mission, consensus on goals and the principal's role in goal-setting processes (e.g. Andrews and Soder, 1987; Bamburg and Andrews, 1990; Brewer, 1993; Cheng, 1994; Goldring and Pasternak, 1994; Hallinger and Murphy, 1986; Heck et al., 1990; Leithwood, 1994; Scott and Teddlie, 1987; Silins, 1994). Researchers often use terms such as vision, mission and goals synonymously in discussions of leadership while operationalising them quite differently in empirical investigations. This lack of conceptual clarity is problematic in that the terms have different theoretical foundations and point towards alternative conceptualisations of how leaders influence school outcomes.

Vision

Personal vision refers to the values that underlie a leader's view of education. The use of the word 'vision' is not accidental. A vision enables one to *see* facets of school life that may otherwise be unclear, raising their importance above other facets. The foundation of vision is moral or spiritual in nature. For example, the use of vision in religious contexts suggests the notion of a sacred calling from within the individual. While in the USA secular education disavows formal religious practice in schools, education itself remains fundamentally a sacred craft in which we offer service to others. Education is above all else a moral enterprise (Barth, 1990; Bolman and Deal, 1992; Deal and Peterson, 1990; Fullan, 1993; Sergiovanni, 1992).

Roland Barth, among the most articulate proponents of vision as a source of inspiration for educational leadership, claims that personal visions grow out of the values we hold most dearly. He suggests several questions (Barth, 1996, personal communication) that may clarify an educator's personal vision:

- In what kind of school would you wish to teach?
- What brought you into education in the first place?
- What are the elements of the school that you would want your own children to attend?
- What would the school environment in which you would most like to work look like, feel like and sound like?
- If your school were threatened, what would be the last things that you would be willing to give up?
- On what issues would you make your last stand?

The power of a personal vision lies both in its impact on the leader's own behaviour and in its potential to energise others. A clearly formed personal vision shapes our actions, invests our work with meaning and reminds us why we are educators. When others share a personal vision, it can become a catalyst for transformation (Barth, 1990; Bolman and Deal, 1992).

Caldwell (1998) draws an explicit linkage between the personal vision of a school leader, school learning, and school improvement. He refers to a variety of data – quantitative and qualitative – suggesting the importance of vision, though he emphasises the need to use a small 'v' in referring to the concept. To support this view, Caldwell references research conducted by Johnston (1997) on 'learning focused leadership.' In the context of her case study research, Johnston described the role of vision as it was enacted in the work of a principal.

> *The principal was clearly influential but, at the same time, was regarded as a team player. She was particularly adept at demonstrating what the current reality was while exposing the school to a vision of what could be. She articulated the creative tension gap and indicated the way forward. In the process the school was infused with an energy and optimism not often seen in schools at this time. The idea that all within the school should be leaders captures the notion of leadership of teams... (Johnston, Leadership and learning in self-managing schools. Unpublished doctoral thesis. University of Melbourne, 1997)*

School mission

An *organisational mission* exists when the personal visions of a critical mass of people cohere into a common sense of purpose within a community. Like 'vision' the word 'mission' often connotes a moral purpose. The moral or spiritual character of a shared mission reaches into the hearts of people and engages them to act on behalf of something beyond their own immediate self-interest. Thus, proponents of the transformational leadership construct often talk about the leader's ability to help others find and embrace new goals individually and collectively. Note that a vision or mission is a *quest* in the sense that success does not necessarily depend upon its achievement. Its power lies in the motivational force of a *shared journey* to work towards the accomplishment of something special.

Achieving commitment to group goals, while more difficult than articulating an individual's vision, is generally viewed as a key factor in organisational effectiveness (Cuban, 1984a, 1984b; Kotter, 1996; Senge, 1990). Where a mission exists, staff will take greater responsibility for managing their own behaviour and making decisions consistent with common norms (Leithwood et al., 1998; Marks et al., 2000; Senge, 1990; Silins et al., 2000).

This type of commitment to a shared mission has been a hallmark of the school effectiveness and improvement literature of the past two decades. For the purposes of understanding school improvement, we are especially interested in how shared vision – a mission – develops and is sustained within a school community. An organisational mission may emerge from varying sources. The catalyst may be the personal vision of an individual leader (Bolman and Deal, 1992; Deal and Peterson, 1990). Alternatively, it may emerge over time out of the shared experiences and aspirations of a community of people (Barth, 1990; Fullan, 1993).

Leithwood and colleagues provide empirical support for the balancing act that leaders play in fostering a shared vision or mission:

> *This leadership dimension... [is] aimed at promoting cooperation among staff and assisting them to work together toward common goals. Although there was at least one teacher comment from every school affirming their principal's role in goal [mission] development, most of the comments simply indicated that the principal initiated the process, was a member of the goal-setting committee, or asked for input...One of the teachers in that school said, 'we all seem to want the same things...we're kind of working towards the same goals.' (Leithwood et al., 1998: 72)*

Leithwood and colleagues provided evidence of small effects of principal behaviour in this domain. They found that principal vision, group goals, high expectations, and individual support have effects on several in-school processes such as goal formulation, school culture, teachers, policy and organisation. In turn, these influence school improvement outcomes including commitment to professional change, achievement of school reform goals, policy and organisational change.

Finally, Wiley investigated the relationships among principal leadership, professional community and school improvement using multi-level modelling. Her results are of special interest because they derive from a particularly sophisticated modelling of leadership effects. She found:

> *This evidence suggests that transformational leadership with minimal professional community is influential in facilitating improvement of student achievement in mathematics in a school, while professional community is an influential factor only in combination with above average transformational leadership. (Wiley, 1998: 14)*

Wiley's analysis is interesting in two respects. First, her findings reinforce the importance of vision as a behavioural attribute of successful school leadership. Leaders who were able to articulate their vision for learning were able to contribute to learning even where the degree of professional community was not high. Second, leaders who were able to foster a shared vision via development of a professional community created a synergy that had even greater effects. The conceptual and methodological frameworks laid out in this study are good examples for other researchers in this domain.

Goals

In contrast to vision and mission, a *goal* is a functional target. An educational goal might describe the state that staff in a school wish to achieve by the end of the year in relation to student learning, attendance, graduation rates or school climate. We often define success by whether or not the school's functional goal(s) has been achieved. Unlike vision or mission, the power of a 'goal' lies not in its inspirational force, but in its ability to focus the attention of people on a limited frame of activity.

A distinction between the school effectiveness and school improvement research traditions is apparent with respect to the investigation of goals. In school effectiveness research, goals have often been operationally defined in general terms such as 'clear goals' and 'high expectations'. As noted earlier, publication of the effective schools research identified a 'clear academic mission' as a key component of school effectiveness.

Policy-makers came to view this finding as a key point of leverage for school improvement and devised ways of conveying it to school leaders through training and policies (Barth, 1990; Edmonds 1979, 1982; Honig, 1984; Purkey and Smith, 1983). Scholars and practitioners subsequently translated this work into school improvement programmes and practices that drew widespread attention and dissemination during the ensuing period (e.g. Edmonds, 1982). It is not inaccurate to say that developing a clear school mission soon became a new leadership mantra for superintendents and principals.

Notable critiques of this approach were forthcoming (e.g. Barth, 1990; Cuban, 1984a, 1984b). These critiques focused in part on the assumptions of rational organisation behaviour made by proponents of the 'goal-setting' strategy. These critics questioned whether educational organisations really met the assumptions of rational decision-making and action embedded in the goal-driven approach to improvement (Cuban, 1984a).

In contrast, school improvement research has been more focused on how schools can move toward greater productivity over time (Barth, 1990; Cuban, 1984a; Fullan, 1993; Ouston, 1999; Teddlie and Reynolds, 2000). Outcomes have been generally conceptualized more broadly, for example, as 'increased academic performance', or included perceptions such as 'teacher commitment to', 'agreement with', or 'resistance to' proposed changes. Within the British context, a debate ensued over the 'possible' goals of education against the limited 'official' goals as part of the process of implementing improvement (Teddlie and Reynolds, 2000).

As Ouston (1999) argued, there was no reason for the theory and practice of changing and improving schools to be related to the research on school effectiveness – in fact, many theories of change were built on quite different foundations. Where the effectiveness literature emphasised 'clear mission' and 'clearly-defined goals', the school improvement literature also included the importance of vision, school culture, leadership and pedagogy. These were examined in somewhat different ways, however. In the school improvement literature, greater emphasis was placed on how school leaders facilitated staff planning, goal setting and self-evaluation. Unfortunately, there have been few attempts to develop a dynamic model of school processes that might indicate how improvement would be accomplished within differing school contexts. Moreover, the focus was often the school, despite knowledge of the importance of classroom effects and the need to change teacher practices (Marks et al., 2000; Teddlie and Reynolds, 2000).

In sum, vision, mission building and goal-setting take on different emphases in the practice of school leadership. By way of illustration, we are reminded of Roland Barth's (1986) observation that educators do not jump eagerly out of bed at 6:00 a.m. and rush off to school because they wish to raise scores on achievement tests. Engaging in a shared quest to accomplish something special motivates educators. Yet, school improvement policy frequently mandates that principals engage in goal-setting exercises in the belief that research supports this prescription (Barth, 1986; Cuban, 1988).

Despite the *potential impact* of this leadership function, there remains considerable ambiguity in how leaders shape the school's purposes to foster student learning. At this point in time, we are confident that this avenue is important. However, scholars should view this conclusion as a solid starting point for further elaboration rather than a practical prescription.

Structure and social networks

A second avenue of leadership influence involves the interplay between organisational structures and social networks in and around the school. Ogawa and Bossert (1995) define social structures and networks as the regularised aspects of relationships existing among participants in an organisation. School structures are many and varied. Primary schools now often operate with grade-level teams, cross-grade teams and school management councils, producing new roles and responsibilities. Secondary schools have traditionally operated with academic departments and more varied structures. Principals play a key role by organising these structures proactively in order to achieve the school's mission. It is the principal's role to *make the structures work on behalf of the students*.

Social networks are equally important in leading the school towards its goals. The principal must access the social network of the school in order to gain important information, to communicate values as well as information and to gain support for the school's vision and strategies. The social network is also a source of additional leaders who can help move the school forward.

Empirical evidence from our review supports this view of leadership. For example, Leithwood (1994) found that the principal's leadership shapes three distinct psychological dispositions of teachers: their perceptions of various school characteristics, their commitment to school change and their capacity for professional development. Weil and colleagues (1984) found that principal support of teachers and a proactive stance on problem-solving differentiated leadership in effective versus typical elementary (primary) schools. Leithwood and colleagues and also Silins (1994) determined that leadership which provides individualised support and challenging work, and which fosters a shared mission in the school, contributes to successful school improvement.

Studies across several national contexts found that greater involvement from stakeholders in decision-making is characteristic of higher producing schools. For example, Heck (1993) found that collaborative decision-making and more flexible rule structures were associated with higher achieving secondary schools in Singapore. Cheng (1994) concluded that strong primary school principal leaders in Hong Kong schools tended to promote participation in decision-making. This resulted in stronger and more cohesive social interactions, greater staff commitment and higher morale. In a Canadian study, Leithwood (1994) reported greater implementation of school improvement outcomes where there was greater collaboration in decision-making.

A recent trend towards viewing the school as a learning organisation represents a noteworthy approach to invigorating structure and social networks with educational content. The principal's role in a learning organisation involves creating structures that facilitate communication and collaboration among staff around the school's valued purposes. This conceptualisation suggests a different set of intervening variables linking leadership to school effectiveness than predominated during the effective schools era. These include but are not limited to a shared mission, teacher participation in decision-making, scheduling, use of teaming, principal stimulation of staff learning, patterns of collaboration and team learning (see Leithwood et al., 1998).

People

Several frameworks (e.g. Bossert et al., 1982; Bridges, 1977; Leithwood, 1994; Ogawa and Bossert, 1995) propose that administrative activity is largely directed at influencing people in the school organisation. Evidence accumulated from the past twenty years of research on educational leadership provides considerable support concerning this domain of principal leadership.

For example, Leithwood (1994) highlights 'people effects' as a cornerstone of the transformational leadership model. More specifically, Leithwood's (1994) empirical investigation found that principal effects are achieved through fostering group goals, modelling desired behaviour for others, providing intellectual stimulation and individualised support (towards personal and staff development, for example). With respect to outcomes, leadership had an influence on teachers' perceptions of progress with implementing reform initiatives and teachers' perceptions of increases in student outcomes.

Other studies using an instructional leadership model also provide support for principal effects on people as a means to affect outcomes. Heck and colleagues (1990) found that principals in higher producing schools spent more time in direct classroom supervision and support of teachers. At both the primary and secondary levels, they also gave greater attention to working with teachers to coordinate the school's instructional programme, solving instructional problems collaboratively, helping teachers secure resources and creating opportunities for in-service and staff development.

These conclusions reinforce the image of school leadership as a *people-oriented* activity. Strategy, planning and resource management are important facets of the educational manager's role. Yet, in the end, leadership involves working with and through people (Bridges, 1977; Cuban, 1988). Researchers have begun to identify the means by which school leaders put this into practice to foster high-quality learning environments.

The context of school leadership

The assumption that leadership makes a difference is supported by our review. Yet scholars have also noted that leaders operate in different contexts and that these contexts place constraints on leadership behaviour (see Bridges, 1977, 1982; Cuban, 1988; Rowan et al., 1982). While researchers have only begun to include context variables in their empirical models, this is an area that demands greater attention. Initial findings reinforce the hypothesis that a variety of school context factors shape the particular needs for leadership that may exist within a school. Moreover, it appears that the ability to provide leadership that is suited to a particular school context carries over to effects on students.

The school as a context for school leadership

Despite a range of conceptual and methodological problems in incorporating context variables into studies of leadership effects, we discerned an interesting trend among the studies. Socio-economic factors (SES) in the school and community appear to influence principal leadership and its impact on school effectiveness (e.g. Andrews and Soder, 1987; Hallinger and Murphy, 1986; Rowan and Denk, 1984). For example, Andrews and Soder (1987) reported that principal leadership affected reading and mathematics outcomes in elementary schools. When controlling for SES and ethnicity, however, the effects of principal leadership on reading and mathematics outcomes tended to disappear in high SES or predominately Caucasian elementary schools. They remained significant in predominately African-American or low SES schools. This supported their hypothesis of context effects on principal leadership.

Hallinger and Murphy (1986) found that community SES affected how elementary school principals perceived their work. For example, they worked quite differently in defining the school mission in low and high SES effective schools. In low SES schools, principals stressed the mastery of basic skills and did appear to define clear school-wide goal-targets for instruction. They allocated more time to basic skills instruction and built fairly elaborate systems of rewards and recognition for student success. Moreover, principals in low SES schools tended to define their leadership role more narrowly in terms of curriculum coordination, control of instruction and task orientation.

In contrast, principals in high SES effective schools focused more on using mission as a motivational force. Interviews with staff confirmed widespread understanding of the school's mission – their shared values and the school's direction. Yet, in several cases these principals did not even define specific measurable goals for their schools (Hallinger and Murphy, 1986).

This research was unable to untangle whether differences in the use of mission and goals were related to SES or to the life cycle of improvement. It is possible that the low SES effective schools had been in a 'turn-around' phase and goals were used to focus staff attention. In contrast, the high SES effective schools may have passed onto a more mature phase in which the culture of the school was carrying the behaviours that contributed to effectiveness.

Scott and Teddlie (1987) identified a link between SES and elementary school principals' expectations. Principals' expectations, in turn, affected their sense of responsibility. However, Scott and Teddlie determined that principal responsibility was not directly related to outcomes. Although untested by Scott and Teddlie, we noted a possible *indirect* effect (likely to be statistically significant) of principal expectations on school outcomes through principal responsibility.

Contextual influences were also found to impact upon principal behaviour with respect to structures and social networks. For example, Hallinger and Murphy (1986) found that school linkages to the home and parent involvement were weaker in low SES effective schools. In contrast, linkages to the home and parent involvement were strong and pervasive in high SES schools. In the lower SES schools, principals acted as buffers, controlling access to the school and protecting the school's programme from outside influences that might dilute its effectiveness. In higher SES schools, the principal acted as a boundary spanner, constantly seeking ways to involve community members who had a great interest and stake in the school's operation. These findings hint at the relationship between wider community context, the corresponding school culture and the role of the principal. The different extent of contact between school staff and community is important because teacher and administrator attitudes appear to be shaped by expectations and beliefs of the wider community (e.g. Hallinger and Murphy, 1986; Ogawa and Bossert, 1995).

Cheng (1994) noted that other contextual factors (e.g. school size, teacher background) were not generally found to exert any important influence over principal leadership in secondary school settings. Heck (1992) found differences in principal discussion of instructional issues and problems and discussion about how instructional techniques impact on student achievement to be similar across school level, with principals in both effective elementary and high (secondary) schools more involved with these variables than their counterparts at low-achieving schools. There is an interaction with level, however, with principals in effective elementary schools more heavily involved than principals in effective high schools. Heck (1992) also noted that principals in elementary schools (controlling for effectiveness) spend more time attempting to communicate goals to teachers and others than principals in secondary schools.

Again, research in this domain has barely begun to identify patterns of effective leadership. It is only with the recent advent of better statistical tools that researchers are able empirically to study comprehensive models that incorporate context variables along with leadership and school outcomes

(Hallinger and Heck, 1996b). We would encourage the conduct of mixed-methods studies as qualitative data have the potential to tease out important patterns identified in quantitative research (Heck and Hallinger, 1999).

The cultural context of school leadership

Another feature of context that begs for systematic investigation is the cultural context in which leaders act. It is possible – even likely – that differences in the social construction of the leadership role differ across societies (Hofstede, 1980). As Getzels and colleagues (1968) theorised and researchers outside educational administration have empirically investigated, organisational culture is only a portion of a broader social culture (Brislin, 1993; Hofstede, 1980; Ralston et al., 1991). The broader societal culture exerts an influence on administrators beyond the influence exerted by a specific organisation's culture (Getzels et al., 1968; Gerstner and Day, 1994; Hofstede, 1976, 1980). Surprisingly, scholars in educational administration have devoted little effort towards uncovering the cultural foundations of leadership when used in this broader sense (Bajunid, 1996; Cheng, 1995; Dimmock and Walker, 1998; Hallinger, 1995; Hallinger and Heck, 1996b; Heck and Hallinger, 1999).

Gerstner and Day (1994: 123) assert: 'Because leadership is a cultural phenomenon, inextricably linked to the values and customs of a group of people, we do not expect differences in leadership prototypes to be completely random. Rather they should be linked to dimensions of national culture.' Their own cross-cultural research in the business sector found significant differences in how different nationalities perceive the traits of leadership. Additional analyses found that these perceptual differences were also significant when countries were grouped as reflecting an eastern or western culture. Unfortunately, less empirical data is available concerning the impact of culture on the behaviour, as opposed to the perceptions, of leaders.

Culture is the source of values that people share in a society. As such, culture can be viewed as having effects on multiple features of the school and its environment. Culture shapes the institutional and community context within which the school is situated by defining predominant value orientations and norms of behaviour (Getzels et al., 1968). It influences the predilections of individual leaders as well as the nature of interactions with others in the school and its community. Moreover, it determines the particular educational emphasis or goals that prevail within a culture's system of schooling. Since cultural values vary across nations, we would expect cross-cultural variation in the educational goals of societies as well as the normative practices aimed towards their achievement (Getzels et al., 1968).

Current conceptualisations of administrative practice represent a useful point of departure for better understanding the relationships between leadership and societal culture. Frameworks such those proposed by Bossert and colleagues (1982) point to important antecedents of leadership – variables that shape the needs and requirements of leadership within the organisation – as well as paths by which leaders may achieve an impact on the organisation.

What remains is to make the social culture explicit in such frameworks in order to explore its impact on the social and institutional system in which leadership is exercised. Theoretical work in educational administration (e.g. Getzels et al., 1968; Cheng, 1995; Cheng and Wong, 1996) and research in the general leadership literature provide useful direction in this quest (e.g. Brislin, 1993; Hofstede, 1976, 1980).

Given the general trends of globalisation and broader, faster access to information, we expect that investigations of the nature of leadership across cultures will assume a central place in the research community in the coming decade. Investigations of the cultural context of schooling and the subsequent roles played by leaders at different organisational levels (such as district administrators, principals, senior teachers) represent a rich vein for future exploration (Bajunid, 1996; Cheng, 1995; Cheng and Wong, 1996; Hallinger, 1995; Hallinger and Leithwood, 1996; Heck, 1996; Wong, 1996).

The trend towards globalization makes it even more critical that we ground future leadership development efforts in a 'knowledge base' that is not only relevant to global trends in educational development but also grounded in the norms of local cultures (Bajunid, 1996; Cheng, 1995; Hallinger and Leithwood, 1998).

Future directions for research in educational leadership and management

Research conducted over the past two decades answers the question *'can leadership enhance school effectiveness?'* in the affirmative. Over the two decades since the advent of school effectiveness research, scholarship has benefited from improvements in the application of both theory and methodology. Consequently, we have increasing confidence in the belief that school leaders – especially principals – do make a difference in schooling outcomes.

While our review supports the belief that principal leadership influences school effectiveness, we temper this conclusion in two important respects. First, school leaders achieve effects on their schools *indirectly*. Skilful school leaders influence school and classroom processes that have a *direct* impact on student learning. Second, school leaders themselves are subject to considerable influence via the norms and characteristics of the school and its environment.

The fact that leadership effects on school achievement appear to be indirect is cause for neither alarm nor dismay. As noted previously, achieving results through others is the essence of leadership. A finding that principal effects are mediated by other in-school variables does nothing whatsoever to diminish the principal's importance. Understanding the routes by which principals can improve school outcomes through working with others is itself a worthy goal for research. Most importantly with respect to this point, the res these effects appear to *compound* as principals pursue school-

The fact that the effects noted in these studies remain s concern. In the words of Ogawa and Hart (1985: 65):

[The study's] most important finding was that the principal variable accounted for between 2 and 8 percent of the variance in test scores. While such figures may seem small, there are at least two reasons they should not be dismissed as unimportant...findings of research on school effectiveness suggest that even small proportions of variance are important. Jencks and his associates demonstrate that only about 15 percent of the total variance in student achievement is attributable to between school differences. Further, Rowan and his associates conclude that about 5 percent of the total variance in student achievement can be attributed to stable state-level properties. In light of these results, the discovery that 2–8 percent of variance in student performance is attributable to principals takes on a glow of relative importance.

Thus, although the findings reinforce the notion that leadership makes an important difference in school effectiveness, they do not support the image of the heroic school leader. School leaders do not *make* effective schools. Rather the image we draw from this review is that of leaders who are able to work with and through the staff to shape a school culture that is focused yet adaptable. They work with staff to foster development of a school culture in which staff find meaning in their work and are motivated to learn and solve problems with a greater degree of collaboration than typifies many schools.

Our satisfaction of seeing significant progress towards answering a potentially important question for policy and practice is moderated, however, by continuing limitations in this knowledge base. Persisting blind spots and blank spots (Heck and Hallinger, 1999) in the research base form the basis for our identification of priorities in this field.

1 *Untangle the conceptual confusion concerning how school leaders employ vision, mission, and goals to influence school effectiveness.*

Both the frequency with which vision/mission/goals appeared as a significant intervening variable and the general popularity of this construct among scholars and practitioners suggest that it ought to receive high priority in the next phase of investigation. Attacking this problem will require researchers to link their conceptual and operational definitions of variables more clearly. For example, researchers have at times operationalised vision and mission as functional goal targets. The absence of clarity in language has led to confusion in interpretation of results.

Scholars must also extend this research by clearly explicating *in advance* of investigation the theoretical rationale for relationships among variables. We found a tendency among researchers to offer a framework of commonly used variables (for example mission, teacher expectations, principal supervision), without fully elaborating on how and why these variables would interact to result in the proposed effects (see Rowan and Denk, 1984; Weil et al., 1984; Wiley, 1998 as worthy exceptions to this tendency). For example, if vision is part of a model of leadership effects, *how* would the researcher expect leaders to employ vision and *why* would this interaction be likely to influence other variables in the model?

2 *Broaden investigation of school leadership and its effects beyond the principalship.*

The notion of distributed leadership is not only theoretically attractive, but also potentially powerful in practice. The past decade witnessed a normative shift away from the dominant leader and towards an egalitarian model of leadership. Yet the fact remains that school principals occupy a position of significance in the structural hierarchy of schools.

In the year 2002 it is as foolish to think that *only* principals provide leadership for school improvement as to believe that principals *do not* influence school effectiveness. Unfortunately, whether out of inconvenience or conceptual ambiguity, few researchers have undertaken empirical investigation of alternative sources of leadership in educational management. With some notable exceptions, rhetoric, prescription and advocacy continue to dominate discussions of distributed leadership in schools (see Leithwood et al., 1998). Concerted effort is needed to define and investigate leadership more broadly while simultaneously maintaining a focus on leadership that emanates from the principal's office.

3 *Incorporate the construct of the school as a learning organisation into explorations of school leadership and its effects.*

The bulk of published research in our review was theoretically grounded in the school effectiveness research (e.g. Andrews and Soder, 1987; Cheng, 1994; Heck et al., 1991), reflecting the general popularity of this framework during the 1980s and 1990s. Although it remains a useful heuristic, scholars in educational management would benefit from expanding their approach to conceptualising and studying school leadership effects.

We believe in the potential efficacy of the learning organisation construct for research in this domain. It is notable that the main avenues of leader influence identified in this review – shared mission, structure and social networks, people – are hallmark components of the learning organisation (Senge, 1990). These represent a complementary perspective for viewing the manner by which leaders contribute to school effectiveness. Use of this construct in empirical research is already evident in the work of Leithwood and colleagues (1997) and appears worthy of a wider effort.

4 *Study leadership in its cultural context with an intention to explicate the influence of cultural norms on the conceptualisation and exercise of leadership.*

While the studies included in our review were conducted in numerous different countries, none was conducted with a specific eye towards the influence of that nation's culture. In each case, culture was an assumed background variable; in effect, it was 'held constant'.

There is much to learn through explicit attention to the exploration of leadership within its *cultural* context. Theoretical and practical advances in the field will derive from two sources. First, the ready dissemination of knowledge and educational policies internationally makes it imperative to understand how local culture reshapes globally popularised policies and practices (Cheng,

1995; Hallinger, 1995; Hallinger and Leithwood, 1998; Heck, 1996). For example, the means by which leaders share decision-making, provide instructional leadership, articulate a vision and set goals may well differ across cultures. These differences have practical implications for achieving school effectiveness (see Cheng and Wong, 1996).

Second, differences in cultural construction of leadership that researchers may identify in practice will have acute implications for theory. To date, the international knowledge base in educational management reflects a severely limited set of conceptions grounded in Judeo-Christian notions of human motivation (Bajunid, 1996; Cheng, 1994). The field will benefit from further development of this perspective via exploration of this potentially rich vein.

These directions by no means represent the only ones suggested by this research. They do, however, represent priority directions by virtue of their theoretical and practical significance. It is this intersection of theoretical and practical concerns that will continue to make research in this domain exciting in the coming decade.

References

Andrews, R. and Soder, R. (1987) 'Principal instructional leadership and school achievement', *Educational Leadership*, 44: 9–11.

Bajunid, I. A. (1996) 'Preliminary explorations of indigenous perspectives of educational management: the evolving Malaysian experience', *Journal of Educational Administration*, 34 (5): 50–73.

Bamburg, J. and Andrews, R. (1990) 'School goals, principals and achievement', *School Effectiveness and School Improvement*, 2 (3): 175–91.

Barth, R. (1986) 'On sheep and goats and school reform', *Phi Delta Kappan*, 68 (4): 293–6.

Barth, R. (1990) *Improving Schools from Within*. San Francisco: Jossey-Bass.

Bolman, L. and Deal, T. (1992) *Reframing Organizations*. San Francisco: Jossey-Bass.

Bossert, S., Dwyer, D., Rowan, B. and Lee, G. (1982). 'The instructional management role of the principal', *Educational Administration Quarterly*, 18 (3): 34–64.

Brewer, D. (1993) 'Principals and student outcomes: evidence from US high schools', *Economics of Education Review*, 12 (4): 281–92.

Bridges, E. (1977) 'The nature of leadership', in L. Cunningham and R. Nystrand (eds), *Educational Administration: The Developing Decades*. Berkeley, CA: McCutchan.

Bridges, E. (1982) 'Research on the school administrator: the state-of-the-art, 1967–1980', *Educational Administration Quarterly*, 18 (3): 12–33.

Brislin, R. (1993) *Understanding Culture's Influence on Behaviour*. New York: Harcourt Brace.

Caldwell, B. (1998) 'Strategic leadership, resource management and effective school reform', *Journal of Educational Administration*, 36 (5): 445–61.

Cheng, K. M. (1995) 'The neglected dimension: cultural comparison in educational administration', in K. C. Wong and K. M. Cheng (eds), *Educational Leadership and Change: An International Perspective*. Hong Kong: Hong Kong University Press.

Cheng, K. M. and Wong, K. C. (1996) 'School effectiveness in east Asia: concepts, origins and implications', *Journal of Educational Administration*, 34 (5): 32–49

Cheng, Y. C. (1994) 'Principal's leadership as a critical factor for school performance: evidence from multilevels of primary schools', *School Effectiveness and School Improvement*, 5 (3): 299–317.

Cuban, L. (1984a,) 'The sham of school reform: sleight of hand with numbers', *San Jose Mercury*, 1c, 2c, 24 April.

Cuban, L. (1984b) 'Transforming the frog into a prince: effective schools research, policy, and practice at the district level', *Harvard Educational Review*, 54: 129–51.

Cuban. L. (1988) *The Managerial Imperative and the Practice of Leadership in Schools*. Albany, NY: SUNY Press.

Deal, T. and Peterson, K. (1990) *The Principal's Role in Shaping School Culture*. Washington, DC: US Government Printing Office.

Dimmock, C. and Walker, A. (1998) 'Transforming Hong Kong's schools: trends and emerging issues', *Journal of Educational Administration*, 36 (5): 476–91.

Edmonds, R. (1979) 'Effective schools for the urban poor', *Educational Leadership*, 37, 15–24.

Edmonds, R. (1982) 'Programs of school improvement: an overview', *Educational Leadership*, 40, 4–11.

Fullan, M. (1993) *Change Forces: Probing the Depths of Educational Reform*. New York: Teachers College Press.

Gerstner, C. and Day, D. (1994) *Leadership Quarterly*, 5 (2): 121–34.

Getzels, J., Lipham, J. and Campbell, R. (1968) *Educational Administration as a Social Process*. New York: Harper and Row.

Goldring, E. and Pasternak, R. (1994) 'Principals' coordinating strategies and school effectiveness', *School Effectiveness and School Improvement*, 5 (3): 239–53.

Hallinger, P. (1995) 'Culture and leadership: developing an international perspective in educational administration', *UCEA Review*, 36 (1): 3–7.

Hallinger, P. (2001) *A review of studies of principal leadership using the Principal Instructional Management Rating Scale*, paper presented at the annual meeting of the American Educational Research Association, Seattle, WA.

Hallinger, P. and Heck, R. (1996a) 'Reassessing the principal's role in school effectiveness: a review of empirical research, 1980–1995', *Educational Administration Quarterly*, 32 (1): 5–44.

Hallinger, P. and Heck, R. (1996b) 'The principal's role in school effectiveness: a review of methodological issues, 1980–95', in K. Leithwood, J. Chapman, D. Corson, P. Hallinger and A. Hart (eds), *International Handbook of Educational Leadership and Administration*. Dordrecht: Kluwer.

Hallinger, P. and Heck, R. (1997) 'Exploring the principal's contribution to school effectiveness', *School Effectiveness and School Improvement*, 8 (4): 1–35.

Hallinger, P. and Heck, P. (1999) 'Can leadership enhance school effectiveness?', in T. Bush, R. Glatter, R. Bolam, P. Ribbins, and L. Bell (eds), *Redefining Educational Management*. London: Paul Chapman/Sage.

Hallinger, P. and Heck, R. (2002) 'What do you call people with visions? The role of vision, mission and goals in school leadership and improvement', in K. Leithwood, P. Hallinger, G. Furman, P. Gronn, J. MacBeath, B. Mulford and K. Riley, *International Handbook of Educational Leadership and Administration*, (2nd edn). Dordrecht: Kluwer.

Hallinger, P. and Kantamara, P. (2001) 'Learning to lead global changes across cultures: designing a computer-based simulation for Thai school leaders', *Journal of Educational Administration*, 39 (3): 197–220.

Hallinger, P. and Leithwood, K. (1994). 'Exploring the impact of principal leadership', *School Effectiveness and School Improvement*, 5 (3): 206–18.

Hallinger, P. and Leithwood, K. (1998) 'Unseen forces: the impact of social culture on leadership', *Peabody Journal of Education*, 73 (2): 126–51.

Hallinger, P. and Murphy, J. (1986) 'The social context of effective schools', *American Journal of Education*, 94 (3): 328–55.

Hallinger, P., Bickman, L. and Davis, K. (1996) 'School context, principal leadership and student achievement', *Elementary School Journal*, 96 (5): 321–44.

Heck, R. (1992) 'Principal instructional leadership and the identification of high- and low-achieving schools: the application of discriminant techniques', *Administrator's Notebook*, 34 (7): 1–4.

Heck, R. (1993) 'School context, principal leadership, and achievement: the case of secondary schools in Singapore', *Urban Review*, 25 (2): 151–66.

Heck, R. (1996) 'Leadership and culture: conceptual and methodological issues in comparing models across cultural settings', *Journal of Educational Administration*, 30 (3): 35–48.

Heck, R. and Hallinger, P. (1999) 'Conceptual models, methodology, and methods to study school leadership', in J. Murphy and K. S. Louis (eds), *The Second Handbook of Research on Educational Administration*. New York: Longman.

Heck, R. and Marcoulides, G. (1996a) 'School culture and performance: testing the invariance of an organizational model', *School Effectiveness and School Improvement*, 7 (1): 76–95.

Heck, R. and Marcoulides, G. (1996b) 'The assessment of principal performance: a multilevel approach', *Journal of Personnel Evaluation in Education*, 10 (1): 11–28.

Heck, R., Larsen, T. and Marcoulides, G. (1990) 'Principal instructional leadership and school achievement: validation of a causal model', *Educational Administration Quarterly*, 26, 94–125.

Heck, R., Marcoulides, G. and Lang, P. (1991) 'Principal instructional leadership and school achievement: the application of discriminant techniques', *School Effectiveness and School Improvement*, 2 (2): 115–35.

Hofstede, G. (1976) 'Nationality and espoused values of managers', *Journal of Applied Psychology*, 61 (2): 148–55.

Hofstede, G. (1980) *Culture's Consequences: International Differences in Work-Related Values*. Newbury Park, CA: Sage.

Honig, B. (1984) 'School reform is working: what's wrong with goal setting and measurement?', *San Jose Mercury*, 1c, 2c, 6 May.

Kotter, J. (1996) *Leading Change*. Boston: Harvard Business School Press.

Leithwood, K. (1994) 'Leadership for school restructuring', *Educational Administration Quarterly*, 30 (4): 498–518.

Leithwood, K. and Hallinger, P. (1993) 'Cognitive perspectives on educational administration: an introduction', *Educational Administration Quarterly*, 24 (3): 296–301.

Leithwood, K. and Jantzi, D. (1990) 'Transformational leadership: how principals can help reform school cultures', *School Effectiveness and School Improvement*, 1 (1): 249–80.

Leithwood, K. and Montgomery, D. (1982) 'The role of the elementary principal in program improvement', *Review of Educational Research*, 52 (3): 309–39.

Leithwood, K., Leonard, L. and Sharratt, L. (1997) *Conditions fostering organizational learning in schools*, paper presented at the annual meeting of the International Congress on School Effectiveness and Improvement, Memphis, TN.

Leithwood, K., Jantzi, D., Ryan, S. and Steinbach, R. (1998) *Distributed leadership and student engagement in school*, paper presented at the annual meeting of the American Educational Research Association, San Diego.

Marks, H., Seashore Louis, K. and Printy, S. (2000) 'The capacity for organizational learning: implications for pedagogical quality and student achievement', in K. Leithwood (ed.), *Understanding Schools as Intelligent Systems*. Stamford, CT: JAI Press.

Miskel, C. (1982) 'An analysis of principal effects'. Unpublished speech to the National Graduate Student Seminar in Educational Administration, Princeton, New Jersey.

Murphy, J., Hallinger, P. and Mitman, A. (1983) 'Research on educational leadership: issues to be addressed', *Educational Evaluation and Policy Analysis*, 5 (3): 297–305.

Ogawa, R. and Bossert, S. (1995) 'Leadership as an organizational quality', *Educational Administration Quarterly*, 31 (2): 224–43.

Ogawa, R. and Hart, A. (1985) 'The effect of principals on the instructional performance of schools', *Journal of Educational Administration*, 22 (1): 59–72.

Ouston, J. (1999) 'School effectiveness and school improvement: critique of a movement', in T. Bush, R. Glatter, R. Bolam, P. Ribbins and L. Bell (eds), *Redefining Educational Management*. London: Paul Chapman/Sage.

Purkey, S. and Smith, M. (1983) 'Effective schools – a review', *Elementary School Journal*, 83, 426–52.

Ralston, D., Elissa, P., Gustafson, D. and Cheung, F. (1991) 'Eastern values: a comparison of managers in the United States, Hong Kong, and the People's Republic of China', *Journal of Applied Psychology*, 77 (5): 664-71.

Rowan, B. and Denk, C. (1984) 'Management succession, school socio-economic context and basic skills achievement', *American Educational Research Journal*, 21 (3): 517–37.

Rowan, B., Dwyer, D. and Bossert, S. (1982) *Methodological considerations in the study of effective principals*, paper presented at the Annual Meeting of the American Educational Research Association, New York.

Rowan, B., Raudenbush, S. and Kang, S. (1991) 'Organizational design in high schools: a multilevel analysis', *American Journal of Education*, 99 (2): 238–66.

Scott, C. and Teddlie, C. (1987) *Student, teacher, and principal academic expectations and attributed responsibility as predictors of student achievement: a causal modeling approach*, paper presented at the Annual Meeting of the American Educational Research Association, Washington, DC.

Senge, P. (1990) *The Fifth Discipline*. New York: Doubleday.

Sergiovanni, T. (1992) *Moral Leadership: Getting to the Heart of School Improvement*. San Francisco: Jossey Bass.

Sheppard, B. and Brown, J. (2000) 'The transformation of secondary schools into learning organizations', in K. Leithwood (ed.), *Understanding Schools as Intelligent Systems*. Stamford, CT: JAI Press.

Silins, H. (1994) 'The relationship between transformational and transactional leadership and school improvement outcomes', *School Effectiveness and School Improvement*, 5 (3): 272–98.

Silins, H., Mulford, B., Zarins, S. and Bishop, P. (2000) 'Leadership for organizational learning in Australian schools', in K. Leithwood (ed.), *Understanding Schools as Intelligent Systems*. Stamford, CT: JAI Press.

Sirois, H. and Villanova, R. (1982) *Theory into practice: a theoretical and research base for the characteristics of effective schools*, paper presented at the annual meeting of the American Educational Research Association, New York.

Teddlie, C. and Reynolds, D. (eds) (2000) *The International Handbook of School Effectiveness Research*. London: Falmer Press.

van de Grift, W. (1987) 'Zelfpercepties van onderwijskundig leiderschap', in F. J. Van der Krogt (ed.), *Schoolleiding en Management*. Lisse: Swets & Zeitlinger.

van de Grift, W. (1989) 'Self perceptions of educational leadership and mean pupil achievements', in D. Reynolds, B. Creemers and T. Peters (eds), *School Effectiveness and Improvement*, Cardiff/Groningen: School of Education/RION.

van de Grift, W. (1990) 'Educational leadership and academic achievement in elementary education', *School Effectiveness and School Improvement*, 1 (3): 26–40.

Weil, M., Marshalek, B., Mitman, A., Murphy, J., Hallinger, P. and Pruyn, J. (1984) *Effective and typical schools: how different are they?*, paper presented at the annual meeting of the American Educational Research Association, Chicago.

Wiley, S. (1998) *Contextual effects on student achievement: school leadership and professional community*, paper presented at the annual meeting of the American Sociological Association.

Wong, K. C. (1996) *Developing the moral dimensions of school leaders*, invited paper presented at the meeting of the APEC Educational Leadership Centers, Chiang Mai, Thailand.

Appendix 1

Useful sources of guidance

The following books are sources of guidance on reviewing literature and other aspects of research relevant to conducting a small-scale investigation. The annotated list is by no means comprehensive: there are numerous other books that address specific methodologies and approaches. However, these texts are a useful starting point for doctoral and masters projects.

Bell, J. (1999) *Doing Your Research Project: A Guide for First-Time Researchers in Education and Social Science*, 3rd edn. Buckingham: Open University Press.
This book has become a well-known text for first-time researchers in education. It serves as a guide to practice for the novice researcher embarking on masters or doctoral study. It takes a step-by-step approach to the research process and the writing up and presentation of a project. There are plentiful examples of research practice and also helpful checklists to help readers monitor the progress of their projects.

Black, T. (2001) *Understanding Social Science Research*, 2nd edn. London: Sage.
The book aims to help students to evaluate research and is clear and straightforward. It is more strongly focused on measurement than other methodologies and research designs.

Blaxter, L., Hughes, C. and Tight, M. (2001) *How to Research*. Buckingham: Open University Press.
This is a new edition of a book that many masters and doctoral students have found useful. It is primarily about the practice and experience of doing small-scale research in social science. There are sections on using Internet sources for literature searches and for other aspects of the research process.

Cohen, L., Manion, L. and Morrison, K. (2000) *Research Methods in Education*, 5th edn. London: Routledge.
Something of a classic among the research methodology textbooks in education, this book is comprehensive, covering a wide range of approaches to research. It is also accessible and a useful introductory text for masters and doctoral students.

Coleman, M. and Briggs, A.J. (eds) (2002) *Research Methods in Educational Leadership and Management*. London: Paul Chapman.

>   A comprehensive and accessible guide to researching educational management and leadership aimed at relatively inexperienced researchers. There are chapters by a range of well-known people in the field that address topics such as designing a project, reliability and validity, ethics, research methods and instruments, analysing data and presentation.

Denscomb, M. (1997) *The Good Research Guide*. Buckingham: Open University Press.

>   Aimed at those undertaking small-scale research projects, the book provides a pragmatic approach to the research process. It aims to help readers with limited time to conduct a rigorous small-scale project, highlighting aspects of good research practice and offering checklists for monitoring research. There is also a companion volume: Denscomb, M. (2002) *Ground Rules for Good Research*. Buckingham: Open University Press.

Fink, A. (1998) *Conducting Research Literature Reviews*. London: Sage.

>   A guide to the process of searching and reviewing research literature, this book examines not only the practicalities of literature review, but also how to become a critical reader of research reports. It addresses issues such as research design and sampling strategy, and also data collection, analysis and presentation.

Gorard, S. (2001) *Quantitative Methods in Educational Research: The Role of Numbers Made Easy*. London: Continuum.

>   This book provides an excellent introduction to research involving numbers. It is very readable and clear. The author presents examples from his own and other work. There are useful chapters on designing a study, using data from existing sources and on sampling techniques. A helpful appendix lists sources of statistical and numerical data. Strongly recommended for anyone considering doing a study involving survey, experimental or multi-method designs.

Hart, C. (1998) *Doing a Literature Review: Releasing the Social Science Imagination*. London: Sage.

>   A thorough examination of the process of reviewing literature. The book makes connections between the literature review in a masters or doctoral study and methodology and research design. It addresses the principles underpinning any literature review and there is a useful chapter on how to analyse ideas and undertake argumentation analysis. In addition, it covers practical aspects of reviewing literature, such as searching bibliographic databases, and contains a chapter on writing. Examples are taken from a range of sources in social science, and the book is clear and readable. There is now also a companion volume specifically addressing literature searches: Hart, C. (2001) *Doing a Literature Search*. London: Sage

Knight, P. T. (2001) *Small-Scale Research*. London: Sage.

>   Very much focused on the needs of a graduate student readership, this book is a guide to conducting small-scale research projects for theses or dissertations. It presents systematically the main modes of enquiry and considers the main strengths and limitations of different approaches. Understanding that small-scale researchers are often short on time and resources, it gives pragmatic practical advice.

Miles, M. and Huberman, M. (1994) *Qualitative Data Analysis: An Expanded Sourcebook*. Thousand Oaks, CA: Sage.
> A classic text on qualitative research approaches. The book is practical and comprehensive – going far beyond data analysis. There are excellent sections on research design, sampling, data reduction, coding and display for qualitative studies. Strongly recommended for anyone considering a study with a qualitative element.

Potter, S. (ed.) (2002) *Doing Postgraduate Research*. London: Sage.
> This book aims to help make the research process as explicit and clear as possible. It addresses the increasing importance of formal research training for graduate students. Taking a practical approach, it provides examples and material to help students develop a range of research skills.

Punch, K. (1998) *An Introduction to Social Research*. London: Sage.
> A comprehensive introduction to both qualitative and quantitative methodologies. It is good on research design, and is very clearly written and presented with good examples of different kinds of research. An excellent all-rounder. There is also a companion volume: Punch, K. (2000) *Developing Effective Research Proposals*. London: Sage. It addresses all aspects of designing a research proposal, and would be useful for planning masters or doctoral research.

Rudestam, K. and Newton, R. (2001) *Surviving your Dissertation: A Comprehensive Guide to Content and Process*, 2nd edn. London: Sage.
> This book covers all dimensions of writing a dissertation or thesis: from choosing a topic and defining research questions through to writing up. A useful section deals with the process of moving from a topic to specifying research questions, something that many masters and doctoral students find quite challenging. Students outside the USA might find the terminology associated with the supervision process a little strange, but otherwise a useful guide to the research and writing process.

Walliman, N. (2000) Your Research Project: *A Step-by-Step Guide for the First-time Researcher*. London: Sage.
> A helpful guide to planning, designing and structuring a research enquiry from the very first stages onwards, which also aims to develop the necessary research skills to conduct a project and considers what makes a successful research project. Another purpose of the book is to help develop skills in critical analysis.

Appendix 2

Blank form for the critical analysis of a text

1. **What review question am I asking of this text?** (e.g. what is my central question? why select this text? does the critical analysis of this text fit into my investigation with a wider focus? what is my constructive purpose in undertaking a critical analysis of this text?)

2. **What type of literature is this?** (e.g. theoretical, research, practice, policy? are there links with other types of literature?)

3. **What sort of intellectual project for study is being undertaken?**
(a) *How clear is it which intellectual project the authors are undertaking?* (e.g. knowledge-for-understanding, knowledge-for-critical evaluation, knowledge-for-action, instrumentalism, reflexive action?)

(b) *How is the intellectuall project reflected in the authors' mode of working?* (e.g. a social science or a practical orientation? choice of methodology and methods? an interest in understanding or in improving practice?)

(c) *What value stance is adopted towards the practice or policy investigated?* (e.g. disinterested, critical, positive, unclear? what assumptions are made about the possibility of improvement? whose practice or policy is the focus of interest?)

(d) *How does the sort of project being undertaken affect the research questions addressed?* (e.g. investigating what happens? what is wrong? how well does a particular policy or intervention work in practice?)

(e) *How does the sort of project being undertaken affect the place of theory?* (e.g. is the investigation informed by theory? generating theory? atheoretical? developing social science theory or a practical theory?)

(f) *How does the authors' target audience affect the reporting of research?* (e.g. do the authors assume academic knowledge of methods? criticise policy? offer recommendations for action?)

4. What is being claimed?

(a) *What are the main kinds of knowledge claim that the authors are making?* (e.g. theoretical knowledge, research knowledge, practice knowledge?)

(b) *What is the content of the main claims to knowledge and of the overall argument?* (e.g. what, in a sentence, is being argued? what are the three to five most significant claims that encompass much of the detail? are there key prescriptions for improving policy or practice?)

(c) *How clear are the authors' claims and overall argument?* (e.g. stated in an abstract, introduction or conclusion? unclear?)

(d) *With what degree of certainty do the authors make their claims?* (e.g. do they indicate tentativeness? qualify their claims by acknowledging limitations of their evidence? acknowledge others' counter-evidence? acknowledge that the situation may have changed since data collection?)

(e) *How generalised are the authors' claims – to what range of phenomena are they claimed to apply?* (e.g. the specific context from which the claims were derived? other similar contexts? a national system? a culture? universal? implicit? unspecified?)

(f) *How consistent are the authors' claims with each other?* (e.g. do all claims fit together in supporting an argument? do any claims contradict each other?)

5. To what extent is there backing for claims?

(a) *How transparent are any sources used to back the claims?* (e.g. is there any statement of the basis for assertions? are sources unspecified?)

(b) *What, if any, range of sources is used to back the claims?* (e.g. first-hand experience? the authors' own practice knowledge or research? literature about others' practice knowledge or research? literature about reviews of practice knowledge or research? literature about others' polemic?)

(c) *If claims are at least partly based on the authors' own research, how robust is the evidence?* (e.g. is the range of sources adequate? are there methodological limitations or flaws in the methods employed? do they include cross-checking or 'triangulation' of accounts? what is the sample size and is it large enough to support the claims being made? is there an adequately detailed account of data collection and analysis? is a summary given of all data reported?)

(d) *Are sources of backing for claims consistent with degree of certainty and the degree of generalisation?* (e.g. is there sufficient evidence to support claims made with a high degree of certainty? is there sufficient evidence from other contexts to support claims entailing extensive generalisation?)

6. How adequate is any theoretical orientation to back claims?

(a) *How explicit are the authors about any theoretical orientation or conceptual framework?* (e.g. is there a conceptual framework guiding data collection? is a conceptual framework selected after data collection to guide analysis? is there a largely implicit theoretical orientation?)

(b) *What assumptions does any explicit or implicit theoretical orientation make that may affect the authors' claims?* (e.g. does a perspective focus attention on some aspects and under-emphasise others? if more than one perspective is used, how coherently do the different perspectives relate to each other?)

(c) *What are the key concepts underpinning any explicit or implicit theoretical orientation?* (e.g. are they listed? are they stipulatively defined? are concepts mutually compatible? is use of concepts consistent? is the use of concepts congruent with others' use of the same concepts?)

7. **To what extent does any value stance adopted affect claims?**

(a) *How explicit are the authors about any value stance connected with the phenomena?* (e.g. a disinterested, critical or positive stance? is this stance informed by a particular ideology? is it adopted before or after data collection?)

(b) *How may any explicit or implicit value stance adopted by the authors affect their claims?* (e.g. have they pre-judged the phenomena discussed? are they biased? is it legitimate for the authors to adopt their particular value stance? have they overemphasised some aspects of the phenomenon while underemphasising others?)

8. **To what extent are claims supported or challenged by others' work?**

(a) *Do the authors relate their claims to others' work?* (e.g. do the authors refer to others' published evidence, theoretical orientations or value stances to support their claims? do they acknowledge others' counter-evidence?)

(b) *How robust is any evidence from others' work used to support claims?* (e.g. see question 5(c))

(c) *How robust is any evidence from others' research and practice that challenges the authors' claims?* (e.g. see question 5(c))

9. **To what extent are claims consistent with my experience?**

10. **What is my summary evaluation of the text in relation to my review question or issue?**

(a) *How convincing are the authors' claims, and why?*

(b) *How, if at all, could the authors have provided stronger backing for their claims?*

Author index

General index

Paul Chapman Publishing

Research Methods in Educational Leadership and Management

Edited by **Marianne Coleman** and **Ann R J Briggs**
both at EMDU, University of Leicester

An essential guide to research in educational leadership and management, this book brings together expert original contributions to present a comprehensive and accessible guide for new and experienced researchers in the field.

This book is a core text for master's level courses in educational management. It is accessible for the beginning researcher while at the same time providing stimulating reading for students and practitioners with some research experience.

Abridged Contents

Marlene Morrison What Do We Mean by Educational Research? \ **Clive Dimmock** Cross-Cultural Differences in the Meaning and Conduct of Research in Education Management \ **Roy Kirk** Exploring the Existing Body of Research \ **Tony Bush** Authenticity in Educational Management Research: Reliability, Validity and Triangulation \ **Hugh Busher** Ethics of Research in Education \ **Ken Fogelman** Surveys and Sampling \ **Michael Bassey** Case Study Research \ **Pam Lomax** Action Research for Educational Management and Leadership \ **Ted Wragg** Interviewing \ **Judith Bell** The Troubles with Questionnaires... \ **Janet Moyles** Seeing is Believing? \ **Martin Cortazzi** Developing a Double Vision: Analysising Narrative and Documents in Educational Research \ **Marlene Morrison** Using Diaries in Research \ **Anthony Pell and Ken Fogelman** Analysing Quantative Data \ **Rob Watling** The Analysis of Qualitative Data \ **Ann R J Briggs** Academic Writing: Process and Presentation

June 2002 • 298 pages
Cloth (0-7619-7184-X) • Paper (0-7619-7185-8)

Paul Chapman Publishing, A SAGE Publications Company,
6 Bonhill Street, London, EC2A 4PU, UK
Order post-free **www.PaulChapmanPublishing.co.uk**